ORSON WELLES

INTERVIEWS

CONVERSATIONS WITH FILMMAKERS SERIES
PETER BRUNETTE, GENERAL EDITOR

Courtesy of BFI Films: Stills, Posters, and Designs

ORSON
WELLES
INTERVIEWS

EDITED BY MARK W. ESTRIN

UNIVERSITY PRESS OF MISSISSIPPI / JACKSON

www.upress.state.ms.us

Copyright © 2002 by University Press of Mississippi
All rights reserved
Manufactured in the United States of America

10   09   08   07   06   05   04   03   02   4   3   2   1
∞
Library of Congress Cataloging-in-Publication Data

Orson Welles : interviews / edited by Mark W. Estrin.
        p.   cm.—(Conversations with filmmakers series)
     Includes index.
     ISBN 1-57806-208-X (cloth : alk. paper)—ISBN 1-57806-209-8 (pbk. : alk. paper)
     1. Welles, Orson, 1915——Interviews.   2. Motion picture producers and
directors—United States—Interviews.   I. Welles, Orson, 1915–   II. Estrin, Mark
W.   III. Series.

PN1998.3.W45 A5   2001
791.43′2233′092—dc21
     [B]   2001045513

British Library Cataloging-in-Publication Data available

CONTENTS

INTRODUCTION

''H AVE YOU ANY THEORIES ABOUT WHAT will happen to you after death?'' Kenneth Tynan asks Orson Welles in the course of a 1967 interview included in this volume. "I don't know about my soul," Welles responds, tongue characteristically in cheek, "but my body will be sent to the White House. American passports ask you to state the name and address of the person to whom your remains should be delivered in the event of your death. I discovered many years ago that there is no law against putting down the name and address of the President. This has a powerful effect on the borders of many countries and acts as a sort of diplomatic visa. During the long Eisenhower years, I would almost have been willing to die, in order to have my coffin turn up some evening in front of his television set."

No coffin containing the Welles body ever did turn up at the White House bearing witness to his decease. After his death in 1985, he was cremated, his ashes later interred on a Spanish farm a three-hour drive from Seville. His remarks to Tynan are funny and, of course, they are outrageous, a word naturally suited to the off-screen (and off-stage and off-air) persona Welles nurtured, then tenaciously relished well into the television era, when his frequent guest appearances and occasional commercials distorted perceptions of his prodigious talent.

As the interviews and profiles collected in this volume repeatedly attest, the Welles career and the Welles personality became rapidly entangled, locked in permanent resistance to his periodic appeals for their separation. Beyond the scripts he wrote, directed, and enacted for stage, screen, and radio, the words Orson Welles spoke in his own articulate voice—in inter-

views, syndicated newspaper columns, weekly radio commentaries, campaign speeches for Franklin D. Roosevelt—fostered the development of a
complex public presence. By 1938, at the age of twenty-three, he was on the
cover of *Time* magazine and the subject of a *New Yorker* profile.

In the final year of World War II, about a decade after he burst upon the
American scene, a *New Yorker* writer prefaces news that Welles is about to
embark on a lecture tour of American cities in this way: "Until the other day,
we regarded Orson Welles simply as an actor, producer, costumer, magician,
Shakespearean editor, and leading prodigy of our generation, and then out
of our mail fluttered an announcement that he was about to become a new-
day Bryan by delivering an oration called 'The Nature of the Enemy.' " One
year later, in 1946, a *New York Times* reporter interviewing him on a *Lady from
Shanghai* sound stage prefaces *his* profile with references to Welles's "titanic
battle with RKO" over the uncompleted film *It's All True* and prods him to
deny any "bitterness" over *Citizen Kane*. By the mid-forties, in other words,
hyperbolic praise was already coexisting with veiled implications of unkept
promise.

With rare lapses, interviewers treat Welles with utter respect and admiration, even wonder, but as the years pass and the number of uncompleted
projects accumulates, the veiled implications occasionally turn into pointed
assertions, especially in the background information selected for inclusion
by profilers. The persistent accusation that "awesome Orson" (as one British
headline writer identified him) squandered his talent—that (in the words of
Kenneth Tynan) he grew "fat spreading himself thin"—commonly includes
the contention that he wasted too much time in conversation. Refuting that
charge in an interview, Welles dismisses advice he once received from playwright Thornton Wilder, who told him to stop frittering his time away in
talk: "He used to say to me, 'You must stop wasting your energy, Orson. You
must do what I do—have capsule conversations.' Just as a comic can do three
minutes on his mother-in-law, Thornton could do three minutes on Gertrude Stein or Lope de Vega. That's how he saved his energy. But I don't
believe that you have more energy if you save it. It isn't a priceless juice that
has to be kept in a secret bottle. We're social animals, and good conversation—not just parroting slogans and vogue words—is an essential part of
good living."

Has any filmmaker ever enjoyed "good conversation" as much as Orson
Welles? Has any filmmaker ever been as dazzling a conversationalist? *Orson*

Welles: Interviews brings together a substantial selection of interviews, profiles, and press conferences originally published or broadcast between 1938
and 1989, four years after his death. One of them, an interview televised in
France in 1975, did not reach print until 1998 (also in France) and, like other
material in this collection, is published in English here for the first time.
Transcriptions of two BBC television interviews included here have not been
published at all. Like Welles himself, these pieces are peripatetic, conducted
for newspapers, magazines, specialized film journals, and television broadcasts in assorted locations throughout the United States, Great Britain, and
Europe. Several offer vivid testimony to Welles's grasp on the public imagination in his heyday, including a *New York Times* account of his press conference the day after the *War of the Worlds* broadcast. This report provides one
of the most accurate and lively descriptions of the event available in print.
Newsreel footage of that press conference contains some repetitious and garbled interchanges but does manage to capture the accusatory atmosphere in
ways that no print version can accomplish. Looking and sounding as if they
had stepped directly from the script of *The Front Page,* reporters surround
Welles and bombard him with questions. He is a faux-innocent in a sea of
sharks.

   While individual pieces naturally emphasize specific films of a particular
period, many of them range over his entire career, especially interviews conducted from the late fifties onwards. As the collection repeatedly illustrates,
the Welles career was multidimensional (a fact still insufficiently acknowledged) and thoroughly interwoven with the Welles persona. These interviews, profiles, and press conferences portray the development of that
persona in the public imagination, then go on to confirm the unrivaled talent and intellect of the figure behind it as Welles ages. From the beginning,
Welles triumphantly straddled multiple media whose interaction became a
chief source of his creative energy. Especially for relative newcomers to the
Orson Welles Story, the material gathered here gains further resonance when
read with knowledge of the full range of Welles's work and the extent to
which that work was so often ahead of its time. Such awareness helps to
accomplish the task, but it is Welles's own voice that finally comes closest to
setting a frequently distorted record straight.

In the nearly two decades since his death, fascination with Welles and his
work continues to grow, still propelled by the vivid sense of off-stage drama

they periodically generated. To cite one conspicuous example, the United States History section of the *World Almanac and Book of Facts* lists with equal emphasis just three events for its 1938 entry: passage of the Naval Expansion Act; passage of the national minimum wage; and the national panic triggered by Welles's *War of the Worlds* broadcast. Still, the longstanding misperceptions starkly evident in American obituaries at the time of his death invariably persist. "Don't you think it would have been much better for his reputation today if *Citizen Kane* hadn't been Welles's *first* film?" a highly knowledgeable friend challenged not long ago, expressing a view of Welles commonly articulated even by sophisticated observers of American culture. "Now, really," he continued, "what did he accomplish that is worth anything much after 1941?"

A logical answer to the second question, by far the easier of the two, is, for starters, *The Magnificent Ambersons, The Lady from Shanghai, Othello, Chimes at Midnight, Touch of Evil,* and (although he did not direct that film) his portrayal of Harry Lime in *The Third Man.* Any sensible attempt to respond to the first query, however, is considerably more complicated and, of course, utterly futile, rather analogous to speculating on whether or not Shakespeare might have had a more difficult time earning his reputation if *Hamlet* or *King Lear* had been his first play instead of *Comedy of Errors.* But the question provokes constructive clarification: Contrary to common implicit assumption, *Citizen Kane* did not "just" appear out of a lens magically to catapult its maker to additional fame in yet another creative discipline.

While it *was* (at the age of twenty-six) his first feature film, *Citizen Kane* (and much of his later screen work) grew out of Welles's stage and radio experience in the five years which preceded it. As I particularly attempt to emphasize in the Chronology, the films of Orson Welles are inextricably linked to the theatres and airwaves which he dominated in the late nineteen thirties *and in which he continued to work* long after the completion of *Citizen Kane.* His diverse and alternating media involvement spawned repeated innovation in content and technique, notably evident, for example, in his films' striking experimentation with sound, a clear debt owed to his radio experience.

Welles's visual virtuosity, particularly when he worked with cinematographers Gregg Toland *(Kane)* and Stanley Cortez *(Ambersons)* but also prominently displayed in *Touch of Evil* and *Chimes at Midnight,* owes an analogous debt to his theatre background. He became a montage devotee with his first picture and tells interviewers that editing is far more important to a film's outcome than directing. Nonetheless, his frequent reliance on images of well-populated space conveying a sense of dimensionality through deep focus photography seems influenced by his work in the theatre, where, when warranted, the proscenium arch frames multiple actions and displaced groups of actors to be taken in simultaneously, without, as it were, "editing." Moreover, his special fondness for a tracking camera in long-take sequences frequently prolongs tension "to approximate the intimacy of a theatrical experience," as Joseph McBride points out in a penetrating analysis of Welles's films.

The stage and radio work habitually anticipated film projects—not just Welles's own. He first drew the attention of the national press in 1936 with his Harlem staging of *Macbeth,* a play he would re-imagine as a film a decade later. In 1938, he secured broadcast rights to Daphne du Maurier's just-published novel *Rebecca* and played the part of Maxim de Winter in a CBS radio adaptation. A year later Laurence Olivier starred in that role under the direction of Alfred Hitchcock, whose first American film was *Rebecca.* Also in 1939, three years before he would adapt, direct, and narrate the film version, Welles narrated and played the role of George Minafer (played by Tim Holt in the picture) in a radio broadcast of *The Magnificent Ambersons.*

From the earliest stages of his career Welles sought to extend media boundaries, to link and mix the forms in which he worked, sometimes integrating them, sometimes employing one medium as a potential sounding board for another. As early as 1937, he had his eye on Hollywood, telling a *New York Times* writer that he would like to direct for the screen. As the Chronology shows, he did have some film experience prior to making *Citizen Kane,* including the five-minute, experimental *Hearts of Age* (which he later dismisses as just "a little joke") and the filming he did at the Todd School. In 1938, three years before *Kane* was made, he shot two film sequences in slapstick comedy style, intending to incorporate them into *Too Much Johnson,* a Mercury Theatre stage production he was directing. From late 1939 until early 1940, he engaged in considerable pre-production work on an adaptation of Joseph Conrad's novel *Heart of Darkness,* including shooting some scenes which functioned as actors' screen tests.

Welles excelled at literary adaptation. Originally intended as his first picture for RKO, the *Heart of Darkness* project evolved from his earlier adaptation of the Conrad book for radio, broadcast in 1938 with Welles directing, acting, and narrating. Welles tells the BBC's Leslie Megahey that money worries forced the studio to abandon the project, but another factor almost certainly contributed to the cancellation of *Heart of Darkness:* Welles intended to shoot the picture entirely from the central character's point of view, a radical plan which would have prevented the camera from displaying him directly to the audience, thus eliminating any prospect of the viewer-hero identification typically deemed valuable to a studio picture's success. Always interested in point of view, Welles went one better in his first actual film, where multiple points of view, one of them a newsreel film within the film, are vital to *Citizen Kane*'s narrative structure. And he would continue to employ film in later offscreen projects. For his lavish Broadway stage adaptation of *Around the World in Eighty Days* (1946), Welles shot and edited a considerable amount of film footage which he integrated into the production, whose music and lyrics were composed by Cole Porter.

Numerous conversations illustrate the symbiotic nature of the performing arts throughout Welles's career. Long after he left New York, and then Hollywood, he continued to write and direct for the theatre, to direct and act in films, and (once it had replaced radio as the major broadcast medium) to engage in an extensive array of television projects as writer, director, actor or narrator, or some combination thereof. While directing and starring in his film *Othello,* Welles played the same role onstage in a London production directed by Laurence Olivier. A decade later, in the early sixties, *he* directed Olivier in the London premiere of avant-garde playwright Eugene Ionesco's *Rhinoceros* at the Royal Court Theatre. In this same period, he appeared in Dublin and Belfast in a revised version of *Five Kings,* his theatre cycle of Shakespearean history plays first produced on Broadway in 1939, decades before the Royal Shakespeare Company would undertake such a venture. This reworked *Five Kings* script in turn developed into *Chimes at Midnight* (also titled *Falstaff*), his finest Shakespeare-on-film achievement.

As he discusses in various conversations, perceptions of *time*—how it is used or misused, how reputations are made or unmade for posterity—recur throughout his films. Speaking of himself, not his films, he dismisses any idea of a cultural legacy. "Nothing could be more vulgar than to worry about posterity," he tells an interviewer in 1967. But Welles was also fascinated by the idea of time as technique—of running time and its flow. Because some of his most important films were cut without his authority and others compulsorily abbreviated by budget shortfalls, one gets a more consistent view of his application of this idea in his stagecraft. With the notable exception of his original 132-minute screenplay for *Ambersons,* however, it is clear that he generally preferred a limit of no more than about two hours. As he repeatedly shows in his book (with Roger Hill) *Everybody's Shakespeare* (1934), and as he put into frequent stage practice, Welles was a firm believer in freewheeling, compressed, non-academic productions of classical theatre, including (on the rare occasions when he could get away with it) the performance of plays in under two hours, without an intermission, today a highly popular production method.

Welles was also on the cutting edge in the running time of an individual take. Five years before Hitchcock would make *Rope,* in which every take runs about ten minutes, Welles shot sections of *The Magnificent Ambersons* in complicated long takes. RKO's botch of the picture shriveled or cut those sequences entirely and the studio's subsequent destruction of the deleted footage thus ensures that forties long-take innovation is still credited to Hitchcock. A year before *Rope's* release, Welles experimented with the technique again in *Macbeth.* Those sequences were excised from the released picture but one ten-minute take is included in the restored version (1980).

Numerous articles published between 1936 and 1940 formulated the Welles persona in the popular press. A 1937 *New York Times* summary of his eccentric background and splashy arrival on the New York theatre scene spawned longer features in *Time* and the *New Yorker* the following year, both of them published before the *War of the Worlds* broadcast would heighten journalistic interest even further. The three-part *Saturday Evening Post* series represented in this collection, the longest and most colorful of the early profiles, illustrates the nature of the *wunderkind* image delineated for popular consumption. Published in the winter of 1940, six months before shooting began on *Citizen Kane,* this profile is written in a journalistic style common to the period, one that typically rejects verbatim question-and-answer accounts and rarely quotes its subject directly. Its hyperbolic tone, like that of other Welles profiles, suggests that such omission also represents an attempt to protect him against charges of immodesty, comical as such a notion may now appear. It is certain, however, that Welles was interviewed extensively— note, for example, his explanation for the *War of the Worlds* panic—and that he and Maurice Bernstein, his guardian from the age of fifteen, were the primary information sources. Indeed, the first installment of the series included a photograph of Welles and Fred Smith, one of the two writers, dining together in Hollywood.

The *Post* piece sounds so exaggerated in its portrait of young Orson's genius that it occasionally appears to verge on deliberate parody, a view more easily taken today, I suspect, than at the time of its original publication. Still, though they became the major forces in creating the Welles legend, such articles also planted the lasting notion that their subject exaggerated his accomplishments when certain details later shifted or remained unsubstantiated. Simon Callow, one of his biographers, argues convincingly that the legend of Orson Welles was primarily orchestrated by Welles himself, especially in the early years of its formation. To discover the process by which the Welles legend came to pass is also to consider, in our own media-driven culture, when he thought he might have become its victim. That is another implicit subject in this range of interviews.

Topics discussed in these early pieces follow Welles in interviews for the rest of his life. Writers stress his inventiveness—in, for example, his productions of the Afro-American *Macbeth* for the WPA and the Mercury Theatre's adaptation of *Julius Caesar,* the latter updated to reflect the Fascist threat to Europe. In the 1938 interview which opens this collection, he tells Richard O'Brien that he is determined to upgrade radio drama by extending the inherent "intimacy" of the medium through technical and narrative experimentation. These introductory pieces about the work show that Welles had sprung immediately forth as a pivotal centerpiece within it, a development hastened by the *causes célèbres* some of that work had become, notably the production of *The Cradle Will Rock* and the *War of the Worlds* broadcast. And, of course, Welles himself—brash, articulate, brimming with innovative ideas which he could implement and publicize with maximum flair—made especially good copy. (The *New York Times,* 1937, when Welles was twenty-two years old: "He got up from the table in the bar where all this talk had been going on, adjusted what he called his low comedy scarf and walked down the street—very deliberately, like an old-time actor—toward the Mercury Theatre.")

News of the unique two-picture contract Welles signed with RKO in 1939 was widely reported in the press and highlighted in the *Saturday Evening Post* profile. Speculation over his first RKO project and the subsequent battle over the release of *Citizen Kane* became natural grist for movie-page news and gossip columns, erupting into headlines in early 1941, when the Hearst organization's assault against the picture—and especially against Welles—became known. For the rest of the year, well past the picture's delayed premiere on the first of May, the brouhaha unfolded, with Welles insisting in a lengthy press statement and in a newspaper article ("*Citizen Kane* Is Not about Louella Parsons' Boss") that Charles Foster Kane was a "fictitious" figure. In response to further allegations in Hearst newspapers that one of his radio plays contained Communist propaganda, Welles released yet another, more vociferously worded press statement accusing Hearst of conducting a series of "vicious" personal attacks in retaliation against *Citizen Kane:* "I am not a Communist. I am grateful for our constitutional form of government, and I rejoice in our great American tradition of democracy. Needless to say, it is not necessarily unpatriotic to disagree with Mr. Hearst." Though unbeknownst to Welles at the time, such attacks led to his becoming a featured attraction in the files of the FBI, as material recently released under the Freedom of Information Act substantiates.

In this context, it is all the more surprising to find virtually no interviews in this period. Welles's published statements were vetted by lawyers in anticipation of possible Hearst libel action and formal print interviews were avoided. His public utterances were almost exclusively fleeting, innocuous responses to reporters covering the *Citizen Kane* opening. Once he completed shooting *The Magnificent Ambersons* and acting in *Journey into Fear* in early 1942, he headed for South America, where he spent six months making *It's All True.* Upon his return in August, he granted a jocular, evasive interview to the *New York Times* which never mentions *Kane,* but, by then, there was another controversy to be referenced, however discreetly—the mutilation of *Ambersons* during his absence.

Welles would remain reluctant to discuss *Kane* or Hearst publicly for years to come, primarily because of lingering libel concerns. Citing an incident in Buffalo, New York which made him realize just how far Hearst's "minions were prepared to go," he eventually suggests to interviewers that his silence on the subject had been motivated by fears for his personal safety as well. In a 1946 *Times* interview, he does comment briefly on past troubles with *Kane* and *It's All True* but claims to feel no bitterness toward RKO. Skeptical though one might now be at such an assertion so soon after the RKO experience, it does anticipate the tone of more detailed discussions later in his life where Welles sounds genuinely rueful over his relationship with the studio. The first interview in which he discusses *Kane* in a substantive way does not occur

until 1960, when he responds at length to questions from the BBC's Huw
Wheldon, who remarks that until then, "curiously enough," Welles had
rarely spoken about *Citizen Kane* outside of promotional interviews. Readers
who have heretofore accepted the shibboleth that he was incapable of shar-
ing creative credit for the picture will be surprised to discover Welles's
emphatic expression of gratitude to cinematographer Gregg Toland in this
BBC transcription, an attribution he reiterates in other interviews.

His fascination with politics, a subject to which he returns repeatedly, is
first featured in John McCarten's *New Yorker* interview announcing Welles's
lecture tour on the dangers of Fascism. One might quizzically suggest that
January 1945 was a tad late to be warning the nation about Fascist evil but (as
the Chronology shows) Welles had been active in American political life for
some time, speaking at anti-Fascist rallies as early as 1938 and campaigning
intensively for Franklin Roosevelt's re-election in 1944. Throughout his life,
he wrote commentaries and made speeches on a broad range of political and
cultural subjects. In 1982, three years before his death, he was among the
featured speakers at an anti-nuclear rally in Central Park.

Welles genuinely came to regret that he did not enter the world of politics
more directly. Among the refrains running through these pieces is his stated
disappointment that he never sought political office. Maintaining that he
planned to run for the U.S. Senate out of California in 1946, and that shortly
before his death in 1945 Roosevelt had encouraged him to do so, Welles
claims he was dissuaded from running by Alan Cranston, then a young political activist who eventually became a Democratic U.S. Senator from that
state. Welles also gave serious consideration to running for the seat of junior
Senator from Wisconsin but decided against it. His opponent in that race
would have been Joseph McCarthy, whose subsequent reign of political terror led Welles to declare, with some embellishment, that he blamed himself
for McCarthy's devastating impact on American life. "I'm basically an independent radical," he tells the BBC's Bernard Levin in 1967. "So I would have
belonged to the Democratic Party and would have been on its left wing."

Such revelations are intriguing in the context of the Welles ego and public
persona. But they also relate to his films, in which links between politics and
individual egos appear in both explicit and encoded form, most evident in
Kane, his Shakespeare adaptations (especially *Chimes at Midnight*), and his
screenplay (with Oja Kodar) for *The Big Brass Ring.* J. Edgar Hoover's now
documented fear that Welles was a dangerous Communist confirms that he

had become a logical target for the McCarthy witch-hunting crowd in Congress as well. Although IRS tax trouble was another contributing factor, it cannot have been entirely coincidental that Welles worked in Europe from 1948 until 1955, "almost exactly the arch of the most virulent Red-baiting blacklist years," as Peter Bogdanovich writes in *This Is Orson Welles*. In those years and again from 1958 to 1975, Welles lived abroad, returning to the U.S. sporadically for various projects, just as he would return to Europe periodically in the last decade of his life.

The first important interview conducted outside the United States (*Sight and Sound*, 1950) is also the first to elicit explicit consideration of cinema as *medium* and assessments of other filmmakers. Published by the British Film Institute, *Sight and Sound* is the oldest of respectable film journals still publishing today, but, unsurprisingly, it was in France where Welles was accorded the most intense level of serious attention. As the 1950s progressed, Welles and Hitchcock became key directorial pivots in the development of film *studies*—the serious scrutiny of film as an academic subject grounded in theory. Although in 1958 film studies was still in its infancy, its rise triggered the growth of scholarly journals devoted to the subject, none of which was more influential than *Cahiers du Cinéma*.

Although he occasionally mocks the high minded seriousness of French interviewers to reporters outside France, he clearly revels in the sophisticated level of appreciation he finds there and responds in kind. Welles's conversations with French critics, filmmakers, and scholars are notable for their range and depth, despite the occasional intrusive sycophancy in a questioner's tone. The two-part *Cahiers du Cinéma* interview (1958), conducted by the eminent French film critic André Bazin and others during the Cannes Film Festival and in Paris, coincided with the release of *Touch of Evil*, the last film Welles would direct for a Hollywood studio. This is the first time that the entire *Cahiers* interview has been published in English.

Welles was only forty-three in 1958, but a surprising number of his interviews from that year onward are characterized by an increasingly pronounced collective stocktaking. His later interviews contrast significantly in spirit and tone with the persona-establishing pieces of the thirties and forties, which were published almost exclusively in the popular press for a general audience. While Welles the man still figures centrally in the *Cahiers* interview, for example, his films and, especially, their visual style—matters relating to montage, camera lenses, shot duration—assume sustained priority. In a period when notions of *auterism* and the incontrovertible power of the director were arguably at their zenith, Welles denigrates the director's role in favor of the editor's: "For my vision of film," he tells Bazin and Charles Bitsch, "editing is not an aspect, it is *the* aspect. Directing is an invention of people like you." However disingenuous his position may sound, it is a consistent Welles refrain, one which was already on the record by 1937, when he was quoted by a *New York Times* reporter: "Now a front-rank director himself, he thinks the importance of directors is apt to be overrated." Two decades later, he tells his *Cahiers* interviewers: "The only place where I have absolute control is in the editing studio. Consequently, that's where the director is, potentially, a true artist." Elsewhere in this conversation, with no apparent trace of irony, he says, "I could work for an eternity editing a film." "The real filmmaker is a writer," he tells yet another interviewer, this time elevating not the authority of the editor to which he usually points, but the essential connection between writer and director, ideally, he says, one and the same person.

In the 1950 *Sight and Sound* interview, Francis Koval maintains that "although in the course of conversation Orson underlines several times that he is essentially a theatre man and 'rather hazy on the subject of movies,' the continuous flow of ideas cascading from his lips with fervor and conviction belies these affirmations." Assorted interviews in this volume lend special testimony to Koval's description. In the second part of the 1958 *Cahiers* interview, for instance, the subjects hurtle from *Touch of Evil* (particularly Welles's character of Quinlan and its relationship to other Welles roles) to Shakespeare to matters of philosophy and religion to his films' representation of American society. Typically, Welles's remarks are peppered with informed contextual allusions to Gide, Marlowe, Kyd, Montaigne, Nietzsche, and (of course) Shakespeare.

One interview was commissioned by an American publication (*Playboy*), but the major ones of the 1960s, like those of the previous decade, were conducted outside the United States. They feature *The Trial* and *Chimes at Midnight,* Welles's primary films of this decade, but the conversations are characteristically broad in subject matter, branching out from his films into discussions of social and political issues, religion, British history, advertising and, naturally enough, the conflict between art and economics. These interviews contain typically incisive observations about his own work. "I believe," he tells Juan Cobos and Miguel Rubio, "I have never made a film without having a solid ethical point of view about the story. Morally speaking, there is no ambiguity in what I do." He re-enforces that position in a 1969 London *Observer* profile when he declares his detestation of "agnosticism, people who do not *choose.*" In "A Trip to Don Quixoteland," he rejects a visual style dependent on a static camera: "I do not believe in the cinema unless there is movement on the screen. This is why I am not in agreement with certain directors who content themselves with a static cinema. For me, these are dead images. I hear the noise of the projector behind me and, when I see these long, long walks along streets, I am always waiting to hear the director's voice, saying, 'Cut!' "

This piece is also among the first interviews to confront Welles directly with John Houseman's claim that Herman Mankiewicz was the true author of *Citizen Kane.* In 1958, Welles had told *Cahiers du Cinéma:* "The only film I wrote from the first to the last word is *Citizen Kane.*" To Cobos and Rubio in 1964, he responds this way: "He [Mankiewicz] wrote several important scenes. Houseman is an old enemy of mine. I was very lucky to work with Mankiewicz; everything concerning Rosebud belongs to him." In a 1967 conversation, he tells BBC interviewer Kathleen Halton, "All of my own films are my own scripts," stating that he never has used writers, only "a couple of collaborators." Four years later, in "Raising Kane," her *New Yorker* essay subsequently reprinted in *The Citizen Kane Book,* film critic Pauline Kael substantially heightened the *Kane* authorship stakes with additional persuasive evidence intended to portray Mankiewicz as the picture's principal screenwriter. The controversy, which lingers to this day, prompted Welles to write a letter to the London *Sunday Times* (17 November 1971) seeking to clarify the evolution of *Kane*'s screenplay and maintaining that the final version was drawn from "two screenplays, one written by Mr. Mankiewicz, in Victorville [California], and the other in Beverly Hills by myself." By 1982, in the BBC's *Orson Welles Story,* Welles alludes to Mankiewicz as his "co-author."

For Welles, acting is a consistently inviting subject. He makes penetrating comments about The Method, contrasts the demands of stage acting with those of acting before the camera, and, in a press conference at the Brussels World's Fair in 1958, distinguishes between directors who are technicians and those who are actors' directors, maintaining that few of them combine both talents. In a (London) *Sunday Times* interview with film critic Dilys Powell in 1963, he analyzes movie stardom: "When the camera falls in love, what is begotten is the authentic movie star, and there are very few of those. Spencer

Tracy, James Cagney, Gary Cooper, James Dean, Marlene Dietrich, and Marilyn Monroe were not necessarily great actors but they were great stars. . . . Abbott and Costello were box-office champions. Not so Buster Keaton. But who was the real movie star—Costello or Keaton? Most of Garbo's pictures scarcely made back their cost, and Garbo is the greatest movie star of all time. . . . Laurence Olivier [is] to be named with Garrick and Kean, not with Tracy and Cooper. Olivier is a very great actor, but his star quality is an achievement, and the camera doesn't fall in love with achievement. . . . Actors like Peter O'Toole, Albert Finney and Tom Courtenay are going to make quite a new British cinema and theatre. We have some good young people in America too, of course. Geraldine Page—I've never seen a better actress. And I've never worked with a better actor than Anthony Perkins."

Despite some evidence of anecdotal exaggeration or inconsistency and an occasional tendency to flatter his audience, Welles reacts candidly even to uncomfortable subjects. In "Welles on Falstaff," an interview published in 1967 by *Cahiers du Cinéma in English,* he rejects the charge that he is an obsessive perfectionist: "I am in a certain way a maniac, a 'perfectionist,' but in many other aspects, not at all. I always leave some things unelaborated. I do not believe that a film is to be made like those pictures in which people paint the leaves of a tree one by one." A *New York Times* interview conducted in 1972 during rehearsals for a television production of *The Man Who Came to Dinner* highlights another negative trait. Alluding to his intimidating reputation, the producers of the telecast tell the interviewer that "the chance of employing Welles seemed like an offer to go along on D-Day with a guarantee you wouldn't be shot." The production floor manager defends Welles, remarking that he could indeed be difficult, "but only if you weren't doing your job properly."

The sound of money also jangles uncomfortably in pockets of these conversations. The degree of authority he gained and lost so early in his filmmaking career led to the conviction that Welles was an utterly undisciplined filmmaker, incapable (especially after he lost control of *Touch of Evil*) of exercising financial prudence and therefore unable to acquire adequate financing for his projects. His responses to questions on this topic and his exquisitely detailed descriptions of his filmmaking process dilute such a judgment but they do not diminish the sadness implicit in the frequent allusions to his financial predicaments. Speaking of his unfinished picture *Don Quixote* he cheerfully tells interviewers that when he does release the picture, "It will be called *When Will You Finish Don Quixote?"* Occasionally, the subject prompts a flash of anger, evident in these remarks to Leslie Megahey: "Since it's my own little picture that I put my own money on, I don't know why they don't bug authors and say, 'When are you gonna finish *Nellie,* that novel you started ten years ago?' You know, it's my business."

Coming from a man often attacked as a monomaniac, the self–deprecation and candid stocktaking pervasive in these interviews are frequently startling. In 1946, he is characteristically hard on himself as he talks about his acting style to a *New York Times* interviewer: "No critic has ever liked my acting. I have an unfortunate personality. I can show you, frame for frame, that my eyebrows move less than Ray Milland's in *The Lost Weekend.* If I permitted myself one-tenth of his expressions in that excellent performance, I would be howled out of the theatre. I have only to walk into camera range and the critics are convinced that I am a hambone. I am an actor of the old school. That is the only way I can explain it." He continues that refrain to the end of his life, insisting to Leslie Megahey in 1982 that his performance in *Journey into Fear* a half century earlier was "very hammy." When asked by Kenneth Tynan in 1967 to name his major vice, he responds, "*Accidia*—the medieval Latin word for melancholy, and sloth."

Over the years, he is generous in his praise for a limited group of directors which includes Griffith, Lubitsch, De Sica, Renoir, Kubrick, Hawks and (especially) Ford, but he is also capable of scathing comments about others. In a 1960 *Sight and Sound* interview, he dismisses the work of an unnamed Oscar-winning director, clearly William Wyler, who "tells the actors nothing. He does about forty-five takes of every scene, then prints the right one. His taste is perfect, but the actors have to be very patient. In the end, they do what he wants and has never told them." He dislikes Antonioni, Bergman, and Resnais (among various others explicitly condemned or damned with faint praise), but reserves his most stinging comments for DeMille, Kazan, Minnelli, and Hitchcock. He tells *Cahiers du Cinéma* that he walked out on Nicholas Ray's *Rebel Without a Cause* and still becomes "angry just thinking about that film." He expresses admiration for Kazan's directorial skill, but is unable to restrain his angry dismissal of a Cinémathèque française student's query: "*Chère mademoiselle,* you have chosen the wrong *metteur en scène* because Elia Kazan is a traitor. He is a man who sold to McCarthy all his companions at a time when he could continue to work in New York at high salary, and having sold all his people to McCarthy, he then made a film called *On the Waterfront* which was a celebration of the informer. And therefore no question which uses him as an example can be answered by me."

In 1964 he refers to Hitchcock as "an extraordinary director" but subsequently attacks him in remarks which smack of petty jealousy or, possibly, undisclosed personal animus. None of Hitchcock's "pictures will be of any interest a hundred years from now," he tells Kenneth Tynan in 1967. Two years after Hitchcock's death, in 1982, Welles makes other cruel generalizations during appearances in Paris. At the Cinémathèque française: "There have only been two directors in the history of the world who have brought the public [into cinema houses] in large quantity because of their names. I will name the two, and when I tell you that I detest both of them I will shock you to your bones . . . Cecil B. DeMille and Alfred Hitchcock." To *L'Avant-Scène Cinéma* interviewers: "A long time ago, Hitchcock made a marvelous film called *The Thirty-Nine Steps*. Everything he did in America is dry, empty, weak. It's nothing. He gave in to Hollywood, and he lost all the charm of his English style, which came from the semi-bohemian, semi-poor atmosphere of the small film industry. As soon as he became a cog in the Hollywood machine, he graced us with those Ingrid Bergmans and those *Birds,* that whole mess which I don't want to talk about. . . . He's exactly the opposite of a director like Renoir, whose first concern was the actor, the people, and that is my concern too. . . . He was only interested in the camera. It was so organized, his *mise en scène,* that one could almost do without him. I detest that."

Richard Marienstras's interview, published in English here for the first time, was conducted for a French television project focusing on key stage and screen "mediators" of Shakespeare. The two-hour conversation, filmed in 1974 and broadcast on French television the following year, was excerpted in print but not fully published until 1998, when it appeared in *Positif.* Nowhere else in his numerous discussions of Shakespeare is it as plainly evident that Shakespearean drama comprised one of the central passions of Welles's life. He is in dazzling conversational form here, in the company of a highly perceptive interviewer, not only in his insights into Shakespearean drama and its transference to stage and screen, but also in the range, depth, and fluidity of his responses.

Even including his 1975 American Film Institute tribute, in 1982 Welles was celebrated as he had not been since the heady days of the late '30s and early '40s. In that year, the BBC broadcast *The Orson Welles Story,* a luminous exposition of Welles's life on the world stage. Telecast in the United Kingdom, this program would not be shown in the United States until 1990—in abbreviated form on the TNT cable channel. Leslie Megahey's exceptional interview, the centerpiece of the original BBC documentary and probably the most honest and comprehensive of Welles's television dialogues, is extracted from that production and published here for the first time. He becomes progressively more introspective, even elegiac at times, but typically suppresses evidence of bitterness. Among its greatest pleasures is (once again) Welles's candor, by turns wry, self-deprecating, rueful. "I would have sold my soul to play The Godfather," he tells Megahey, referring to Marlon Brando's role as Don Corleone.

The most elaborate celebration that year occurred in France, where Welles continued to be lionized as nowhere else, and where President François Mitterand appointed him a Commander of the French Legion of Honor. In February and March 1982, Welles was honored at that keynote event, at luncheons and dinners, at press conferences, and at that year's César awards ceremony, France's equivalent to the Oscars, over which Welles presided. These events are represented with "Five Days in the Life of Commander Welles," which appeared in a special Welles issue of *L'Avant-Scène Cinéma* (July 1982) and is published in English here for the first time. Leslie Megahey's BBC interview and this summary of the Paris proceedings conclude the interviews on a note of triumph near the end of Welles's life. For its part, Gore Vidal's "Remembering Orson Welles" provides the coda four years after his death, returning us full circle to those early profiles which formulated the original Welles legend—validating it, debunking it, immortalizing it all at the same time. "I have made an art form of the interview," Vidal recalls Welles telling him.

"Most people aren't afraid of death when it comes," Welles said to *L'Avant-Scène Cinéma* interviewers in 1982. "They fear pain, age, solitude, being abandoned. Death is only real for a few poets in the world. For the others, it isn't real. Because if death really meant something to human sensibility, we wouldn't have the atomic bomb, because the bomb is, quite simply, death." When he died in 1985, typical obituaries and career summaries (especially in the American press) dwelled as much on the failures and regrets, on the bloated image of dissipated prospects captured on television gab shows, as on the formidable range of achievements or the majestic voice, mind, and talent. In the intervening years, the pendulum has swung dramatically around and today the man and his work are a perpetual source of dramatic energy—in restored or reconstructed versions of his films; in biographical and critical studies; in documentary film compilations; in stage plays, films, and television dramas in which Welles himself is a major character. A recent television adaptation of *The Magnificent Ambersons* showcases his original screenplay. Ongoing projects to circulate his unreleased films and to publish collections of his writings continue.

Read the Chronology. Scan the Filmography. Browse through the interviews at the heart of this volume. Orson Welles's creative juices never stopped flowing, a fact repeatedly verified in his own strong voice throughout these "good conversations."

Consistent with policies established for the Conversations with Filmmakers series, interviews are published in their entirety, with minimal, silent editorial changes when warranted for clarity or correction of identifiable error. Each of the three parts of the *Saturday Evening Post* profile is self-contained and a substantial portion of the biographical coverage in the first two segments is repeated elsewhere in this volume. I have therefore included only the final installment which uniquely tracks the *War of the Worlds* aftermath and takes Welles to Hollywood. In rare instances, some redundant information included in the introductions to interviews has been omitted. Leslie Megahey's interview has been extracted from the 1982 BBC documentary *The Orson Welles Story* which originally included extensive film clips and interviews with other figures in Welles's life. The Megahey-Welles interchanges are published here in full. Some information is repeated in various pieces, in part because writers often relied on earlier articles as source material. That is especially true of anecdotes establishing the Welles legend, certain hyperbolic details of which he later attempts to correct. Some overlap also occurs when topics become natural refrains: aspects of individual Welles films, his passion for Shakespeare, his regret at never having run for political office, his money woes.

I have especially sought to bring together difficult-to-find, scattered conversations originally published or telecast outside the United States along with American material notable for its documentation of Welles's emergence as a public figure. Most of the French interviews published here or cited in the introduction have been newly translated by Alisa Hartz expressly for this volume. Welles was, of course, an exquisitely garrulous man and many interviews exist. Several of those cited in this introduction and numerous others considered for inclusion have been omitted for a variety of reasons, including space limitations, content duplication and transcript unavailability.

In the Chronology, I have attempted to synopsize the continuous influence of other media on Welles's film career, an understanding of which is vital for an objective appreciation of his work. I have omitted many details, including most of his unrealized projects. The Chronology cites only the titles of films he directed and the most important among those in which he otherwise participated. Production particulars are listed in the Filmography and are not, therefore, usually repeated in the Chronology.

Within the vast amount of Wellesiana, several works deserve special mention for easing the burden of this venture by aiding in the identification of material for possible inclusion and, especially, in navigating the daunting maze of detail charting the Welles career. They include biographies by Barbara Leaming (*Orson Welles: A Biography.* New York: Viking, 1985), Frank Brady (*Citizen Welles.* New York: Scribner's, 1989), Simon Callow (*Orson Welles: The Road to Xanadu.* London: Jonathan Cape, 1995), and David Thomson (*Rosebud.* New York: Knopf, 1996); scholarly studies by James Naremore (*The Magic World of Orson Welles.* Dallas: Southern Methodist University Press, 1989) and Joseph McBride (*Orson Welles.* New York: Da Capo Press, 1996); the Special Issue on Orson Welles published by the film journal *Persistence of Vision* (1989); and numerous reference sources, particularly Brett Wood's meticulous survey (*Orson Welles: A Bio-Bibliography.* Westport, CT: Greenwood Press, 1990) and Jonathan Rosenbaum's "Welles's Career," the most detailed Welles chronology published to date. The Rosenbaum chronology appears as an appendix to Peter Bogdanovich's *This Is Orson Welles* (New York: Da Capo Press, 1998), another indispensable volume for Welles research which Rosenbaum edited. Interviews and profiles cited in the Introduction but not included in this collection were telecast on the BBC ("The Bernard Levin Interview," 17 March and 3 April 1967; and Kathleen Halton's "Movies Interview," unspecified 1967 date) and published in the *New York Times* (28 November 1937; 30 August 1942; and 26 November 1972); *Time* (9 May 1938); the *New Yorker* (8 October 1938); *Cahiers du Cinéma* ("A Press Conference," September 1958); *Sight and Sound* (Spring 1960); the (London) *Sunday Times* (3 February 1963); *Cahiers du Cinéma in English* (September 1967); the (London) *Observer* (7 December 1969); and *L'Avant-Scène Cinéma* (July 1982; and January–February 1986).

I want to express my sincere thanks to the people who made significant contributions in bringing this collection into print: Kevin Costa, Sidney Gottlieb, Alisa Hartz, Natalie DiRissio, Matthew McDonough, Leonard Fleischer, Joseph Plut, Kevin Harty, and Matt Wolf; those who granted permission to publish this material (including interviews eventually omitted) with a particular note of appreciation to Leslie Megahey, Oja Kodar, Matthew Tynan, Richard Marienstras, and Hugh McCarten; my film studies students and colleagues, especially Joan Dagle, Kathryn Kalinak, and Claudia Springer; others at Rhode Island College, particularly John Nazarian, John Salesses, Richard Weiner, James McCroskery, and Jason Blank; Wendolyn Weber, Merfyn Williams, Peter Pullan, Edward Brooks, Lyndon Van Der Pump, Roberta and Alex deJoia, Jimmy Mullick, Hannah Barr, and Mark Julevich; reference and inter-library loan staff of Adams Library at Rhode Island College, especially Myra Blank; the college's Faculty Research Committee; Damon McCollin-Moore and untold staff members at the British Film Institute, the British Library newspaper branch, the Westminster Reference Library, and the Theatre Museum Library, all in London; Vicky Mitchell at the BBC; Rebecca Cape at the Lily Library of Indiana University; and John Harris at the Museum of Modern Art in New York City. I also extend personal thanks to Abe Estrin, a remarkable Wellesian figure in my own life; to my daughter and son-in-law, Robin Estrin and Seamus Kelly, for the meals, the mails, and so much else; and, especially, to Seetha Srinivasan and Anne Stascavage at the University Press of Mississippi for their advice and confidence.

Most of all, I offer my inexpressible gratitude to my wife Barbara L. Estrin for absolutely everything. She creates rainbows and finds, as Gore Vidal writes of Orson Welles, "new ways of seeing things that others see not at all." This book is dedicated to her.

Mark W. Estrin

CHRONOLOGY

1915   George Orson Welles born 6 May, in Kenosha, Wisconsin, to Beatrice Ives Welles and Richard Head Welles. One sibling, Richard, Jr., aged ten.

1918   Mother's cultural absorption exposes OW to the arts at an early age and influences the family's decision to move to Chicago. They are joined there by mother's friend Dr. Maurice Bernstein, whom OW calls "Dadda."

1919   Beatrice and Richard Welles separate.

1924   Beatrice Welles dies at the age of forty-three, four days after OW's ninth birthday.

1926   OW enters the highly progressive Todd School for Boys, in Woodstock, Illinois, where he acts and writes extensively, performs magic, and adapts, directs, and designs an array of classical and contemporary plays and musical productions.

1929   Writes theatre column for *Highland Park* [Illinois] *News*. Travels through Europe with friends.

1930   Journeys with father to China and Japan. Richard Welles dies in December, aged fifty-eight.

1931–32 Maurice Bernstein is named OW's legal guardian. Upon graduation from Todd, briefly attends Chicago Art Institute. Sketching tour to Ireland and the Aran Islands. Acts with Dublin's Gate Theatre company, followed by an interval with the Abbey Theatre. While in Dublin, OW produces several plays independently, acts in local productions, and writes "Chitchat and Criticism" column for a weekly paper under the pseudonym Knowles Noel Shane.

1933   Tries unsuccessfully to secure acting work in London and New York. Travels in Morocco and Spain; writes detective potboilers in Seville. Directs production of *Twelfth Night* for Todd School, filming a dress rehearsal in color with a silent-movie camera. Signed by stage star Katharine Cornell and her husband, director Guthrie McClintic, for repertory productions in New York and on U.S. tour; plays Mercutio in *Romeo and Juliet* and major roles in *Candida* and *The Barretts of Wimpole Street.*

1934   Todd Press publishes *Everybody's Shakespeare,* OW's collaboration with Todd School headmaster Roger Hill, featuring edited acting versions of *The Merchant of Venice, Julius Caesar,* and *Twelfth Night,* commentaries, and OW's sketches for potential set and costume designs. Obtains first radio acting job, a CBS weekday series of dramatizations aimed at schoolchildren. Organizes and acts in summer drama festival at Todd. Makes his first film, the five-minute, 16mm *The Hearts of Age.* Marries Virginia Nicolson. Recast as Tybalt in revised New York production of the Cornell-McClintic *Romeo and Juliet.*

1935   Earns living primarily from radio drama, including participation (which continues until 1939) in the landmark series *The March of Time.* Adapts and stars in CBS broadcast of *Hamlet.* Appears in Broadway production of Archibald MacLeish's verse drama *Panic.*

1936   Conceives and directs the "voodoo" *Macbeth* for the Negro Theatre Unit of the Federal Theatre Project. Funded by the U.S. government's Works Progress Administration, the production plays for two months in Harlem, transfers to Broadway, then tours the U.S.

1937   Directs and plays title role in Federal Theatre production of Marlowe's *Dr. Faustus.* Continues to play numerous roles on radio, including Jean Valjean in his own adaptation of *Les Miserables.* Assumes title role in the weekly radio series *The Shadow,* which he plays to 1939. With John Houseman, produces *The Cradle Will Rock,* Marc Blitzstein's political musical, for the Federal Theatre Project but WPA marshals padlock the theatre to block its opening. Another theatre is found, the audience is encouraged to walk the twenty-one block distance to the new venue, and *Cradle,* now a *cause célèbre,* is performed there without sets or costumes. OW and Houseman form The Mercury Theatre, a repertory "people's theatre" which opens in New York (November) with *Caesar,* a modern dress version of Shakespeare's *Julius Caesar,* adapted and directed by OW, who also plays Brutus.

1938   Daughter Christopher is born to OW and Virginia Nicolson Welles. Mercury Theatre productions include Dekker's *Shoemaker's Holiday* and Shaw's *Heartbreak House.* OW is subject of *Time* magazine cover story ("Marvelous Boy: Shadow to Shakespeare, Shoemaker to Shaw," 9 May) and a *New Yorker* profile ("This Ageless Soul," 8 October). For another Mercury production, *Too Much Johnson,* OW shoots two film sequences in the manner of slapstick comedy, intending to incorporate them into the play but never uses the footage. *The Mercury Theatre on the Air,* a series of literary adaptations featuring OW, begins weekly CBS radio broadcasts. On 30 October, the series broadcasts an adaptation of H. G. Wells's novel *The War of the Worlds,* precipitating widespread panic among listeners convinced that a Martian invasion of America is underway. The following week, the program broadcasts OW's adaptation of Joseph Conrad's novella *Heart of Darkness.* Renamed *The Campbell Playhouse* for its new soup company sponsor in December, the Mercury radio series continues to March 1940. OW secures radio rights to Daphne du Maurier's new novel *Rebecca,* then plays Maxim de Winter in the *Campbell Playhouse* adaptation (9 December). Begins to make appearances at political rallies, including a protest against German religious persecution and a benefit supporting anti-Franco Loyalists fighting in the Spanish Civil War. Publishes several magazine articles. Continues to write and to lecture on a range of political and cultural subjects throughout his life.

1939   *The Mercury Shakespeare,* revised edition of *Everybody's Shakespeare,* is published by Harper. *Five Kings,* OW's epic adaptation of Shakespeare's Falstaff-centered history plays, performs in Boston, Washington, D.C., and Philadelphia. In August, signs contract with RKO Pictures to write, produce, direct, and act in two films. Narrates and plays role of George Minafer in *Campbell* broadcast of his adaptation of Booth Tarkington's novel *The Magnificent Ambersons.*

Engages in pre-production work on *Heart of Darkness,* initially intended as his first RKO picture (unrealized). Appears on NBC's *Fred Allen Show,* and continues in subsequent years to guest-star regularly on popular radio variety programs.

1940   Three-part profile, "How to Raise a Child," published in *Saturday Evening Post.* OW and Virginia Nicolson Welles are divorced. Herman J. Mankiewicz, John Houseman, and a secretary spend two months in Victorville, California, working on a screenplay for OW's first RKO film, entitled, in turn, *Orson Welles #1; American;* and, finally, *Citizen Kane.* "Pat Hobby and Orson Welles," a short story by F. Scott Fitzgerald, is published in *Esquire* (May). Filming of *Citizen Kane* begins in July and is completed in October; editing and other post-production tasks continue. OW lectures on "The New Actor" in U.S. cities, including San Antonio, Texas, where he participates in *H. G. Wells Meets Orson Welles,* a radio conversation between the two men broadcast 28 October, almost two years to the day since the Mercury *War of the Worlds* dramatization.

1941   The convoluted controversy over *Citizen Kane's* alleged portrait of newspaper titan William Randolph Hearst erupts in the American press in January. Pressured by threats of libel suits and other efforts to suppress the film—including Louis B. Mayer's offer to buy all *Citizen Kane* prints in order to destroy them—RKO studio head George Schaefer stalls for time, delaying the release of the picture while marshaling support with covert screenings for select audiences. Mercury Theatre production of *Native Son,* adapted from Richard Wright's novel, directed by OW and co-produced by OW and John Houseman, opens on Broadway (March) to glowing reviews. Hearst newspapers allege that an OW radio play, *His Honor the Mayor,* contains Communist propaganda and that OW is himself a Communist sympathizer, thus triggering an OW FBI file which persists through the 1950s. *Citizen Kane* is released on 1 May to overwhelmingly positive reviews but to a disappointing box-office response from wary filmgoers intimidated by the picture's avant-garde reputation. Later nominated in nine Academy Award categories (including Best Picture, Director, and Actor), *Citizen Kane* wins only one for Best Original Screenplay; the award is

shared by OW and Herman Mankiewicz. With his companion
Dolores Del Rio serving as his aide, OW debuts professionally as
magician at county fairs and in theatres around the country (summer). *The Orson Welles Show* premieres on CBS radio in September,
continuing until February 1942. *The Magnificent Ambersons* enters
production.

1942   After completing principal shooting on *Ambersons* and his acting
role in *Journey into Fear,* OW spends six months in Rio de Janeiro
and other South American locales under State Department sponsorship making the omnibus film *It's All True,* but the project is
terminated. While he is in Rio, RKO re-cuts and re-shoots scenes
from *The Magnificent Ambersons* and releases the 132-minute film in
an 88-minute version despite OW's vain attempts to preserve his
picture's integrity. The studio also evicts OW's Mercury staff from
its premises and later destroys all deleted *Ambersons* footage. Upon
his return to U.S., OW resumes extensive radio work, including participation in NBC's stump-the-experts quiz show, *Information
Please.* Participates in "The Artists' Front to Win the War," a Carne-
gie Hall rally featuring Charlie Chaplin, Lillian Hellman, and other
celebrities.

1943   *Journey into Fear* is released. OW writes guest columns in the *New
York Post* and the first of twelve "editorials" for *Free World* magazine. Makes speech attacking racism at a Chicago rally. Guest hosts
The Jack Benny Program for several weeks. Directs, co-produces, and
stars in *The Mercury Wonder Show,* showcasing his magic tricks,
staged free-of-charge for wartime servicemen; films a segment from
this show for the picture *Follow the Boys.* Marries Rita Hayworth.
Jane Eyre is released.

1944   Begins a weekly CBS variety series entitled *Orson Welles Almanac.*
Makes numerous appearances for the Armed Forces Radio Service
which continue through the celebration of V-J Day. Campaigns
actively for Franklin D. Roosevelt's reelection as President, giving
speeches at rallies and on radio, and, in September, substituting for
FDR in a debate with his Republican opponent, Thomas Dewey.
Daughter Rebecca is born to OW and Rita Hayworth. Initiates

another radio program, *This Is My Best,* adaptations of published stories performed before a live audience.

1945   National lecture tour, "The Nature of the Enemy," on the topic of Fascism. From January to November, writes periodic column for the *New York Post* on a range of issues. Participates in CBS broadcasts mourning the death of FDR. While continuing his regular radio programs and guest appearances for other networks, he introduces *Orson Welles Commentaries,* a series of social and political essays for ABC. Completes shooting *The Stranger.*

1946   OW adapts Jules Verne's novel *Around the World in Eighty Days* as a lavish Broadway musical, which he also directs; music and lyrics are by Cole Porter. A considerable amount of film footage, shot and edited by OW, is integrated into the production, which opens in New York in May to mixed reviews. *Mercury Summer Theatre of the Air* (CBS) and numerous other radio appearances. *The Stranger* is released. Shooting begins on *The Lady from Shanghai.*

1947   Charlie Chaplin's film *Monsieur Verdoux,* "based on an idea by Orson Welles," is released. *Duel in the Sun,* narrated by OW, premieres. OW and Rita Hayworth divorce.

1948   *The Lady from Shanghai* and *Macbeth* are released. From 1948 to 1955 OW works almost exclusively outside the United States.

1949   *The Third Man,* from Graham Greene's novel, directed by Carol Reed and featuring OW as Harry Lime, wins Grand Prix at the Cannes Film Festival. OW accepts assorted acting roles primarily to fund his film adaptation of Shakespeare's *Othello,* which he is shooting in Italy and Morocco. Plagued by money woes, the *Othello* project falters in and out of production for another two years.

1950   *The Blessed and the Damned,* the collective title for two plays by OW in which he also appears, enjoys critical acclaim in Paris. Tours Germany in *An Evening with Orson Welles.*

1951   In London, initiates a BBC radio series, *The Adventures of Harry Lime,* prompted by his role in *The Third Man;* he appears in all thirty-nine episodes, several of which he also writes; the program is later broadcast in the U.S. Publishes article, "Thoughts on Germany," in the British journal *The Fortnightly.* Narrates another U.K. radio series, *The Black Museum,* with stories adapted from Scotland Yard files. Stars in *Othello,* a production directed by Laurence Olivier which plays at the St. James Theatre, London.

1952   Film of *Othello* is screened in May at the Cannes Film Festival, where it wins the Palme d'Or. OW co-stars (as Moriarty) with John Gielgud (as Holmes) and Ralph Richardson (as Watson) in "The Final Problem," the closing episode in a BBC radio adaptation of *Sherlock Holmes.*

1953   Works on projects in London, Rome and Paris, including a ballet, "The Lady in the Ice." Delivers lecture at the Edinburgh Film Festival. Returns briefly to the U.S. to make his first television appearance, playing the title role in Peter Brook's adaptation of Shakespeare's *King Lear* on CBS.

1954   Films *Mr. Arkadin* in various European locations. Plays roles in other pictures produced in Europe.

1955   *Mr. Arkadin* is released in March and, later, in London, under the title *Confidential Report. Orson Welles's Sketch Book,* a six-week series of television commentaries for the BBC, premieres in April. Begins to work on his film adaptation of Cervantes' novel *Don Quixote,* which he shoots and edits intermittently in Mexico and Europe for many years but does not complete. Marries Paola Mori in London. Adapts, directs, and plays multiple roles in *Moby Dick—Rehearsed,* a stage version of Melville's *Moby Dick,* at the Duke of York's Theatre, London. Films *Around the World with Orson Welles,* a series of travelogues shot in European locales for British television. Returns to the U.S. in October. Daughter Beatrice is born to OW and Paola Mori in New York.

1956   Directs and stars in production of *King Lear* staged at New York's City Center, playing most performances from a wheelchair as a result of a broken ankle. Performs a variety act for six weeks in Las Vegas, Nevada. Moves temporarily to Hollywood, OW's first visit there in many years. Acts in John Huston's film of *Moby Dick,* released in June. Appears in television drama and variety shows, including an episode of *I Love Lucy* entitled "Lucy Meets Orson Welles."

1957   Spends much of the year filming and editing *Touch of Evil.*

1958   *Touch of Evil* is released and wins the grand prize at the Brussels World's Fair Film Festival, where OW conducts a press conference. *The Long Hot Summer* and *The Roots of Heaven* are released. Directs his first film for television, *The Fountain of Youth,* which he also narrates; telecast on NBC's *Colgate Palmolive Theatre* (16 September); *Fountain of Youth* wins a Peabody Award for creative achievement.

1959   At the Cannes Film Festival, OW shares acting honors with his co-stars Dean Stockwell and Bradford Dillman for *Compulsion,* released in April. Narrates and acts in other films.

1960   Acts in several films, including *Crack in the Mirror* which is released this year. *Chimes at Midnight,* OW's stage composite of Shakespeare's Falstaff plays—*Henry IV, Parts 1 and 2,* and *Henry V,* with brief excerpts from *Richard II* and *The Merry Wives of Windsor*—is produced in Belfast and Dublin; the text reworks OW's *Five Kings* (1939) and is revised again by OW for a forthcoming film version. Directs avant-garde playwright Eugene Ionesco's *Rhinoceros,* starring Laurence Olivier, which opens at the Royal Court Theatre, in London and, following critical acclaim, moves to the West End.

1962   While shooting *The Trial,* his adaptation of Franz Kafka's novel, OW meets Olga Palinkas (renamed Oja Kodar), who later becomes his lifelong companion and professional collaborator. *The Trial* is released in December.

1966   *Chimes at Midnight,* also distributed under the title *Falstaff,* is released. Films *The Immortal Story* in Paris and Madrid. *A Man for All Seasons* is released.

1968–71   *The Immortal Story (Une Histoire immortelle)* is released simultaneously in France in movie houses and on television. Spends much time in Europe filming *Orson's Bag,* a CBS television special which never airs. Along with considerable other material shot for that aborted telecast, OW completes a condensed color adaptation of Shakespeare's *Merchant of Venice* (1969), in which he also plays Shylock. Guest stars on American television variety and talk shows, as he will continue to do frequently until his death. Narrates and appears in numerous films, including adaptations of Sophocles' play *Oedipus the King* and Joseph Heller's novel *Catch-22*. Works on *The Deep*, which is nearly completed but never released. Begins working on *The Other Side of the Wind*, a project he pursues until 1976 but does not complete. Receives a special Academy Award for "superlative artistry and versatility in the creation of motion pictures" (1970). Publication of Pauline Kael's "Raising Kane" (1971) triggers intense debate on *Citizen Kane* authorship.

1972   Stars in television production of Kaufman and Hart's comedy *The Man Who Came to Dinner* for NBC.

1974   *F for Fake*, shot in France and the U.S. in 1973, opens at film festivals in New York and London.

1975   OW is honored by the American Film Institute with its Life Achievement Award. At the tribute, telecast on CBS as *The American Film Institute Salute to Orson Welles*, clips from *The Other Side of the Wind* are screened. Moves to Beverly Hills.

1976   The last year OW works on the heavily autobiographical *Other Side of the Wind*, the most stylistically and thematically promising of his uncompleted projects. Although actual shooting and a good deal of the editing are completed, ensuing efforts to release the footage are stymied by legal and other entanglements.

1978   OW is honored by the Directors Guild of America, in Hollywood. *Filming Othello*, intermittently shot and edited since 1974, premieres at the Berlin Film Festival.

1980   Begins shooting *The Dreamers*, based on stories by Isak Dinesen; filming continues sporadically for several years but the picture is uncompleted. OW's film of *Macbeth* is restored.

1982   President François Mitterand appoints OW a Commander of the

French Legion of Honor, in a Paris ceremony. *The Orson Welles Story*, a two-part BBC documentary, is telecast in the U.K. Delivers speech at an antinuclear rally in Central Park. With Oja Kodar, completes screenplay for *The Big Brass Ring*, posthumously published in 1987; the screenplay is eventually filmed by George Hickenlooper and released under the same title in 1999.

1984   Invited to direct *Rocking the Cradle*, a film dramatizing events surrounding the 1937 production of *The Cradle Will Rock*, OW spends six months revising the screenplay while production plans proceed, but financing collapses. The OW screenplay is posthumously published in 1994. Another version of the *Cradle* story, written and directed by Tim Robbins, is eventually filmed under the title *The Cradle Will Rock* and released in 1999.

1985   On 10 October, following an appearance on a television talk show the previous evening, OW dies of a heart attack at his Hollywood home. In the years since his death, restored or reconstructed versions of *Othello, Touch of Evil, It's All True,* and *Don Quixote* have been released. The original OW screenplay for *The Magnificent Ambersons* has been reconstructed, published, and newly re-filmed for cable television. Similar projects continue.

FILMOGRAPHY

As Director

1934
THE HEARTS OF AGE
Producer: William Vance
Directors: **Orson Welles**, William Vance
Screenplay: **Orson Welles**
Cinematography: William Vance
Cast: **Orson Welles** (Death), Virginia Nicolson, William Vance, Edgerton
Paul, students at the Todd School
16mm, B&W
5 minutes

1938, uncompleted
TOO MUCH JOHNSON
Mercury Theatre
Producer: **Orson Welles**, John Houseman
Director: **Orson Welles**
Screenplay: **Orson Welles**, from the play by William Gillette
Cinematography: Harry Dunham, Paul Dunbar
Editors: **Orson Welles**, William Alland, Richard Wilson
Cast: Joseph Cotten (Augustus Billings), Anna Stafford [Virginia Nicolson]
(Lenore Faddish), Edgar Barrier (Leon Dathis), Arlene Francis (Mrs. Dathis),
Ruth Ford (Mrs. Billings), Mary Wickes (Mrs. Battison), Eustace Wyatt (Fad-
dish), Guy Kingsley (MacIntosh), George Duthie (purser), **Orson Welles**

(Keystone Kop), John Berry, Howard Smith, Augusta Weissberger, John
Houseman, Marc Blitzstein, Herbert Drake, Richard Wilson, Judith Tuvim
[Judy Holliday]
16mm, B&W
40 minutes
Intended for incorporation into a planned Mercury Theatre stage production
of *Too Much Johnson,* which was canceled. Unedited; never publicly screened;
sole copy of completed footage destroyed in fire at Orson Welles's home in
Madrid in 1970.

1941
CITIZEN KANE
Mercury Productions / RKO Radio Pictures
Producer: **Orson Welles**
Director: **Orson Welles**
Screenplay: Herman J. Mankiewicz, **Orson Welles,** (John Houseman, uncred-
ited)
Cinematography: Gregg Toland
Art Director: Van Nest Polglase
Editor: Robert Wise
Music: Bernard Herrmann
Costumes: Edward Stevenson
Cast: **Orson Welles** (Charles Foster Kane), Joseph Cotten (Jedediah Leland;
also newsreel reporter), Everett Sloane (Bernstein), Dorothy Comingore
(Susan Alexander Kane), Ray Collins (James W. Gettys), William Alland (Jerry
Thompson; also newsreel narrator), Agnes Moorehead (Mary Kane), Ruth
Warrick (Emily Monroe Norton Kane), George Coulouris (Walter Parks
Thatcher), Erskine Sanford (Herbert Carter; newsreel reporter), Harry Shan-
non (Jim Kane), Philip Van Zandt (Rawlston), Paul Stewart (Raymond), For-
tunio Bonanova (Matisti), Georgia Backus (Bertha Anderson, curator of
Thatcher Library), Buddy Swan (Charles Foster Kane, age 8), Sonny Bupp,
(Charles Foster Kane, Jr.), Gus Schilling (head waiter), Richard Baer (Hill-
man), Joan Blair (Georgia), Al Eben (Mike), Charles Bennett (entertainer),
Milt Kibbee (reporter), Tom Curran (Theodore Roosevelt), Irving Mitchell
(Dr. Corey), Edith Evanson (nurse), Arthur Kay (orchestra leader), Tudor Wil-
liams (chorus master), Herbert Corthell (city editor), Benny Rubin (Smather),
Edmund Cobb (reporter), Frances Neal (Ethel), Robert Dudley (photogra-

pher), Ellen Lowe (Miss Townsend), Gino Corrado (Gino, the waiter), Alan
Ladd, Louise Currie, Eddie Coke, Walter Sande, Arthur O'Connell, Katherine
Trosper, and Richard Wilson (reporters), Gregg Toland (newsreel interviewer), Herman J. Mankiewicz (newspaperman), Jean Forward (Susan Alexander's singing voice)
B&W
119 minutes

1942
THE MAGNIFICENT AMBERSONS
Mercury Productions / RKO Radio Pictures
Producer: **Orson Welles**
Director: **Orson Welles** (additional scenes directed by Robert Wise, Freddie
Fleck, and Jack Moss)
Screenplay: **Orson Welles** (additional scenes written by Jack Moss and
Joseph Cotten), from the novel by Booth Tarkington
Cinematography: Stanley Cortez
Art Director: Mark-Lee Kirk
Editor: Robert Wise
Music: Bernard Herrmann
Costumes: Edward Stevenson
Cast: **Orson Welles** (narrator), Tim Holt (George Amberson Minafer), Joseph
Cotten (Eugene Morgan), Dolores Costello (Isabel Amberson Minafer), Agnes
Moorehead (Fanny Minafer), Anne Baxter (Lucy Morgan), Ray Collins (Jack
Amberson), Richard Bennett (Major Amberson), Don Dillaway (Wilbur
Minafer), Erskine Sanford (Roger Bronson), J. Louis Johnson (Sam, the but-
ler), Charles Phipps (Uncle John Minafer), Dorothy Vaughn (Mrs. Johnson),
Ann O'Neal (Mrs. Foster), Elmer Jerome, Maynard Holmes, Edwin August,
Jack Baxley, Harry Humphrey (townspeople), Jack Santoro (barber), Lyle
Clement, Joe Whitehead, Del Lawrence (men in barbershop), Katherine Shel-
don, Georgia Backus (women in sewing room), Bobby Cooper (George as a
boy), Heenan Elliott (terrorized laborer), Drew Roddy (Elijah), Bert LeBaron,
Jim Fawcet, Gil Perkins (idle men), Henry Rocquemore (man in apron), Nina
Gilbert, John Elliot (ball guests), Helen Thurston (Lucy's stunt person), Dave
Sharp (George's stunt person), Jess Graves (servant in dining room scene),
Olive Ball (Mary, the maid), Gus Schilling (drugstore clerk), James Westerfield
(Irish policeman), William Blees (young driver at accident), Philip Morris

(second policeman), Hilda Plowright (nurse), Billy Elmer (house servant); [in deleted scenes] Mel Ford (Fred Kinney), Bob Pittard (Charlie Johnson), Ken Stewart (club member), Ed Howard (Eugene's driver), Lil Nicholson (boarding house landlady), B. Emery (man in boarding house)
B&W
88 minutes (originally 131 minutes)

1942; revised 1943
JOURNEY INTO FEAR
Mercury Productions / RKO Radio Pictures
Producer: **Orson Welles**
Director: Norman Foster (and **Orson Welles**, uncredited)
Screenplay: Joseph Cotten (and **Orson Welles**, uncredited), from the novel by Eric Ambler
Cinematography: Karl Struss
Art Directors: Albert D'Agostino, Mark-Lee Kirk
Editor: Mark Robson
Music: Roy Webb
Costumes: Edward Stevenson
Cast: Joseph Cotten (Howard Graham), Dolores Del Rio (Josette Martel), **Orson Welles** (Colonel Haki), Ruth Warrick (Stephanie Graham), Agnes Moorehead (Mrs. Mathews), Everett Sloane (Kopeikin), Jack Moss (Banat), Jack Durant (Gogo), Eustace Wyatt (Dr. Haller), Frank Readick (Mathews), Edgar Barrier (Kuvetli), Stefan Schnabel (purser), Hans Conreid (Oo Lang Sang, the magician), Robert Meltzer (steward), Richard Bennett (ship's captain), Shifra Haran (Mrs. Haklet), Herbert Drake, Bill Roberts
B&W
69 minutes (originally 91 minutes)

1946
THE STRANGER
Haig Corporation / International Pictures / RKO Pictures
Producer: S. P. Eagle [Sam Spiegel]
Director: **Orson Welles**
Screenplay; Anthony Veiller (and John Huston, **Orson Welles**, uncredited)
Cinematography: Russell Metty

Art Director: Perry Ferguson
Editor: Ernest Nims
Music: Bronislaw Kaper
Costumes: Michael Woulfe
Cast: **Orson Welles** (Franz Kindler, alias Charles Rankin), Loretta Young (Mary Longstreet), Edward G. Robinson (Inspector Wilson), Philip Merivale (Judge Longstreet), Richard Long (Noah Longstreet), Byron Keith (Dr. Lawrence), Billy House (Mr. Potter), Martha Wentworth (Sarah), Konstantin Shayne (Konrad Meinike), Theodore Gottlieb (Farbright in cut scenes), Pietro Sosso (Mr. Peabody), Isabel O'Madigan
B&W
95 minutes (originally 115 minutes)

1948
THE LADY FROM SHANGHAI
Columbia
Executive Producer: Harry Cohn
Director: **Orson Welles**
Screenplay: **Orson Welles** (and William Castle, Fletcher Markle, Charles Lederer, uncredited), from the novel *If I Die Before I Wake* by Sherwood King
Cinematography: Charles Lawton, Jr. (and Rudolph Maté, Joseph Walker, uncredited)
Art Directors: Stephen Goosson, Sturges Carne
Editor: Viola Lawrence
Music: Heinz Roemheld
Costumes: Jean Louis
Cast: **Orson Welles** (Michael O'Hara), Rita Hayworth (Elsa Bannister), Everett Sloane (Arthur Bannister), Glenn Anders (George Grisby), Ted de Corsia (Sidney Broom), Gus Schilling (Goldie), Louis Merrill (Jake), Erskine Sanford (judge), Carl Frank (District Attorney Galloway), Evelyn Ellis (Bessie), Wong Show Chong (Li), Harry Shannon (horse cab driver), Sam Nelson (captain), Richard Wilson (district attorney's assistant), Mandarin Theatre of San Francisco Players
B&W
86 minutes

1948; restored 1980
MACBETH
Mercury Productions / Literary Classics Productions / Republic Pictures
Executive Producer: Charles K. Feldman
Producer: **Orson Welles**
Director: **Orson Welles**
Screenplay: **Orson Welles,** from the play by William Shakespeare
Cinematography: John L. Russell
Art Director: Fred Ritter
Editor: Louis Lindsay
Music: Jacques Ibert
Costumes: **Orson Welles,** Fred Ritter, Adele Palmer
Cast: **Orson Welles** (Macbeth), Jeanette Nolan (Lady Macbeth), Dan O'Her-
lihy (Macduff), Edgar Barrier (Banquo), Roddy McDowall (Malcolm), Erskine
Sanford (Duncan), Alan Napier (a Holy Father), John Dierkes (Ross), Keene
Curtis (Lennox), Peggy Webber (Lady Macduff / witch), Lionel Braham
(Siward), Archie Heugly (Young Siward), Christopher Welles (Macduff child),
Brainerd Duffield (1st murderer / witch), William Alland (2nd murderer),
George Chirello (Seyton), Gus Schilling (porter), Jerry Farber (Fleance), Lur-
ene Tuttle (gentlewoman / witch), Charles Lederer (witch), Robert Alan (3rd
murderer), Morgan Farley (doctor)
B&W
107 minutes (later shortened to 86 minutes; restored to original length in
1980)

1952; restored 1992
OTHELLO
Mercury Productions / Marceau Films / United Artists
Producer: **Orson Welles**
Director: **Orson Welles**
Screenplay: **Orson Welles,** from the play by William Shakespeare
Cinematography: Anchise Brizzi, G. R. Aldo, George Fanto, with Obadan
Troiani, Alberto Fusi
Art Director: Alexandre Trauner
Editors: Jean Sacha, John Shepridge, Renzo Lucidi, William Morton
Music: Alberto Francesco Lavagnino, Alberto Barberis
Costumes: Maria de Matteis

Cast: **Orson Welles** (Othello / narrator), Micheál MacLiammóir (Iago), Suzanne Cloutier (Desdemona), Robert Coote (Roderigo), Michael Laurence (Cassio), Hilton Edwards (Brabantio), Fay Compton (Emilia), Nicholas Bruce (Lodovico), Jean David (Montano), Doris Dowling (Bianca), Joseph Cotten (senator), Joan Fontaine (page), Abdullah Ben Mohamet (page to Desdemona)
B&W
91 minutes

1955
MR. ARKADIN (released in Britain as CONFIDENTIAL REPORT)
Mercury Productions / Filmorsa / Cervantes Films / Sevilla Film Studios
Executive Producer: Louis Dolivet
Director: **Orson Welles**
Screenplay: **Orson Welles**
Cinematography: Jean Bourgoin
Editor: Renzo Lucidi
Art Director: **Orson Welles**
Music: Paul Misraki
Costumes: **Orson Welles**
Cast: **Orson Welles** (Gregory Arkadin / narrator), Paola Mori (Raina Arkadin), Robert Arden (Guy Van Stratten), Akim Tamiroff (Jacob Zouk), Michael Redgrave (Burgomil Trebitsch), Patricia Medina (Mily), Mischa Auer (The Professor), Katina Paxinou (Sophie), Jack Watling (Marquis of Rutleigh), Gregoire Aslan (Bracco), Peter Van Eyck (Thaddeus), Suzanne Flon (Baroness Nagel), Tamara Shane (woman in apartment), Frédéric O'Brady (Oskar), and Gert Frobe
B&W
100 minutes

1958, telecast
THE FOUNTAIN OF YOUTH
Welles Enterprise / Desilu
Executive Producer: Desi Arnaz
Director: **Orson Welles**
Screenplay: **Orson Welles**, from the short story "Youth from Vienna" by John Collier

Cinematography: Sidney Hickcox
Art Director: Claudio Guzman
Editor: Bud Molin
Cast: **Orson Welles** (host / narrator), Dan Tobin (Humphrey Baxter), Joi Lansing (Carolyn Coates), Richard Jason (Alan Brody), Billy House (Albert Morgan), Nancy Kulp (Mrs. Morgan), Marjorie Bennett (journalist)
B&W
25 minutes

1958; restored 1975; re-edited and restored 1998
TOUCH OF EVIL
Universal-International
Producer: Albert Zugsmith
Director: **Orson Welles** (with Harry Keller, uncredited)
Screenplay: **Orson Welles** (additional scenes written by Franklin Coen, uncredited), from a screenplay (by Paul Monash, uncredited) adaptation of the novel *Badge of Evil* by Whit Masterson
Cinematography: Russell Metty
Art Directors: Alexander Golitzen, Robert Clatworthy
Editors: Virgil W. Vogel, Aaron Stell (with Edward Curtiss and Ernest Nims, uncredited)
Music: Henry Mancini
Costumes: Bill Thomas
Cast: **Orson Welles** (Hank Quinlan), Charlton Heston (Ramon Miguel "Mike" Vargas), Janet Leigh (Susan Vargas), Joseph Calleia (Pete Menzies), Akim Tamiroff ("Uncle Joe" Grandi), Valentin De Vargas ("Pancho"), Ray Collins (District Attorney Adair), Dennis Weaver (motel clerk, "The Night Man"), Joanna Moore (Marcia Linnekar), Mort Mills (Schwartz), Marlene Dietrich (Tanya), Victor Millan (Manolo Sanchez), Lalo Rios (Risto), Michael Sargent (Pretty Boy), Mercedes McCambridge (gang leader), Joseph Cotten (coroner), Zsa Zsa Gabor (manager of strip club), Phil Harvey (Blaine), Joi Lansing (Zita), Harry Shannon (Police Chief Gould), Rusty Wescoatt (Casey), Gus Schilling (Eddie Farnham), Wayne Taylor, Ken Miller, Raymond Rodriguez (gang members), Arlene McQuade (Ginnie), Domenick Delgarde (lackey), Joe Basulto (young delinquent), Jennie Dias (Jackie), Yolanda Bojorquez (Bobbie), Eleanor Dorado (Lia), John Dierkes (plainclothes cop)
B&W
93 minutes (1975 and 1998 versions: 108 minutes)

1962
THE TRIAL
Paris-Europa Productions / Hisa Films / FI-C-IT / Globus-Dubrava
Producers: Alexander Salkind, Michael Salkind
Director: **Orson Welles**
Screenplay: **Orson Welles**, from the novel by Franz Kafka
Cinematography: Edmond Richard
Art Director: Jean Mandaroux
Editors: Yvonne Martin, Denise Baby, Fritz Mueller
Music: Jean Ledrut (*Adagio for Organ and Strings* by Tomaso Albinoni and,
uncredited, jazz by Martial Solal, Daniel Humair)
Costumes: Hélène Thibault
Cast: Anthony Perkins (Joseph K.), **Orson Welles** (Hastler, the Advocate),
Jeanne Moreau (Miss Burstner), Romy Schneider (Leni), Elsa Martinelli
(Hilda), Suzanne Flon (Miss Pittl), Madeleine Robinson (Mrs. Grubach), Akim
Tamiroff (Block), Arnoldo Foa (inspector), Fernand Ledoux (clerk of the
court), Maurice Teynac (director of K.'s office), Billy Kearns (1st police officer),
Jess Hahn (2nd police officer), William Chappell (Titorelli), Raoul Delfosse,
Karl Studer, Jean-Claude Romoleux (executioners), Wolfgang Reichmann
(usher), Thomas Holtzmann (student), Maydra Shore (Irmie), Max Haufler
(Uncle Max), Michel Lonsdale (priest), Max Buchsbaum (judge), Paola Mori
(librarian), Van Doude (archivist), Katina Paxinou (scientist in cut scenes)
B&W
120 minutes

1966
CHIMES AT MIDNIGHT (released in U.S. as *Falstaff;* in Spain as *Campanadas
a medianoche*)
Internacional Films Española / Alpine Productions
Executive Producers: Alessandro Tasca di Cuto; Harry Saltzman
Producers: Emiliano Piedra, Angel Escolano
Director: **Orson Welles**
Screenplay: **Orson Welles**, adapted from plays by William Shakespeare *(Rich-
ard II, Henry IV Parts I and II, Henry V,* and *The Merry Wives of Windsor);* narra-
tion drawn from *The Chronicles of England* by Raphael Holinshed
Cinematography: Edmond Richard
Art Directors: José Antonio de la Guerra, Mariano Erdorza

Editor: Fritz Mueller
Music: Alberto Francesco Lavagnino
Costumes: **Orson Welles**
Cast: **Orson Welles** (Sir John Falstaff), Keith Baxter (Prince Hal, later King Henry V), John Gielgud (King Henry IV), Jeanne Moreau (Doll Tearsheet), Margaret Rutherford (Mistress Quickly), Norman Rodway (Henry Percy, called Hotspur), Marina Vlady (Kate Percy), Alan Webb (Justice Shallow), Walter Chiari (Silence), Michael Aldrich (Pistol), Tony Beckley (Poins), Fernando Rey (Worcester), Andrew Faulds (Westmoreland), José Nieto (Northumberland), Jeremy Rowe (Prince John), Beatrice Welles (Falstaff's page), Paddy Bedford (Bardolph), Julio Peña, Fernando Hilbeck, Andrés Mejuto, Keith Pyott, Charles Farrell
B&W
119 minutes

1968
THE IMMORTAL STORY (world premiere in France, where it was televised and released in theatres simultaneously as *Une Histoire immortelle*)
ORTF / Albina Films
Producer: Micheline Rozan
Director: **Orson Welles**
Screenplay: **Orson Welles,** from the novella by Isak Dinesen
Cinematography: Willy Kurant
Art Director: André Piltant
Editors: Yolande Maurette, Marcelle Pluet, Françoise Garnault, Claude Farny
Music: Erik Satie
Costumes: Pierre Cardin
Cast: **Orson Welles** (Mr. Clay / narrator), Jeanne Moreau (Virginie Ducrot), Roger Coggio (Elishama Levinsky), Norman Eshley (Paul), Fernando Rey (merchant)
COLOR
58 minutes

1967–69, uncompleted
THE DEEP
Producer: **Orson Welles**
Director: **Orson Welles**

Screenplay: **Orson Welles**, from the novel *Dead Calm* by Charles Williams
Cinematography: Willy Kurant, Ivica Rajkovic
Cast: Laurence Harvey (Hughie Warriner), Jeanne Moreau (Ruth Warriner),
Orson Welles (Russ Brewer), Oja Kodar (Rae Ingram), Michael Bryant (John
Ingram)
COLOR

1969; filmed for television; completed but never fully screened
THE MERCHANT OF VENICE
Director: **Orson Welles**
Screenplay: **Orson Welles**, condensed from the play by William Shakespeare
Cinematography: Giorgio Tonti, Ivica Rajkovic, and Tomislav Pinter
Cast: **Orson Welles** (Shylock), Charles Gray (Antonio), Irena Maleva (Jessica)
COLOR
40 minutes

1970–76, uncompleted
THE OTHER SIDE OF THE WIND
SACI / Les Films de l'Astrophore
Producer: Dominique Antoine
Director: **Orson Welles**
Screenplay: **Orson Welles**, Oja Kodar
Cinematography: Gary Graver
Cast: **Orson Welles** (narrator); John Huston (Jake Hannaford), Peter Bogda-
novich (Brooks Otterlake), Norman Foster (Billy Boyle), Howard Grossman
(Charles Higgam), Oja Kodar (The Actress), Geoffrey Land (Max David),
Cathy Lucas (Mavis Henscher), Joseph McBride (Mr. Pister), Mercedes
McCambridge (Maggie), Cameron Mitchell (Zimmer), Edmond O'Brien (Pat),
Lilli Palmer (Zarah Valeska), Bob Random (John Dale), Benny Rubin (Abe
Vogel), Tonio Selwart (The Baron), Gregory Sierra (Jack Simon), Susan Stras-
berg (Juliette Rich), Paul Stewart (Matt Costello), Dan Tobin (Dr. Bradley
Pease Burroughs), Cassie Yates (Cassie), Gene Clark (projectionist), Stéphane
Audran, John Carroll, Claude Chabrol, Gary Graver, Curtis Harrington,
Felipe Herba, Dennis Hopper, Henry Jaglom, Peter Jason, Paul Mazursky, Eric
Sherman, Richard Wilson
COLOR AND B&W

1974
F FOR FAKE
SACI / Les Films de l'Astrophore / Janus Film und Fernsehen
Producers: Dominique Antoine, François Reichenbach
Director: **Orson Welles**, with material from an earlier film by François
Reichenbach
Screenplay: **Orson Welles**, Oja Kodar
Cinematography: Christian Odasso, Gary Graver
Editors: Marie-Sophie Dubus, Dominique Engerer
Music: Michel Legrand
Costumes: Oja Kodar
Cast: **Orson Welles**, Oja Kodar, Elmyr de Hory, Clifford Irving, Edith Irving,
François Reichenbach, Joseph Cotten, Richard Drewett, Laurence Harvey,
Jean-Pierre Aumont, Nina Van Pallandt, Richard Wilson, Paul Stewart, How-
ard Hughes, Gary Graver, Sašsa Devcic, Andrées Vincent Gomez, Julio Palin-
kas, Christian Odasso, François Widoff (as themselves), offscreen voices of
Peter Bogdanovich, William Alland
16mm, COLOR
85 minutes

1978
FILMING *OTHELLO*
Producers: Klaus Hellwig, Juergen Hellwig
Director: **Orson Welles**
Screenplay: **Orson Welles**
Cinematography: Gary Graver
Editor: Marty Roth
Music: Francesco Lavagnino, Alberto Barbaris
Cast: **Orson Welles**, Micheál MacLiammóir, Hilton Edwards, others from the
1952 *Othello*
COLOR AND B&W
84 minutes

1978–85
THE DREAMERS, uncompleted
Director: **Orson Welles**
Screenplay: **Orson Welles**, from stories by Isak Dinesen

Cinematography: Gary Graver
Cast: **Orson Welles** (Marcus Kleek), Oja Kodar (Pellegrina), other roles not cast
COLOR
About 20 minutes of footage shot

filmed 1955–73; the uncompleted film is released 1992
DON QUIXOTE (also released as DON QUIXOTE BY ORSON WELLES)
  Original Shoot
Producer: Oscar Dancigers
Director: **Orson Welles**
Screenplay: **Orson Welles**, from the novel by Miguel de Cervantes
Cinematography: José Garcia Galisteo, Juan Manuel de Lachica, Edmond Richard, Jack Draper, Ricardo Navarette, Manuel Mateos, Giorgio Tonti, Gary Graver
Editors: Maurizio Lucidi, Renzo Lucidi, Peter Parasheles, Ira Wohl, Alberto Valenzuela
  Released Version
Production company: El Silencio
Producer: Patxi Irigoyen
Editors: Jess Franco, Rosa Maria Almirall, Fatima Michalczik
Dialogue adaptation: Javier Mina, Jess Franco
Music: Daniel J. White
General Supervisor: Oja Kodar
Cast: Francisco Reiguera (Don Quixote), Akim Tamiroff (Sancho Panza), Patty McCormack (Dulcinea), **Orson Welles** (himself; narrator), Dubbing: **Orson Welles**, José Mediavilla (voices of Don Quixote), **Orson Welles**, Juan Carlos Ordonez (voices of Sancho Panza)
B&W
118 minutes

filmed 1942; released 1993 (a documentary and partial restoration of **Orson Welles**'s uncompleted three-part film *It's All True*)
IT'S ALL TRUE: BASED ON AN UNFINISHED FILM BY ORSON WELLES
  Original shoot of IT'S ALL TRUE
Mercury Productions, for the U.S. State Department Coordinator of Inter-American Affairs and RKO Radio
Executive Producers: Nelson Rockefeller, George Schaefer

Producer: **Orson Welles**
Director: **Orson Welles**, Norman Foster (*Bonito* episode)
Cinematography: W. Howard Greene
Editor: José Noriega
Script: **Orson Welles**, Norman Foster, John Fante
  FOUR MEN ON A RAFT
Director: **Orson Welles**
Cinematography: George Fanto
Cast: Manuel (Jacaré) Olimpio Meira, Jeronimo André de Souza, Raimundo (Tatá) Correia Lima, Manuel (Preto) Pereira da Silva (the jangadeiros), Francisca Moreira da Silva (young bride), José Sobrinho (her husband)
  THE STORY OF SAMBA (CARNAVAL)
Director: **Orson Welles**
Screenplay: Robert Meltzer
Cinematography: Harry J. Wild
Cast: Grande Othelo, Pery Ribeiro (performers)
  MY FRIEND BONITO
Producer: **Orson Welles**
Director: Norman Foster
Story: Robert Flaherty
Cinematography: Floyd Crosby
Cast: Jesús Vásquez (Chico)
  released version of IT'S ALL TRUE: BASED ON AN UNFINISHED FILM BY ORSON WELLES
Paramount Pictures / Les Films Balenciaga / The French Ministry of Education and Culture / French National Center for Cinematography / Canal + / R. Films / La Fondation GAN pour le Cinema
Producers: Régine Konckier, Richard Wilson, Bill Krohn, Myron Meisel, Jean-Luc Ormieres
Associate Producer/ Senior Research Executive: Catherine Benamou
Directors: Richard Wilson, Myron Meisel, Bill Krohn
Screenplay: Bill Krohn, Richard Wilson, Myron Meisel
Cinematography: Gary Graver
Editor: Ed Marx
Music: Jorge Arriagada
Narrator: Miguel Ferrer

COLOR AND B&W
86 minutes

As Actor Only

JANE EYRE (1943) As Rochester; d. Robert Stevenson
FOLLOW THE BOYS (1944) As Himself; d. Edward Sutherland
TOMORROW IS FOREVER (1945) As Erich Kessler / John MacDonald;
d. Irving Pichel
BLACK MAGIC (1947) As Cagliostro; d. Gregory Ratoff
PRINCE OF FOXES (1948) As Cesare Borgia; d. Henry King
THE THIRD MAN (1949) As Harry Lime; d. Carol Reed
THE BLACK ROSE (1950) As General Bayan; d. Henry Hathaway
RETURN TO GLENNASCAUL (1951) As Himself; d. Hilton Edwards
TRENT'S LAST CASE (1953) As Sigsbee Manderson; d. Herbert Wilcox
SI VERSAILLES M'ÉTAIT CONTÉ (1953) As Benjamin Franklin; d. Sacha Guitry
L'UOMO, LA BESTIA E LA VIRTÙ (1953) As the Beast; d. Stefano Vanzina
NAPOLEON (1954) As Hudson Lowe; d. Sacha Guitry
TROUBLE IN THE GLEN (1954) As Samin Cejador y Mengues; d. Herbert
Wilcox
THREE CASES OF MURDER (1954) As Lord Mountdrago; episode d. George
More O'Ferrall
MOBY DICK (1956) As Father Mapple; d. John Huston
MAN IN THE SHADOW (1957) As Virgil Renchler; d. Jack Arnold
THE LONG HOT SUMMER (1958) As Will Varner; d. Martin Ritt
THE ROOTS OF HEAVEN (1958) As Cy Sedgwick; d. John Huston
COMPULSION (1959) As Jonathan Wilk; d. Richard Fleischer
FERRY TO HONG KONG (1959) As Captain Hart; d. Lewis Gilbert
DAVID AND GOLIATH (1959) As Saul; d. Richard Pottier, Fernando Baldi
AUSTERLITZ (1960) As Fulton; d. Abel Gance
CRACK IN THE MIRROR (1960) As Hagolin / Lamorcière; d. Richard Fleischer
THE TARTARS (1960) As Burundai; d. Richard Thorpe
LAFAYETTE (1961) As Benjamin Franklin; d. Jean Dreville
ROGOPAG (1963) As the Director; episode d. Pier Paolo Pasolini
THE V.I.P.S (1963) As Max Buda; d. Anthony Asquith
MARCO THE MAGNIFICENT (1964) As Ackermann; d. Denys de la Patellière,
Noël Howard

IS PARIS BURNING? (1966) As Consul Raoul Nordling; d. René Clément

A MAN FOR ALL SEASONS (1966) As Cardinal Wolsey; d. Fred Zinnemann

THE SAILOR FROM GIBRALTAR (1967) As Louis from Mozambique; d. Tony Richardson

CASINO ROYALE (1967) As Le Chiffre; episode d. Joseph McGrath

I'LL NEVER FORGET WHAT'S 'IS NAME (1968) As Jonathan Lute; d. Michael Winner

OEDIPUS THE KING (1968) As Tiresias; d. Phillip Saville

THE LAST ROMAN (1968) As Emperor Justinian; d. Robert Siodmak

HOUSE OF CARDS (1969) As Charles Leschenhaut; d. John Guillermin

THE SOUTHERN STAR (1969) As Plankett; d. Sidney Hayers

TEPEPA [*VIVA LA REVOLUCIÓN*] (1969) As General Cascorro; d. Giulio Petroni

THE BATTLE OF NERETVA (1969) As Senator; d. Veljko Bulajic

MIHAI VITIEAZU [MICHAEL THE BRAVE] (1969) role; d. Sergui Nicolaescu

12 + 1 (1969) As Markau; d. Nicholas Gessner

THE KREMLIN LETTER (1970) As Aleksai Bresnavitch; d. John Huston

START THE REVOLUTION WITHOUT ME (1970) As Himself / Narrator; d. Bud Yorkin

CATCH-22 (1970) As General Dreedle; d. Mike Nichols

WATERLOO (1970) As Louis XVIII; d. Sergei Bondarchuk

UPON THIS ROCK (1970) As Michelangelo; d. Harry Rasky

MALPERTIUS (1971) As Uncle Cassavius; d. Harry Kumel

A SAFE PLACE (1971) As Magician; d. Henry Jaglom

LA DÉCADE PRODIGIEUSE [TEN DAYS' WONDER] (1971) As Theo Van Horn; d. Claude Chabrol

THE CANTERBURY TALES (1971) As Old January; d. Pier Paolo Pasolini

GET TO KNOW YOUR RABBIT (1972) As Mr. Delasandro; d. Brian de Palma

SUTJESKA (1972) As Winston Churchill; d. Stipe Delic

THE TOY FACTORY [NECROMANCY / THE WITCHING] (1972) As Mr. Cato; d. Bert Gordon

TREASURE ISLAND (1973) As Long John Silver; d. John Hough, Andrea Bianchi; includes material shot in 1965, d. Jesus Franco. Screenplay credited to Wolf Mankowitz and O.W. Jeeves [**Orson Welles**] from the novel by Robert Louis Stevenson

VOYAGE OF THE DAMNED (1976) As Raoul Estedes; d. Stuart Rosenberg

NEVER TRUST AN HONEST THIEF [GOING FOR BROKE / HOT MONEY] (1979) As Sheriff Paisley; d. George McCowan. Never released.

THE MUPPET MOVIE (1979) As Lew Lord; d. James Frawley

THE DOUBLE MCGUFFIN (1979) As Himself; d. Joe Camp

THE SECRET OF NIKOLA TESLA (1980) As J. P. Morgan; d. Krsto Papic

BUTTERFLY (1981) As Judge Rauch; d. Matt Cimber

THE MUPPETS TAKE MANHATTAN (1982) As Himself; d. Frank Oz

WHERE IS PARSIFAL? (1984) As Klingsor; d. Henri Helman

THE TRANSFORMERS (1986) As voice of Planet Unicron; d. Nelson Shin

SOMEONE TO LOVE (1987) As Himself; d. Henry Jaglom. The film is "dedicated with love to **Orson Welles.**"

As Narrator Only

SWISS FAMILY ROBINSON (1940) d. Edward Ludwig

DUEL IN THE SUN (1947) d. King Vidor

OUT OF DARKNESS (1955) d. Albert Wasserman

LE SEIGNEURS DE LA FORÊT [LORDS OF THE FOREST] (1956) d. Henry Brandt, Heinz Sielmann

THE VIKINGS (1958) d. Richard Fleischer

HIGH JOURNEY (1959) d. Peter Baylis

SOUTH SEAS ADVENTURE (1959) d. Carl Dudley

KING OF KINGS (1961) d. Nicholas Ray

DER GROSSER ATLANTIK [RIVER OF THE OCEAN] (1962) d. Peter Baylis

THE FINEST HOURS (1963) d. Peter Baylis

A KING'S STORY (1965) d. Harry Booth

AROUND THE WORLD OF MIKE TODD (1968) d. Saul Swimmer

BARBED WIRE (1969) d. Adrian J. Wensley-Walker

START THE REVOLUTION WITHOUT ME (1969) d. Bud Yorkin

TO BUILD A FIRE (1970) d. David Cobham

SENTINELS OF SILENCE (1971) d. Robert Amram

DIRECTED BY JOHN FORD (1971) d. Peter Bogdanovich

TO KILL A STRANGER (1971) d. Peter Collinson

THE CRUCIFIXION (1972) d. Robert Guenette

FUTURE SHOCK (1973) d. Alex Grasshoff

BUGS BUNNY SUPERSTAR (1975) d. Chuck Jones

THE CHALLENGE OF GREATNESS (1975) d. Herbert Kline

THE OTHER SIDE OF THE MOUNTAIN (1975) d. Larry Peerce
THE LATE GREAT PLANET EARTH (1977) d. Robert Amram
HISTORY OF THE WORLD—PART I (1981) d. Mel Brooks
THE MAN WHO SAW TOMORROW (1981) d. Robert Guenette
GENOCIDE (1981) d. Arnold Schwartzman
SLAPSTICK (OF ANOTHER KIND) (1984) d. Steven Paul
ALMONDS AND RAISINS (1984) d. Russ Kavel

ORSON WELLES

INTERVIEWS

"The Shadow" Talks

RICHARD O'BRIEN / 1938

A CONVICTION THAT RADIO DRAMA lends itself better to a narrative than to a strictly dramatic form was the inspiration for the "first person singular" technique employed by Orson Welles, actor-producer of the Mercury Theatre, in the current series of Monday night performances on WABC's stage.

Mr. Welles, who is doing the adaptations of the stories as well as doubling in brass as director and star, believes that not enough creative effort has been brought to drama projected over the air; the broadcasters, he maintains, have been content to borrow material indiscriminately from the stage and screen and to present it in emasculated form, embellished with a plethora of sound effects.

"Our idea, in presenting these plays in 'first person singular,' is to bring not the theatre to radio, but our own individual interpretation of radio to the listener," Mr. Welles explained. "The idea is only experimental. It may prove a failure but it is only by trying new methods that radio drama will ever achieve any independence and eventually discover a satisfactory art form of its own. Understand, it is not our purpose in any sense to be 'arty'; the experiment is based on a distinct belief that an original treatment of microphone drama is better than the old haphazard method of clinging to a technique designed for the stage. Broadcast drama, if it ever hopes to arrive anywhere, must stand on its own feet, even if it is necessary for some time to grope in the dark.

"There is nothing that seems more unsuited to the technique of the microphone, it seems to me, than to tune in a play and hear an announcer say: 'The curtain is now rising on a presentation of—' and then for him to set the stage, introduce the characters and go on with the play. The curtain is not rising at all, as everybody well knows, and this method of introducing the characters and setting the locale seems hopelessly inadequate and clumsy.

"Then, too, when one listens to a drama presented in this manner, it strikes me his attitude is a very impersonal one," said Mr. Welles. "The effect of eavesdropping is somewhat akin to overhearing a conversation, let's say, in the next apartment; the listener seems to be entirely out of the picture.

"That brings me to another point; while I have no quarrel with the commercial sponsorship of radio programs (the system seems entirely logical), I do find fault with the fact that the broadcasters, in presenting a program, develop it along lines pleasing to the sponsor, rather than to the radio audience itself, for whom it is really intended.

"There seems to be another mistaken idea that, while the intelligence of the radio audience has been estimated at 11 years old, that does not mean that those who write for the microphone should be of a similar mental stature. *Alice in Wonderland* and *Treasure Island* were written for children, but their appeal is so widespread that they have delighted grown-ups and lovers of literature as well.

"It also seems important to me to remember that in presenting entertainment over the air the thought should always be kept in mind that the invisible audience should never be considered collectively, but individually. While our aim is to reach many thousands of people, the listeners should be considered as small groups of two or three, and then the idea of intimacy can be best achieved. For intimacy is one of radio's richest possessions."

It was the idea of intimacy, Mr. Welles confessed, that first caused him to hit upon the idea of the "story-teller" or "first-person-singular" technique which he introduced in *Dracula, Treasure Island* and *A Tale of Two Cities,* and which he intends employing in *Hamlet,* Wilkie Collins's *Blow Up the Brig* and other stories to be broadcast later in the series.

"The added appeal of a narrator introduced as a 'story-teller' brings more intimacy to the dramatic broadcast," he said. "When a fellow leans back in his chair and begins: 'Now, this is how it happened'—the listener feels that the narrator is taking him into his confidence; he begins to take a personal interest in the outcome.

"While sound effects are very necessary in a medium that deals entirely with sound," Mr. Welles continued, "I believe that they are overdone in most radio plays, having a tendency to clutter up the action. Sound effects which are usually employed merely to paint the scenery should be used intelligently and economically and should have as much value to the play as the spoken word. I don't wish to be misunderstood. Sound effects and music are essential to any air drama; we are using all the equipment that radio offers, but economically and, we hope, intelligently."

Mr. Welles is of the opinion that not as great strides have been made in broadcast drama as other allied forms of ethereal entertainment, such as sports, news and public events. Greater showmanship has gone into these branches of broadcasting than the drama, he believes.

"Radio is a popular, democratic machine for disseminating information and entertainment, but as regards drama it is still in the experimental stage," said Mr. Welles. "However, there is a heart-warming indication that it is beginning to attract writers of the top rank. In the last five years its technical progress has not been as great as in the beginning, because the more obvious shortcomings and drawbacks have been ironed out. But to my mind radio is taken too lightly. The highbrows are still sniffing at it. But when television comes—and I understand it is not far off—they will be the first, in all probability, to hail it as a new art form."

Mr. Welles, whose rapid rise as a figure of importance in the theatrical world was based upon such popular Mercury Theatre experiments as *Julius Caesar* in mufti, *The Shoemaker's Holiday* and *Heartbreak House,* is very curious about radio. And he has reason to be. When he sent a road unit of *Caesar* into the hinterlands, he found that his claim to fame as producer-star of the Mercury Theatre was dwarfed among the playgoers by the overshadowing fact that he had played "The Shadow" on the air waves. He hopes that his nine-week dramatic experiment in the Summer Theatre of the Air may efface the memory of that sinister figure from the listener's mind. But he is not so sure.

The War of the Worlds Press Conference: FCC to Scan Script of War Broadcast

NEW YORK TIMES/1938

THE FEDERAL COMMUNICATIONS COMMISSION requested yesterday a transcript and electric recording of the radio broadcast Sunday night which dramatized H. G. Wells's 41-year-old novel, *The War of the Worlds,* and spread panic among thousands of Americans convinced that fiction in the form of tensely spoken "news" bulletins was stark fact.

Pending receipt of the script from the Columbia Broadcasting System, Frank R. McNinch, chairman of the commission, called the program "regrettable," but was silent as to the course of action the FCC might take. It was made plain that a thorough study of the text would precede any decision.

Meanwhile, with large sections of the radio-listening public incensed over what they regarded as a dangerous hoax, the broadcasting system and Orson Welles, the 23-year-old star of the disputed show, joined in issuing statements of regret. CBS, through W. B. Lewis, vice president in charge of programs, reiterated that announcements of the nature of the presentation had been made "before, after and twice during" the feature but added:

"In order that this may not happen again the program department hereafter will not use the technique of a simulated news broadcast within a dramatization when the circumstances of the broadcast could cause immediate alarm to numbers of listeners."

Along similar lines was a statement from Neville Miller, president of the

National Association of Broadcasters. It was made public in Washington, where interest in the broadcast and the problem it posed was surprisingly great. With a wide variety of conversational controversies arising from the situation, Commissioner T. A. M. Craven, New Jersey member of the body headed by Mr. McNinch, raised the question of censorship.

Mr. Craven agreed the investigation should be held, but asked "utmost caution" to avoid censorship and declared that the public "does not want a spineless radio."

Another development of the day came from H. G. Wells himself, who is in London. His local agent, Jaques Chambrun of 745 Fifth Avenue, hinted at legal trouble for the sponsors of the broadcast if a "retraction" was not forthcoming. Mr. Chambrun said:

"In the name of Mr. H. G. Wells, I granted the Columbia Broadcasting System the right to dramatize Mr. H. G. Wells's novel, *The War of the Worlds*, for one performance over the radio. It was not explained to me that this dramatization would be made with a liberty that amounts to a complete rewriting of *The War of the Worlds,* and renders it into an entirely different story.

"Mr. Wells and I consider that by so doing the Columbia Broadcasting System and Mr. Orson Welles have far overstepped their rights in the matter and believe that the Columbia Broadcasting System should make a full retraction. Mr. H. G. Wells personally is deeply concerned that any work of his should be used in such a way, and with a totally unwarranted liberty, to cause deep distress and alarm throughout the United States."

When this point was brought up to Mr. Welles, he said he had not considered the possibility of action because he had thought that the program constituted a "legitimate dramatization of a published work." Nothing regarding a step in the nature of a retraction was forthcoming from the broadcasting organization and Mr. Welles indicated he would seek legal advice if it became necessary. He expressed his admiration for the Wells "classic" and implied his appreciation for the right to make use of it in any form.

Copies of the script made available here showed clearly how persons who tuned in just after the opening of the program at 8 P. M. might have heard almost half an hour of a story that, except for its references to residents of Mars and the fantastic nature of the events described, was disconcerting to say the least—before there was any assurance that it was all in fun.

Following the preliminary announcements, listeners heard a few moments of dance music originating from a "hotel," and then an interruption in the long-familiar style of announcers rushing on the air with important news. It was at that point, undoubtedly, that fears began to spread.

Dire reports continued to flash across the country as a well-schooled troupe brought the listeners the story of a supposed meteorite crashing near Trenton, N. J., out of which hideous Martians crawled, armed with a lethal "heat-ray" and ultimately a deadly black smoke that brought all human beings to an appalling doom.

For those who tuned in late, the first announcement of the truth was delayed until the "middle break," listed on the thirty-second page of the script. The whole interruption, which comprised a five-line description of the broadcast, and system and station announcements, was scheduled to take twenty seconds. After it, there was no relapse from make-believe until the close.

The New Jersey area got the worst of the scare not only because the adapters had chosen it as the scene of the alleged catastrophe but because geographical names were taken right off the map, with Princeton, Trenton and Grovers Mill, a well-known landmark, specified.

Names of persons and institutions, on the other hand, were garbled. For what was presumably intended to suggest the American Museum of Natural History, the "National History Museum" was named. And the role taken by Mr. Welles—that of "Professor Richard Pierson, famous astronomer," of Princeton—knowingly or otherwise, inevitably brought to the minds of several persons the name of Dr. Newton L. Pierce, assistant in astronomy at that university.

Undergraduates there, incidentally, were prompt to form a "League for Interplanetary Defense," one of whose platform planks was an embargo on all "Martial"—with a capital M—music.

Although a similar levity pervaded the comments of many persons— mainly those who had not heard any of the broadcast—there could be no question that communities whose telephone service was cluttered during the peak of the fear were in no mood for joking. Such a one was Trenton, where City Manager Paul Morton sent to the FCC one of the twelve protests acknowledge later by Mr. McNinch.

And it was plain that Mr. Welles himself, sleepless and unshaven, was concerned by the turn of events when he appeared at the CBS studios in the afternoon to issue a statement and grant an interview. His statement follows:

"Despite my deep regret over any misapprehension which our broadcast last night created among some listeners, I am even the more bewildered over this misunderstanding in the light of an analysis of the broadcast itself.

"It seems to me that there are four factors which should have in any event maintained the illusion of fiction in the broadcast.

"The first was that the broadcast was performed as if occurring in the future and as if it were then related by a survivor of a past occurrence. The date of the fanciful invasion of this planet by Martians was clearly given as 1939 and was so announced at the outset of the broadcast.

"The second element was the fact that the broadcast took place at our regular weekly Mercury Theatre period and had been so announced in all the papers. For seventeen consecutive weeks we have been broadcasting radio drama. Sixteen of these seventeen broadcasts have been fiction and have been presented as such. Only one in the series was a true story, the broadcast of *Hell on Ice* by Commander Ellsberg, and was identified as a true story within the framework of radio drama.

"The third element was the fact that at the very outset of the broadcast and twice during its enactment listeners were told that this was a play, that it was an adaptation of an old novel by H. G. Wells. Furthermore, at the conclusion a detailed statement to this effect was made.

"The fourth factor seems to me to have been the most pertinent of all. That is the familiarity of the fable, within the American idiom, of Mars and Martians.

"For many decades 'The Man From Mars' has been almost a synonym for fantasy. In very old morgues of many newspapers there will be found a series of grotesque cartoons that ran daily, which gave this fantasy imaginary form. As a matter of fact, the fantasy as such has been used in radio programs many times. In these broadcasts, conflict between citizens of Mars and other planets has been a familiarly accepted fairy-tale. The same make-believe is familiar to newspaper readers through a comic strip that uses the same device."

Seated before a battery of newsreel cameras, Mr. Welles repeated elements of the statement in a dozen ways, then took time to deny with a weary smile that the whole thing was a "plant" to publicize the Mercury Theatre's new play, *Danton's Death,* scheduled to open tomorrow night. A similar denial came subsequently from the firm of Charles Scribner's Sons, when it was pointed out that H. G. Wells's *Apropos of Dolores* had been published yesterday.

Mr. Welles, who did the adaptation himself, said that among the many telegrams he had received regarding the broadcast there were many from listeners saying "how much they liked the show."

How to Raise a Child: The Education of Orson Welles, Who Didn't Need It

ALVA JOHNSTON AND FRED SMITH/ 1940

THE MOST PUZZLED PEOPLE IN THE UNITED STATES on Sunday night, October 30, 1938, were the traffic policemen of New Jersey. There were plenty of frightened citizens in America at that time, but the most confused ones were the motorcycle cops on the highways between New York and Philadelphia. At about 8:15 or 8:20 P.M. most of the traffic over those roads suddenly went wild.

Hundreds of automobiles began to flash along at speeds which normally indicate gangsters leaving scenes of assassination. But there were family parties in most of the cars; the women and children couldn't all be gun molls and child racketeers. When a motorcycle man tried to overhaul one speeding auto, he was passed by two or three others. The stampede was in all directions. Nobody would stop for a policeman's hail. Now and then, a traffic man would catch an incoherent shout that there was an "invasion" or that "the world was coming to an end."

There were puzzled policemen in station houses all over the country, as demands came over the telephone for gas masks and information as to the safest places to hide from the enemy. The second most puzzled group were the switchboard operators, as the telephones suddenly went crazy and began to rave deliriously. Next came the clergy; priests were startled by the rush to get confessions under the wire, and Protestant ministers astonished at the

This profile, the third and final installment of a three-part series, originally appeared in the *Saturday Evening Post*, 3 February 1940. Parts I (20 January 1940) and II (27 January 1940) highlighted Welles's childhood and early theatre experience.

interruption of their sermons by demands for prayers to avert the impending doom of the world. Fourth in the order of puzzlement may well have been hospital attendants who were called on to handle the nervous wrecks and falling-downstairs cases.

The puzzled section of the population was slow in discovering the cause of the panic, because the panic-stricken people had different stories to tell. They had tuned in at different periods during the Columbia network's broadcast of the "invasion" and had many different ideas about the invaders. Some said they were octopuslike Martian monsters armed with poison gas and death rays. Others thought it was merely the world coming to an end, as per schedule. Others identified the invaders as Germans; still others, as Japanese. Princeton sociologists, who interviewed victims of the panic in the interests of science, found one man who had thought the invaders were Chinese.

The wonder boy had broken loose again. Orson Welles, the child wizard, had had another brainstorm. This time the bizarre bratling had gone in for popular science. After having Harlemized and gangsterized Shakespeare, he had decided to put Orson Welles effects into the solar system. The twenty-three-year-old earth shaker had taken *The War of the Worlds,* an old-fashioned thriller written by H. G. Wells in 1898, and given it a modern treatment, using a combination of newscast and newspaper styles. His success in scaring the nation resulted from the capable handling of the old familiar earmarks of credibility. He gave names, addresses, occupations and other minute details; identified each farm, hamlet, turnpike, knoll, swamp and creek in the terrain which the Martian monsters swept over; christened every cop and village loafer who got mixed up in the interplanetary unpleasantness.

It was this change of pace from the particular to the cosmic that paralyzed the reasoning powers of his listeners. The seasoning of little facts of geography and personal identity caused the Welles public to swallow his wildest absurdities. The "specificity of detail" is emphasized as an important factor in the panic in *The Invasion of Martians,* a book to be published early in 1940 by Dr. Hadley Cantril, assistant professor of psychology at Princeton University. This work, in which Doctor Cantril was assisted by Dr. Paul F. Lazarsfeld, Dr. Frank N. Stanton and others, was financed by the General Education Board of the Rockefeller Foundation, which made a grant of $3000 for the study of the episode because of its richness in mass psychology. Doctor Cantril described the Welles uproar as "the first modern panic that has been studied with the research tools now available to the social scientist."

The boy wonder always moves in showers of fireworks, but he was dazzled by his own success in the Martian broadcast. He apparently had had no expectation his little Halloween entertainment would cause people to take to the hills in automobiles loaded with canned goods. The premier infant prodigy had no idea of becoming America's leading *enfant terrible.*

It is Welles' custom to have the original script of his radio shows rehearsed by others and recorded phonographically, so that, as he puts it, "I can hear it fresh aloud." Getting it "fresh aloud," he can grasp the merits and defects of a script better than by reading it. After listening to the recorded version, Welles revises the script. Before he had heard the electrical transcription of the rough draft of *The War of the Worlds,* Welles asked a technician at the Columbia studio what he thought of it.

"Very dull. Very dull," said the technician.

"What don't you like about it?"

"It'll put 'em to sleep."

Welles asked what was wrong.

The technician said: "No human interest. Where's the love interest?"

It was luminously self-evident that the plot was short of love interest. The only action was that the armor-plated superdevils from the red planet exterminated all but three or four earth inhabitants and then died of colds in the head, because the armor, though protecting them against machine guns and cannons, didn't keep out germs. The routine method of introducing the boy-meets-girl angle would be to cause Mr. America to marry the Queen of Mars and spend the honeymoon on Venus, but Welles has too much artistic conscience for such a compromise. He agreed with the technician, however, that the piece was dull.

Albert Schneider, business manager for Welles, predicted that the young maestro would hurt the prestige of his Mercury Theatre and of the Columbia Broadcasting System by putting such insipidities on the air; Schneider later showed the courage of his convictions by going to sleep during the Sunday-night broadcast. Welles was gloomy about it all. Had time permitted, he would probably have discarded the Martian invasion in favor of something lively. While revising the script, it occurred to him that the broadcast would take place on the night before Halloween. Seizing on this as a pretext to excuse the Martian hocus-pocus, he wrote an epilogue saying that the broadcast was the Mercury Theatre's way of "dressing up in a sheet and jumping out the window and saying 'Boo.' " The question whether Welles intended to scare people may eventually be decided by juries. Lawsuits have been filed by persons who claim to have been hurt during the Martian reign of terror. The strongest part of the defense is that the broadcast was announced in the radio columns of newspapers as a dramatization of the H. G. Wells novel and that this was explained at the beginning, in the middle and at the end of the performance.

The dial-twiddling habit was responsible for most of the trouble. The majority of listeners tuned in late and missed the announcement that the broadcast was fiction. Charlie McCarthy was both the hero and the villain. By his near monopoly of the air at this hour, he saved tens of millions from the Welles frightfulness. He is the villain, however, because he held the dial twiddlers with his wisecracks until after the rival network had introduced the Martian invasion as an H. G. Wells fantasy; then, yielding the microphone to singers, Charlie released the dial twiddlers to tune in on the eyewitness picture of world destruction without having advance notice that it all came under the head of entertainment.

According to the Gallup poll, 9,000,000 people heard all or part of the Martian broadcast; according to the estimate of the Princeton sociologists, approximately 1,750,000 people were frightened. At any rate, while Welles was grinding away at what he apparently considered an intolerably dull routine, strange things were happening around the country, samples of which are as follows:

Public-spirited citizens of Providence, Rhode Island, telephoned to the local utility demanding a blackout. A Pittsburgh woman tried to drink poison, saying, "I'd rather die this way than like that." A linotyper of Selma, Louisiana, running in the dark, caught his chin under a neighbor's clothesline and thought he was hit by a death ray. A Mobile woman, getting the news on returning from the Greater Mobile Gulf Coast Fair, said to her husband, "I had a premonition that we should have gone to church instead of the fair." A colored woman, later interviewed by the Princeton sociologists, recalled that there was half a chicken left in the icebox, and said, "We might as well eat it now, because we won't be here in the morning." The staff of the *Memphis Press-Scimitar* rushed to the office to get out an extra. Misled by neon lights in the distance and by the gasoline-and-rubber fumes on the highways, many residents of New Jersey claimed to have seen and smelled the Martians, who were supposed to have landed near Princeton. A man ran into the Press Club at Princeton University saying that he had seen the Martian space ship explode and had observed animals jumping from it. The town of Concrete, Washington, got a double dose of terror, as the local power-and-light plant broke down just as Orson Welles was saying that the poison gas was choking him.

Among those interviewed for the Princeton treatise on mass psychology was a woman who refused to be reassured by her husband. When he demonstrated that jazz bands were broadcasting from other stations, she retorted, "Nero fiddled while Rome was burning." A Jewish woman who had previously come to feel that all catastrophes were aimed at the Jews, told the scientific workers that she had felt a sense of relief on learning that the Martians were mowing down their victims without regard to race or creed. One woman reported that through the blackest moments she kept saying to herself, "Well, anyway, I won't have to pay the butcher bill." A German family, picking up a few things and starting to run, had its plans disorganized when one of the children ran back into the house to rescue a canary. A working girl, who had saved up $3.25 toward a pair of shoes, spent it on a railroad ticket and traveled sixty miles before she learned that it was only an Orson Welles holiday. The least frightened listener was Mrs. H. V. Kaltenborn, who knew, she said, that if anything big were really happening, her husband would be on the air interpreting it.

After Welles had started the stampede, various factors helped it along. Mobs love panics. Persons questioned in the scientific survey confessed that they "derived a certain satisfaction or pleasure" from their terror. Another factor was the news-bearer instinct. A professional nobody enjoys the momentary illusion of being a somebody when he is first with the news. Hardened nonentities never had such a chance of gaining temporary importance as in spreading the tidings that the world was coming to an end. Some commentators thought that Welles had merely exploded latent hysteria over the European situation. Republican philosophers found that the panic resulted from national jitters caused by the epileptic policies of the New Deal. A psychoanalyst, who gave his views to Princeton inquirers, laid the blame on sex imbroglios. One university sociologist said the explanation was that all the intelligent people of the country were listening to Charlie McCarthy. Hitler and the Nazi press traced the uproar to the naïve contents of the American mind.

Orson Welles has a profound theory. The most terrifying thing, he says, is suddenly becoming aware that you are not alone. In this case, the earth, thinking itself alone, suddenly became aware that another planet was prowling around. Welles has another theory—namely, that the last two generations are softened up because they were deprived in their childhood, through mistaken theories of education, of the tales of blood and horror which used to be a part of the routine training of the young. Under the old system, according to Welles, the child felt at home among ghosts and goblins, and did not grow up to be a push-over for sensational canards. But the ban on gruesome fairy tales, terrifying nursemaids and other standard sources of horror has left most of the population without any protection against fee-fi-fo-fum stuff.

Welles had nearly finished the broadcast before he detected that something was wrong. Through a glass partition in the studio he observed the entrance of several policemen, and he also noticed unwonted activity at a battery of telephones.

As soon as the broadcast was over, attendants hurried over to inform him that there were long-distance calls for him.

The first message was a threat of death from a chamber-of-commerce official of Flint, Michigan, who asserted that the population of Flint had been scattered far and wide and that it would take days to reassemble it. The next message gave statistics on the broken tibias and fibulas of Western Pennsylvania. Hundreds of dollars were paid to the A. T. & T. that night for the privilege of swearing at Welles. One telephoner called Welles, "You beauty," but none of the others paraphrased the claim that he was born out of wedlock. The thing grew serious as the death toll mounted. It was around twenty at ten P.M. Later research indicated that there had been no fatalities, but at the time Welles regarded himself as a mass murderer. But whether a wholesale killer or not, he had to get to the Mercury Theatre to direct a dress rehearsal of *The Shoemaker's Holiday.* The infant prodigy has always had the ability to abolish instantly all subjects except the one he is concentrating on. For three or four hours, while he was drilling his cast, he was unconscious of everything else; on walking out to take a smoke, he was surprised to see his name in bright lights racing around the bulletin board which girdles The New York Times Building. Welles mentioned this on returning to the theater; somebody said he was crazy. He sighed and continued with the rehearsal, which went on until three or four A.M. The next day he apologized and explained all day long.

The chief victim of the panic is Welles himself. He is branded for life as the Mars man. People bear down on him like ten thousand Ancient Mariners on one wedding guest and hold him while he listens to their Martian stories. He can detect a glitter in the eye of every stranger; from the nature of the glitter he can figure to the split second how long it will be before the stranger comes over and opens a Martian conversation. Welles sees on nearly everybody a burning time fuse which at a given moment is going to burst into a Martian epigram or question. He is a pathetic figure today.

Out in Hollywood there are four time fuses burning on nearly everybody Welles sees. The first leads up to Mars; the second, to why he wears a beard; the third, to how he landed the most extraordinary contract in Hollywood; the fourth, to how he comes to be only twenty-four years old. No other newcomer's arrival in Hollywood ever caused so much indignation as Welles'. It is difficult to understand why. His beard is considered an intolerable provocation, although Hollywood is the whisker capital of the nation, with its assortment of Vandykes, Burnsides, Dundrearys, Piccadilly weepers and House of Davids, which actors are always growing for period roles. Ordinarily, a man could walk down the street carrying his head in his hand, or drive a chariot drawn by a gnu and an okapi, without attracting attention in the stunt-sated cinema colony. But the picture people take Orson's beard personally. Most of the columnists have foamed at the mouth about it. It worked on the feelings of the easy-going Big Boy Williams to such an extent that he took out a knife and cut off Welles' necktie in Chasen's restaurant.

Somewhat more understandable is the bitter resentment at the fact that Welles has the nerve to be only twenty-four years old. Hollywood today is a sort of Old Infant Prodigies' Home. During its first two decades, the picture business was rich in child colossuses. Thalberg was tremendous before he was old enough to vote, and Zanuck was terrific at twenty-five. But the growing complexity of the business has made it more difficult for baby genius to forge ahead. David Selznick and Pandro Berman were around thirty before they won the infant-prodigy rating. It is in the nature of things that the superannuated infant prodigies and their cohorts should disapprove of a fresh young infant prodigy.

Welles' youth might have been condoned if it had not been for his extraordinary picture contract. Probably more screwball contracts have been written in Hollywood than in the rest of the world put together, and ordinarily, the most fantastic of them attracts no attention, but the Welles contract has caused a furious war of words. It provides that he should write, produce, direct and act in the pictures he makes; it pays him $150,000 a picture plus a percentage of the gross; it stipulates that neither the president nor board of directors or anybody else can interfere with him in any way. No one in authority over Welles has the right to see the work until it is completed.

This would seem to concern only Welles and the picture company, but that is not the way Hollywood sees it. There it is everybody's business. The idea that such a contract should have gone to a twenty-four-year-old carpet-bagger with a beard is considered a menace to the public welfare. The thing has become a branch of California's migratory-worker problem; Welles and the actors he has imported from his Mercury Theatre in New York are looked on as a lot of gilded okies. One cinema-trade paper inquired on its front-cover page, "Can It Be the Beard?" It reviewed the rather imposing list of Welles' Broadway failures; then, by the simple device of classifying all the Welles successes as failures, it gave him an artistic rating of zero and cried out that such things as the Welles contract were not to be borne. Columnists opened fire on Welles for everything that he did. He was simultaneously attacked for being a recluse and a playboy, and was charged with snubbing Shirley Temple.

It was vain for him to protest that he was growing a beard for the purpose of playing a part which required a beard; the overwhelming sentiment was that the beard was a deliberate act of aggression.

Welles' extraordinary contract was a triumph of the policy of being hard to get. Hollywood started after him four years ago with an offer of $300 a week. It gradually raised the bid until it was about thirty times the original offer. Welles pleaded that he was interested in other things, but finally yielded to an incredible bid. Hollywood wanted him because his Broadway productions, both the hits and the failures, have been marked by boldness, originality, and superlative craftsmanship. The hard-to-get policy was easy for Welles to follow, because he had determined in the beginning not to go to Hollywood until he had an idea that he believed in. He finally decided that he could bring his whole artistic equipment into action on a film version of Conrad's *Heart of Darkness*. In addition to his producer-director-actor-writer capacity Welles is his own chief scenic artist and property man; in his two latter roles *Heart of Darkness* was irresistible, with its luxuriant tropical settings and its mysterious jungle business. Production difficulties, however, caused a postponement of this film in favor of a thriller with the tentative title of "The Smiler With the Knife."

Welles is the head boss and the green hand in his unit at the RKO studio. In his capacity of new boy he spends his evenings studying picture technique; in his capacity of big chief he spends his days directing his night-school teachers. This is all in character. From his earliest infant-prodigy days Orson has always lectured teachers and instructed specialists in their specialties.

For his second film, Welles wanted to make *Pickwick* with W. C. Fields, but that great actor was under contract elsewhere to play the part of Dickens' thrice-gorgeous old fuddy-duddy. Welles found himself enthusiastic about Hollywood. When a New York friend asked him about it at the RKO studio, Welles pointed to the wilderness of cameras, lights, sound apparatus and other engines of the talkies.

"It's the greatest railroad train a boy ever had," he said.

The paradox about Welles is that, although only twenty-four years old, he has had a greater experience in the world of make-believe than most old-timers of the theater. Starting as a two-year-old Belasco managing cardboard actors, his subsequent twenty-two years have been mainly devoted to the study and practice of showmanship. He virtually turned his prep school into a repertory theater. After stock-company experience in Dublin at sixteen and road-show experience with Katharine Cornell at eighteen, he reached Broadway at nineteen, and crammed two or three lifetimes of experience into his five years there. His devotion to the theater touched a high when he put in a summer vacation writing a book on the drama solely for his own instruction. After reading the book with great admiration, he destroyed it. Some radio stars regard one performance a week as an intolerable chore; Welles has done as many as twenty-five a week in his spare time between producing, directing and scene-designing Broadway shows.

Welles was twenty when, in 1935, he started on his radio career by appearing on the March of Time with a condensed version of *Panic*, a play in which he had acted on Broadway. He gradually became a member of a select group of anonymous radio artists who shuttle about from station to station, taking part in many programs every day. Grabbing every assignment that he could get at fees ranging from forty dollars to seventy-five dollars an appearance, Welles was earning around $1000 a week within a year after his debut. It is only by intensified chiseling and corner-cutting that the members of this flying squadron can get through their programs: the hardest part of their existence is that of thinking up alibis for failing to appear at rehearsals and conferences when their daily schedules are full of conflicts. Because of the pressure of this life, Orson frequently looked at his script for the first time after the show had started. He didn't know whether he was a hero or a villain until he found himself engaged in good or evil deeds; on some occasions, when he was shot or drowned, it came as a bigger surprise to him than to the audience. In a way, this is the ideal technique for mystery shows; if the actor doesn't know what is going to happen to him, it ought to be difficult for the audience to predict it.

When he started rehearsals for the Negro version of *Macbeth,* early in 1936, Welles was broadcasting off and on from ten A.M. until nearly midnight. He could not start rehearsals for *Macbeth* until after midnight, because the theater was in use in the evening. He would work in Harlem until eight A.M. or thereabouts, then hold a conference breakfast and then speed downtown for a ten o'clock broadcast. For several days running he was never out of his clothes, but this ended with his breakdown at a radio recital of a poem of Browning's. He got not only every word wrong but every syllable wrong, and the station cut in with an organ recital. Welles always tries to top everybody; on this occasion he succeeded in adding obscurity to Browning.

Welles produced the black *Macbeth* in co-operation with John Houseman, who was staging plays for the WPA. The idea of doing the tragedy with a colored cast was suggested by Mrs. Welles. Because Christophe, the famous black emperor of Haiti, had been a man after Macbeth's own heart, the action was transferred from Scotland to Haiti. The Birnam Wood that came to Dunsinane was a jungle of palms and bananas. The three weird women were translated into sixty black witch doctors. Welles, always a prey to an exacting artistic conscience, obtained genuine voodoo practitioners who slew goats with strange rites in order to get sacred skins for the witch drums. Welles made it a point of assembling a cast of persons who knew little or nothing of acting and nothing whatever of Shakespeare. He wanted actors who, after mastering the import of the Elizabethan phraseology, would utter the words in their own way, instead of imitating other actors.

It was an arduous enterprise in various respects. During a rehearsal Welles tried repeatedly to silence one of his colored aids who kept on holding a conversation in the center aisle. Finally, Welles said, "If you won't be quiet,

I'll have to make you," and climbed over the footlights. He was seized and dragged away just in time. During the early stages of the argument the aid had taken out his razor, opened it and thoughtfully tied the handle to his wrist, so it would not slip after the first slash.

There were other troubles. One faction in Harlem thought the whole idea was not only a degradation of Shakespeare but a setback to the cultural progress of the Negro in America. The rehearsals progressed in the midst of threats and intrigues. Welles was compelled to squander most of his large radio earnings on the show because the WPA auditors loved to make a prolonged diplomatic negotiation, with exchanges of notes and ultimatums, over the matter of buying a paper of thumb tacks. But the opening night of April 14, 1936, was a grand one. The police had to be called out to handle one of the furriest and most expensive first-night crowds in history. All was forgiven; Welles became a Harlem hero. Most of the critics were impressed. The supernatural business and the battle scenes were tremendous. The voodoo set proved to be thorough-paced troupers. One dramatic critic had let loose a blast against the Government for blowing the money of taxpayers on this kind of thing. When this was translated to the voodoo doctors, they held ceremonies around a witches' caldron full of their own ingredients. "We fix 'im," explained the head doctor. "Give 'im beri-beri." Voodoo prestige soared when, a few days later, the critic died. An ailment of long standing, however, not beri-beri, was responsible.

Welles and Houseman produced two other WPA successes—*Doctor Faustus* and *Horse Eats Hat*. They encountered trouble in 1937, however, with Marc Blitzstein's operetta, *The Cradle Will Rock*, which undermined the capitalistic system with light music. The operetta had been approved and financed by the WPA, but that organization suddenly lost its nerve. Before this date, the WPA chiefs had been fairly audacious in backing pink theater propaganda, but they became thoroughly frightened when congressmen and others began to murmur. The Blitzstein operetta was supposed to have all the dynamite of Beaumarchais' *Le Mariage de Figaro*, which, according to some historians, touched off the French Revolution. After investing considerable sums in *The Cradle Will Rock*, WPA chiefs began to put obstacles in the way of producing it.

When Welles got ready to stage it anyway, they rushed emissaries to New York and padlocked the theater a few hours before opening time. Welles and his actors found themselves locked out as the audience was arriving. This furnished Welles with a chance for some typical Welles fireworks. Assuring the mob of ticket holders that he would produce the show that night, Welles sent out a general alarm for theater owners, and finally engaged an empty showhouse. A piano was moved in so that Blitzstein could play his world-overturning melodies.

With this exploit Welles again hit the front pages of the New York papers. The formerly audacious left-wingers of the WPA turned out to be a lot of stuffed shirts under the skin. In their zeal to save America from the WPA theater, the WPA sent an ax brigade to chop and smash their own stage set-tings in their own padlocked playhouse. Big glass pillars full of neon lights and the other expensive stage equipment of *The Cradle Will Rock* were destroyed in a Carrie Nation raid. Several weeks later, Welles staged the show under private auspices. America survived, but the operetta didn't. The situa-tion, however, might have been reversed, except for the fact that Welles, by a typical miscalculation, produced the piece in a theater so small that, even if it were filled to capacity at every performance, the box-office receipts would not pay running expenses.

After this experience, Welles refused to use his surplus radio earnings to support the Government any longer, and devoted them to the Mercury The-atre, Inc., which he and Houseman organized. Welles set off the fireworks again with a sceneless plain-clothes *Julius Caesar,* made highly contemporary by the fact that the conspirators appeared to be a lot of golden-tongued Chi-cago mobsters rising against a modern dictator of the Hitler-Mussolini type. He stirred the critics, but not the public, with his impressionistic *Danton's Death.* Presentations of the Elizabethan farce, *The Shoemaker's Holiday,* and Shaw's *Heartbreak House* added to his prestige.

Last spring, in collaboration with the Theatre Guild, Welles made his most ambitious effort. Boiling down *Richard II,* the two parts of *Henry IV, Henry V,* the three parts of *Henry VI* and *Richard III* into one monstrous show called *Five Kings,* he tried to stage the story of England from 1377 to 1485, including the fall of chivalry and the rise of the commoners. The production money ran out before it was half rehearsed, and this half-baked Cardiff Giant of a drama failed in an early stage of a road tour. Welles played Falstaff. Ashton Stevens, who has seen all the Falstaffs of the last forty years, said that Welles was the only actor who had risen to the part during that period. Opinions of other critics varied. They generally agreed that Welles had marvelous gusto.

One of the various departments in which Welles can lick all creation is that of being perpetually penniless with an enormous income. After *Five Kings,* he was full of theatrical projects and in urgent need of $15,000. He sought to hock a $40,000 inheritance which comes to him next May. With his usual eccentric approach to his problems, he took Tallulah Bankhead for his financial agent. Starting after her evening appearance in *The Little Foxes,* she held banking hours from one to six A.M. Marc Connelly, who lived in the same hotel, was summoned to her apartment at three A.M., but could not find $15,000 in his pajama pockets. Sherman Billingsley, summoned from his Stork Club, decided that he was not running a pawn shop for impending inheritances. Miss Bankhead kept on smiting rocks of finance until daybreak, but no bank rolls gushed forth. Dashiell Hammett claimed to have a big bagman staked out at The Plaza. Taking Welles over there after breakfast, Hammett greeted the quarry with "Hello, sucker," and the man froze up like the governor of the Bank of England. Welles took a plane for Chicago, where his guardian, Dr. Maurice Bernstein, arranged to get the loan from a Chicago bank. Welles met two bank executives who behaved like hearts of gold; they were willing to waive technicalities and fork over the $15,000 on easy terms, but during the conference a telephone call from Hollywood came for Welles. A motion-picture magnate had been trying to reach him and Welles had left word to switch the call to the bank if it came at the conference hour. The Hollywood man offered Welles $100,000 to produce a picture. Welles refused. The magnate asked how much he wanted.

"It isn't the money," said Welles. "A hundred thousand would be all right. But there isn't any point in talking about it until I have a story that I think I can do."

The two Chicago bankers eyed each other and smiled sardonically. It looked as if Welles were having himself paged with the $100,000 offer in order to build up his credit. They reconsidered on the spot and wouldn't lend him a cent.

Welles finally raised the money by a brief vaudeville appearance in *The Green Goddess.* Then, hitting on the idea of filming *Heart of Darkness,* he went to Hollywood.

The immediate ambition of Welles is to develop his Mercury Company four ways—in pictures, Broadway shows, radio presentations and phono-graphic recordings of classics for school use. Planning moderate-priced Broadway drama, he needs the Hollywood gains to offset the probable Broad-way losses. His ultimate but concealed ambition, according to some of his associates, is to be a college president.

Dedicated Wunderkind

JOHN MCCARTEN/ 1945

UNTIL THE OTHER DAY, WE REGARDED Orson Welles simply as an actor, producer, writer, costumer, magician, Shakespearean editor, and leading prodigy of our generation, and then out of our mail fluttered an announcement that he was about to become a new-day Bryan by delivering an oration called "The Nature of the Enemy" at the City Center. "Mr. Welles' understanding of international happenings," the announcement stated, "has been widely acknowledged. Not only has he the ability of analysis, but of prophecy, and he also has the master's art of making his statements felt by everyone." We decided we must call on the master, who was holed in at the St. Regis, surrounded by enough publicity operatives to put on a production of *Julius Caesar*. On our arrival, one of the lady publicity agents murmured, "He looks dedicated." To us, however, he looked the same as he did the last time we had a talk with him—moon-faced, girthy, bland, and authoritative. He was wearing a ministerial black broadcloth suit, old-fashioned boots with elastic inserts in the sides, and a pair of monogrammed cuff links as big as half dollars. Only the lack of a black string tie (he was wearing a sharp red bow) marred a considerable resemblance to the Boy Orator of the Platte.

Leaning thoughtfully against the fireplace in his living room, Welles told us that he has had a compulsion to awaken his fellow men to the dangers of Fascism for years and is now delighted to be doing something about it. He

Originally published as an unsigned interview in *The New Yorker*, 27 January 1945. Reprinted by permission of the Estate of John McCarten.

plans to make one-night stands in Chicago, Washington, Baltimore, and elsewhere. "Naturally," he remarked, "a lot of people are going to ask, 'What's a ham actor think he's doing as an expert on world affairs?' But that will help prove that international matters are not as mysterious as Rosicrucianism or something. We've got to outgrow our Tinker Toy stage of anti-Fascism and use a sophisticated approach." At this point two photographers appeared and began shooting off flash bulbs. When Welles hesitated under the barrage, both of them muttered, "Keep talking." He obediently carried on. "I've been reading up on Fascism," he said, "and what I learned will help supplement what I actually saw of it in the year and a half I spent down in Latin America. I've got all kinds of friends subscribing to Fascist papers here, so I keep pretty well posted about local Fascist activities." Rambling along in his impressive baritone, he told us that the William Morris Agency had arranged for the lectures, which will command a $2.40 top and will probably make money. "This lecture in the City Center," said Welles, "reminds me of the days when I did the Wonder Radio Show there for the Wonder Bakers. The audience used to make airplanes out of the programs and throw them at us. They might even be rougher this time."

Welles is so intense about fighting Fascism that he's not only going to orate against it but also will give it hell in the newspaper column he's launching this week in the *Post*. "The column is so important," he said, "that I plan to devote almost all my time to it as soon as I can. I've given up all my Hollywood work except to act in one picture each year." As we talked with Welles, all kinds of people kept drifting in—a lady who wanted to know if actors should participate in politics ("Yes"), a correspondent from *Tass,* who chuckled amiably as he took notes in Russian, several local newspapermen, and three Latin Americans in bright yellow shoes. While the crowd was growing, Orson outlined his program for the next few months. As a sturdy supporter of the President, he was to appear at the inauguration. Then off to the Pan-American Conference in Mexico City, perhaps a short spin around Central America, and presently to work on a picture about Latin America he finished some years ago and which he bought the other day from R.K.O. After that, he figures he'll be in the clear for his column. He's been invited to so many Democratic gatherings in Washington during the coming weeks that he's begun to regard himself, he says, as the Lucius Beebe of the Democratic Party. As we left, we heard a publicity man advise him to keep such cracks off the record.

Welles Hits Old Stride Again

THOMAS F. BRADY/1946

ORSON WELLES HAS RESUMED his film-directing-writing-producing career, which was interrupted four years ago by his titanic battle with RKO over the never-completed *It's All True*—a battle that ended, more or less, with his eviction from the RKO studio in July, 1942. His subsequent cinematic operations were confined to acting in three pictures until he made a profit-participation deal with Columbia this year to fabricate a melodrama, *The Lady From Shanghai* with Rita Hayworth, his wife, as his leading lady.

Last week, after thirty-five days on location in Acapulco, Mexico, Welles went to work on a studio sound stage with his old gusto. By the end of the day he was still prodigal with his vitality, although he complained that he needed a doctor because he could not sleep at night. His own doctor, he said, had refused to attend him and had abandoned him to white nights.

In the midst of this harangue, he looked piercingly at the technicians who were preparing the final camera setup of the day, then cried out: "There is too much stalling around here. Some one go put pressure on those men." When a responsive henchman yelled, "Hey, let's go," Welles said sharply, "That's not enough. Go rub up against them the wrong way."

A moment later, after a quick ride on a camera boom, Welles paused to discuss his past. The fullness of time, he said, has dissipated all the bitterness between him and RKO. The Hearst press, however, still avoids any mention of his name because his first picture, *Citizen Kane*, dealt disrespectfully with the publisher of a chain of newspapers. And, he added, the leading Hearst columnist in Hollywood never speaks to him until after two cocktails, although, despite repeated snubs, he has always treated her with Old World courtesy.

He would like, he said, to buy from RKO the footage he shot for *It's All True* and complete the picture just to prove he was right. The film is still stored in a vault in Salt Lake City because of California taxes, but, he said, he has never amassed enough money to handle the project himself and he has been unable to find a backer who would risk capital in the venture.

He interrupted himself to instruct a jury of twelve extras who were appearing in the scene before the camera to regard Miss Hayworth, who was on a witness stand, "with lecherous interest."

Then he resumed discussion of his own career with the pronouncement that he intends to give up acting as soon as he can persuade the film industry to invest in his talent as a director alone.

"I have a small public now," he said, "whose interest in me is sufficient at the box office to make my appearance on the screen a necessary adjunct to my writing and directing. But no critic has ever liked my acting. I have an unfortunate personality. I can show you, frame for frame, that my eyebrows move less than Ray Milland's in *The Lost Weekend.* If I permitted myself one-tenth of his expressions in that excellent performance, I would be howled out of the theatre. I have only to walk into camera range and the critics are convinced that I am a ham-bone. I am an actor of the old school. That is the only way I can explain it."

He doesn't like acting anyway, he added, because he has to shave regularly when he works before the camera.

Welles turned back to the courtroom set and, apparently satisfied with the lechery on the extras' faces, gave the word to photograph it. Immediately afterward, a business operative brought word that a horse-drawn cab, which had been shipped up from Mexico, was stalled at the border by customs men. The failure of the cab to arrive necessitated a quick shuffle in the projected shooting schedule for the next day. So Welles, followed by twenty-three assistants and technicians in a queue, circumnavigated the sound stage on which he was working, picking out camera setups for the coming day. "At approximately 11:35 A.M. tomorrow we will move to this corner," he announced roundly, but none of the technicians seemed to pay any attention.

When the queue had dwindled to three people, Welles turned and spoke charmingly to a minor actor who thanked him for his engagement in the picture. In answer to a reporter's question, Welles said that Columbia had treated him with the utmost generosity up to that time in matters of fiscal and artistic autonomy.

Then he announced with undiminished enthusiasm that he had to hurry away to get some sleep. To a henchman who had apparently found a doctor for him, he cried, "Have the doctor meet me at the car; he can attend to my needs on the way home. I am to be called at 6:30 tomorrow morning—I must go to the baths." And he wrapped his coat around him after the fashion of a black cape and strode out into the mists of the Hollywood night.

Presumably the doctor, the sleep and the baths did him good. A report from the studio the next day disclosed that he directed the first scene while a barber shaved him and cut his hair, a feat which even Cecil B. DeMille has never equaled.

Interview with Welles

FRANCIS KOVAL / 1950

THAT NIGHT THE CURTAIN ROSE twenty minutes late in the Paris theatre where Orson Welles was the main attraction; Orson Welles, the producer and principal actor of *The Blessed and The Damned* written by himself in collaboration with Milton, Dante and Marlowe, as the programme explains.

The angry audience, stamping their feet impatiently, fortunately never suspected that my own dinner-table interview with Welles had been the cause of that delay; the fact was that, engrossed in conversation, we both completely forgot to look at the time. Much as I regretted the result, I could not help feeling that—from the mere journalistic point of view—this was not exactly a failure, considering that Orson Welles had started our talk with the plain statement: "You highbrows writing on movies are nuts! In order to write about movies you must first make them. . . ."

He was still as unconventional and unafraid of shocking anybody as when I first met him three years ago on his arrival in England. On that occasion, towards the end of a reception given in his honour by Sir Alexander Korda, he started a heated discussion on *Hamlet* with Eileen Herlie (just then playing in Laurence Olivier's film) and myself. When the executives of London Films approached him, pointing out that the reception was practically finished and they were going home, Welles replied undisturbed, "I bid you farewell then, gentlemen, but I am just having a most interesting talk with these folks here, and I would like to continue if you don't mind." And then, while the lights

From *Sight and Sound,* December 1950. Reprinted by permission of *Sight and Sound.*

went out one after another and the waiters were clearing the tables, Welles—with a stunning abundance of Shakespearian quotations—proceeded to psycho-analyse Ophelia and to explain to us his conception of *Hamlet* as Shakespeare's most anti-feminist play.

He must have behaved with the same dazzling self-assurance when in 1932—at the age of 17—he arrived in Dublin and obtained a part at the Gate Theatre, pretending to the manager-director, Hilton Edwards, to be one of the stars of the New York Theatre Guild. Very soon Hilton Edwards—like the rest of the world—discovered that the self-assurance was backed by original genuine talent, and he became one of Welles' closest friends. (As a matter of fact, he is co-producer of the show running in Paris at present, and plans to direct Welles' next film.) The prodigy attracted world-wide attention in 1936 with his production of *Macbeth* with an all Negro cast, and again in 1938 with his radio-play on the invasion from Mars. Its unsurpassed realism created a panic in the United States at the time and led to an abrupt end of the young author's brilliant broadcasting career.

Undismayed by countless failures, Orson Welles founded his own theatre, wrote, produced, acted and concentrated on the study of Shakespeare, poured out new ideas. In 1939 he turned to the cinema and in 1941 produced *Citizen Kane*, one of the most controversial films of the last decade. Admired by a discerning minority, hated and bitterly attacked by more or less inarticulate majorities in most countries, the picture did not bring the financial results expected, but it established Welles' name in the cinema. It cost him that unlimited freedom hardly ever given before to a filmmaker by Hollywood executives; a freedom that is to him an essential condition of creative film work. Lack of this condition is discernible in the pictures that followed: *The Magnificent Ambersons, Journey into Fear, The Lady from Shanghai, The Stranger.*

The derogatory statement about serious cinema journalists coming from a man of such achievements—a man who at 35 still gives the impression of an exuberant, brilliantly seductive child prodigy—did not sound offensive at all. It was pronounced with a twinkling smile and in a perfectly charming manner, so typical of Welles—but when I asked him to substantiate it, he erupted:

"Well, I cannot swallow all the sacrosanct principles and accepted truths underlying the writings of people who try to deal seriously with the problems of films. For one, you all seem to start from the article of faith that a silent picture is necessarily better than a sound one. . . ."

My puzzled expression and a timid attempt at interruption were of no avail. All signs of my disagreement and bewilderment were swept aside by a grandiloquent hand movement.

"What I mean to say," he continued, "is that you always overstress the value of images. You judge films in the first place by their visual impact instead of looking for content. This is a great disservice to the cinema. It is like judging a novel only by the quality of its prose. I was guilty of the same sin, when I first started writing about the cinema. It was the experience of film-making that changed my outlook.

"Now I feel that only the literary mind can help the movies out of that cul-de-sac into which they have been driven by mere technicians and artificers. That is why I think that to-day the importance of the director in film making is exaggerated, while the writer hardly ever gets the place of honour due to him. To me people like Marcel Pagnol or Jacques Prévert mean more than any others in the French cinema. In my opinion the writer should have the first and the last word in film making, the only better alternative being the writer-director, but with the stress on the first word."

When I pressed for actual examples to illustrate this theory (which sounds somewhat startling from a man made famous by the visual impact of *Citizen Kane*), Orson Welles produced one without hesitation:

"Take a picture that has become a classic, and deservedly so: *La Femme du Boulanger*. What have you got there? Bad photography, inadequate cutting and a lot of happenings which are told instead of shown. But there is a story and an actor—both superb—which makes it a perfect movie. The story is not even particularly 'cinema.' I think I could make a play out of it in one evening, if I wanted to.

"This example illustrates perhaps better than anything else what I mean when I talk about the primary importance of the film story. I certainly don't refer merely to the anecdotal value that you can summarise in a brief outline like: 'She slaves for 20 years to repay that pearl necklace, and then it proved to be a fake. . . .' It is really more a combination of human factors and basic ideas that makes a subject worth putting on the screen."

It turns out that Orson has been considerably impressed by the Italian neo-realists, but for reasons which fit into the line of his argument. He was struck by Vittorio De Sica's lyric power, particularly as expressed in *Sciuscia*, while he thinks *Bicycle Thieves* more commercial and slick, but less observed. To him De Sica's greatness lies in his being a *writer*-director in the Chaplin tradition. Together with Carol Reed he has been fighting tooth and nail to get one particular De Sica story which was just "an ideal subject for a great movie." But in the end De Sica decided to make the film himself. Among the younger generation he considers Renato Castellani one of the most promising directors, and is very enthusiastic about his *E Primavera*.

Although in the course of conversation Orson underlines several times that he is essentially a theatre man and "rather hazy on the subject of movies," the continuous flow of ideas cascading from his lips with fervour and conviction belies these affirmations.

"I definitely prefer to act on the stage than before the camera," he says. "I find film acting extremely exhausting, both mentally and physically, and I honestly believe I am not a good movie-actor. Even so, I prefer acting to directing, and I prefer writing to anything. Cinema as a medium of expression fascinates me, of course, but ever so often—when directing—I ask myself, whether we really know what we are doing and whether there is any reasonable proportion between the thousands of man-hours spent on the director's job and the final result. And then, I hate the worries connected with the financial and administrative side of film-making. . . ."

But between statements brought forward with utmost sincerity there are flashes of half humorous exaggeration obviously designed to produce a certain effect. They make me think of André Bazin's most fitting remark: "Welles possède en effet, parmi beaucoup d'autres, le génie du bluff. Il le traite comme l'un des beaux-arts au même tître que la prestidigitation, le cinéma ou le théâtre." ["Welles possesses in effect, among many other talents, the genius of bluff. He treats it as one of the great arts, at the same level as prestidigitation, cinema or theatre."]

When discussing contemporary Italian films, for instance, he suddenly remarks with a mischievous glint in his eyes: "Good as some of them are, they are largely over-estimated by snobs who avidly swallow the sub-titles and don't understand a word of Italian. I can see it, now that I have mastered the language. . . . You would probably like them only half as much, if you understood the dialogue."

At my slow-witted reply that my more than superficial knowledge of Italian led me to disagree, Welles with superb versatility turned his flash of irony into a firework of sarcasm:

"Oh, you know, this is part of a theory I once elaborated with Hitchcock in a happy moment. We decided then that in order to have a sweeping success in all the highbrow cinemas of the Anglo-Saxon world we should make a picture about nothing, in no language at all and with bad photography—but copiously sub-titled. We agreed that people would scream their heads off with delight."

I asked Welles whether his achievements of the last fifteen years or so had satisfied his ambitions. Of course they had not.

"I have lost years and years of my life," he exclaims, "fighting for the right to do things my own way, and mostly fighting in vain. I have wasted five years writing film-scripts which no producer would accept. Among the pictures I have made I can only accept full responsibility for one: *Citizen Kane*. In all the others I have been more or less muzzled, and the narrative line of my stories was ruined by commercially-minded people.

"I came to Europe because in Hollywood there was not the slightest chance for me (or for anybody, at that) to obtain freedom of action. With *Othello* I have now at least made a picture for which I can again accept full responsibility. It is true that I would have never embarked on that project, had I known that my financial backers would withdraw. This will be in any case the last of my 'adaptations,' as I am only interested now in putting my own stories on the screen. But left high and dry in the middle of shooting I have put every ounce of energy into this picture, and also every penny I had earned working on *The Third Man, Black Rose, Prince of Foxes* and *Black Magic*. Many people will certainly not understand why I accepted some of the parts in question. Well, the requirements of *Othello* are the explanation.

"I frankly don't think that I am particularly good as Othello but even so I firmly believe that this will be a remarkable picture. I have kept as closely as possible to the original, and the only change I introduced concerns the character of Iago, as played by the Irish actor Micheál Mac Liammóir; I have taken from him the diabolic quality and made him more human. The motive for his actions is supplied by the implication of impotence."

Orson is, of course, less happy about his previous Shakespeare film, *Macbeth*, which during its extended run in Paris has provoked a variety of comment, most of it not very flattering.

"On the first night there was a fight in the cinema between the supporters and adversaries of the picture," he told me. "Indifference would hurt me much more. After all, the film cannot be worthless if people like Jean Cocteau like it. On the other hand I don't take it as a compliment that the picture is having terrific success in Germany, where people are probably attracted by the medieval savagery of the subject. I now see its many shortcomings, particularly in the re-made version, but I still think that it is better Shakespeare than most stage productions of *Macbeth* I have seen. The worst of all is that nobody seems to judge the picture on its own grounds: as an experiment achieved in 23 days and on an extremely low budget."

Orson Welles looks tired, and he admits he is. It is not so much the actual work on the *Othello* production (that took almost a year) as the worries around it that have led to his feeling of exhaustion.

"Returning to the theatre for a while is to me a relaxation", he says with an ambiguous smile.

But his capacity for work is enormous. He treats his nightly appearances on the stage in two diametrically opposed parts as a welcome change from film-work, but his days are still occupied with the editing and dubbing of *Othello*. And in between he finds the time to prepare his next production.

And new films? Not for a while yet. But he entrusts me with the secret (an open one) that in his free moments (where on earth does he find them?) he is scripting a picture about sexual obsession called "Lovelife."

"Despite the subject, it will not be endangered by any censorship," he proclaims. "It will be so respectable that families will take their children to see it without the slightest hesitation. But if I succeed—the picture will shock every adult with human feelings and social conscience."

Interview with Orson Welles (I)

ANDRÉ BAZIN AND CHARLES BITSCH/1958

Cahiers du Cinéma had been hoping to interview Orson Welles for a long time. Our opportunity came during the Cannes Film Festival, which Welles attended for three days. The receptions, press conferences and cocktail parties were so numerous that this "interview" had to be carried out in a limited amount of time. We therefore resigned ourselves to speaking about a restricted number of films, and occasionally hesitated to pursue certain points which could have been developed in greater detail. However . . . we will try to continue this discussion in Paris when Welles arrives to film *Roots of Heaven*. . . .

Since we had to set ourselves some limits, our first questions were anchored in the period following Mr. Arkadin, *because it is not one of his better-known periods. Our point of entry was to ask Orson Welles what exactly his activities had been in television and theater, knowing that he had directed* Othello, Moby Dick, *and* King Lear.

I was hoping you'd ask me about film in general and not about my work, because the tragedy is that I don't like talking about my work. Maybe it's because I don't work enough! Oh well. As far as theater goes, you've just mentioned everything I've done in the past three years. As for film, you know what I've done, leaving aside the films I've made that are either unfin-

This interview, conducted during the Cannes Film Festival in May 1958, appeared in *Cahiers du Cinéma*, June 1958. Translated for this collection by Alisa Hartz. © *Cahiers du Cinéma*. Reprinted by permission.

ished or not yet distributed, including my *Moby Dick,* my *Don Quixote,* and my own version of a film called *Touch of Evil,* because the edit of *Touch of Evil,* like that of *Arkadin,* was, in the end, redone behind my back.

Moby Dick *is a film based on your play?*
Precisely.

And has this film been broadcast on English television yet?
No, not yet.

Is it finished, edited?
Almost edited.

Do you hope to finish it soon?
That depends on the directors of the television channel. All of us working in the entertainment industry are prodigious bluffers: we always pretend to be masters of our destinies, and journalists, the serious and the frivolous, collaborate in this bluff. The fact is that we don't decide what we're going to do. We're always running around the world trying to find the funding to make something. I think that as far as I'm concerned, I've reached an age at which it's useless to continue pretending that I have any control over these things, because it's not true. Journalists never stop asking me, "Do you intend to etc. etc.?" I intend to, obviously. I always intend to.

Besides Moby Dick, *you've undertaken other films for television. In particular, you were much spoken of in France at the time of the Dominici affair.*
Yes. That film is far from being completed. Now I'm going to finish a film on Italian cinema, on Lollobrigida.

A documentary?
A documentary in a very particular style, with drawings by Steinberg, a lot of still photographs, conversations, little stories . . . In fact, it's not at all a documentary. It's an essay, a personal essay.

An essay based on fact?
Not on fact. It's based on fact as much as any essay, but . . . it's not trying to be factual, it's simply not telling lies. It's in the tradition of a diary, my

reflections on a given subject, Lollobrigida, and not what she is in reality. And it's even more personal than giving my point of view; it truly is an essay.

This essay takes current events as its point of departure, like your film on the Dominici affair. Was that also an essay?
Yes, an essay about water. For me, the substance of the Dominici affair is the story of the problem of getting water. One couldn't say that my ideas about dry countries and the problem of water are appropriate for a factual documentary on the Dominici.

In what way is the story of the Dominici a story of water?
The answer to this question is my film. If I told you, I'd be detracting from my film, and that's all I have. It would take a lot of words to explain it, but to explain it in English, French or in any language would be betraying my film. It's the story of water because it was the night that water was streaming torrentially through the Dominici farm that the crime took place. The role of water in the story of a family like this one is what got me interested. I'd need at least a half an hour to answer your questions, while with images I can do it in fifteen minutes. If it weren't a film but a book by André Gide, for example, you wouldn't be surprised to read that the murder took place because of water. But you expect a film to be factual. I have a passion for films that turn their back on fiction but are nonetheless not of the genre that say, "Here's the truth, such is life, etc." Rather, they are made of opinions, the expression of the personality and ideas of the director.

Your Don Quixote *is in three episodes?*
No, that's imprecise. The film will be presented in a single unit.

It's a modernized version of Don Quixote*?*
Yes, in a way. The anachronism of Don Quixote in relation to his era has lost all its efficacy now, because the differences between the sixteenth and the fourteenth centuries are not very clear in our minds. I've simply translated this anachronism into modern terms. As for Don Quixote and Sancho Panza, they're timeless. In the second volume of Cervantes, when Don Quixote and Sancho Panza arrive at a certain place, the people always say, "Look! There's Don Quixote and Sancho Panza. We read a book about them." In this way, Cervantes gives them an amusing side, as if they were both fictional creatures

and more real than life itself. My Don Quixote and Sancho Panza are exactly and traditionally based on Cervantes, but they're our contemporaries.

The film is an hour and a half long?
An hour and a quarter for the moment. It will be an hour and a half when it's finished and when I've filmed the H-bomb scene.

It was probably filmed more quickly than an ordinary film?
No, not more quickly, but with a degree of liberty that one seeks in vain in normal productions, because it was made without cuts, without even a narrative trajectory, without even a synopsis. Every morning, the actors, the crew and I would meet in front of the hotel. Then we'd set off and invent the film in the street, like Mack Sennett. This is why it's enthralling, because it's truly improvised. The story, the little events, everything is improvised. It's made of things we found in the moment, in the flash of a thought, but only after rehearsing Cervantes for four weeks. Because we rehearsed all the scenes from Cervantes as if we were going to perform them, so that the actors would know their characters. Then we went into the street and performed not Cervantes, but an improvisation supported by these rehearsals, by the memory of the characters. It's a silent film.

Will it stay silent, with only a musical accompaniment?
No, I'll speak a commentary. There will be almost no post-synchronization, only a few words.

Do you perform in the film?
I appear as Orson Welles, I don't play a character. There's also Patty McCormack, an extraordinary actress. She plays a little American tourist, in the hotel.

Why did you opt for this method of improvisation?
Because I'd never done it before. That's the only reason. I could easily invent a reason, an aesthetic reason, according to which a film should be filmed in this way, and then I could say that there's no other way to make a film, etc. But the real reason is that it's a method of filming that I've never used and I know it was used in certain masterpieces of silent film. I was also sure that the story would be fresher and more interesting if I were really improvising,

and it is, there's no question. Obviously one must have complete confidence in the actors. It's a very particular way of working, almost impracticable for commercial films.

This way of working doubtless limited your visual experimentation, and from this point of view, your Don Quixote *is probably very different from your other films?*
No, not at all. It's very stylized, much more so than anything I'd done before. It's stylized from the point of view of the frame, and the use of lenses.

Do you still use wide angle lenses, the 18.5mm?
Yes, everything is in 18.5. For *Touch of Evil,* too, practically everything is in 18.5. That lens has unsuspected possibilities.

I recently saw Arkadin *again in Paris. You used the 18.5 for all the shots?*
No, not for all the shots, but for the majority. In *Don Quixote,* everything is in 18.5.

How long did it take to film Don Quixote?
One two-week period, then another three weeks.

Plus the preparation.
Yes, the preparation of the actors, which was very particular. I still have to do the last two scenes. I had to stop filming because Akim Tamiroff had to work on another film, and then I had to play in *The Fires of Summer* to have enough money for my *Don Quixote,* and it's been like that the whole time. We have to wait for a moment in which the actors and I are free at the same time.

Because you made Don Quixote *with your money?*
Yes, naturally. No one would have given me this opportunity.

Is this also the case with the film on Gina Lollobrigida?
There, too, yes. That project may be slightly more commercial! I'd have no luck if I did otherwise. It's very difficult for me to find work.

What's more, it's been said that it was partly by accident that you made Touch of Evil. *Someone else was supposed to do it?*

No. But there are scenes in the film that I neither wrote nor directed, of which I know absolutely nothing. In *Ambersons* there are three scenes that I didn't write or direct!

You made Touch of Evil *because nothing else turned up?*
It was my eighth film! You know, I've been working for seventeen years, I've directed eight films and I've only controlled the editing for three of them.

Citizen Kane *and . . . ?*
Othello and *Don Quixote,* in seventeen years!

And The Lady from Shanghai?
No, not the final cut. My editing style is still discernible, but the final version of the film is not at all mine. Films are always violently torn from my hands.

Do you think that there are important differences between your version of Touch of Evil *and the studio's?*
For me, almost everything baptized *mise en scène* is an enormous bluff. In film, there are very few people who are truly directors, and, among them, there are very few who actually have the opportunity to direct. The only truly important direction happens during the editing. It took me nine months to edit *Citizen Kane,* six days a week. Yes, I was directing *Ambersons,* despite the fact that there were scenes which were not mine, but my editing was modified. The basic montage is mine, and, when one of the scenes in the film holds together, it's because I edited it. In other words, it's as if a man were painting a picture. He finishes it and someone comes along and retouches it, but clearly he can't add paint on to the whole surface of the canvas. I worked months and months editing *Ambersons* before it was ripped away from me. So all that work is there, on the screen. But for my style, for my vision of film, editing is not an aspect, *it is the aspect.* Directing is an invention of people like you. It's not an art, it's at most an art for one minute per day. This minute is terribly crucial, but it happens only rarely. One can only take control of a film during the editing. Well, in the editing room I work very slowly, which always enrages the producers who tear the film from my hands. I don't know why it takes me so long. I could work for an eternity editing a film. As far as I'm concerned, the ribbon of film is played like a musical score, and this performance is determined by the way it is edited.

Just as one conductor interprets a musical phrase *rubato,* another will play it very dryly and academically, a third romantically, etc. The images alone are insufficient. They are very important, but they are only images. The essential thing is how long each image lasts, what follows each image. All of the eloquence of film is created in the editing room.

Editing does indeed seem essential in your recent films, but in Citizen Kane, *the* Ambersons, Macbeth, *etc., you used many sequence shots.*
Mark Robson was my editor for *Citizen Kane.* Alongside Robson and Robert Wise, the assistant, I worked for almost a year on editing. So it's wrong to think that there was nothing to edit just because I used a lot of long takes. We could still work on it. You might note that in these last few years, the films I've shot are more concerned with short takes, because I have less money and the style of the short take is more economical. For a long take, you need an enormous amount of money to control all the elements in front of the camera.

Othello *is indeed made up of short takes.*
Yes, because I never had all the actors together at the same time. Any time you see someone from the back, with a hood on their head, you can be sure it's a stand-in. So I had to do the whole thing in shot-reverse shot, because I could never get Iago, Desdemona, Roderigo, etc. in front of the camera at the same time.

It seemed to me that this is also the case in Arkadin, *but after seeing it again, I don't think so. The link scenes are quite precise.*
But the link scenes are precise in *Othello* too. I simply filmed them on different types of emulsions. The link scene can be as exact as you will, but if you're filming on Dupont, on French or American Kodak, or on Ferrania, you will have fatal jumps in the tone when you mix them in the edit. For *Arkadin,* once again, I didn't use long shots, because a long shot requires a large and capable technical team. There are very few European teams competent to successfully carry out a long shot, very few men, technicians who can manage it.

Still, in Othello, *there is, for example, the scene between Othello and Iago, on the terrace.*

That's true, but it's a shot that was produced very simply, with a jeep. That shot is a jeep and two actors. And how many jeep shots can you put in a film? In *Touch of Evil,* for example, I did a shot which moved through three rooms, with fourteen actors, where the frame varies between close-ups and long shots etc., and which lasts for nearly a reel. Well, this was far and away the most costly shot of the film. So, if you've noticed that I don't use long takes, it's not because I don't like them, but because no one gives me the necessary means to treat myself to them. It's more economical to make one image, then this image and then that image, and try to control them later, in the editing studio. Obviously I would prefer to control the elements in front of the camera while I'm filming, but that requires money and the confidence of your sponsors.

The idea of montage seems to be linked to short takes. Thinking about the Soviet experiments in this area, it would seem that one can really only take full advantage of montage with short takes. Isn't there a contradiction between the importance you give to editing and the fact that you like long takes?
I don't think that all the work of editing is a function of the brevity of the shots. It's wrong to say that the Russians worked with montage a lot because they were filming short takes. One can spend a good deal of time editing a film of long takes, when one isn't content with simply pasting one scene to another.

What goal are you pursuing by using the 18.5 lens so systematically and pushing the techniques of editing as far as you do?
I work, and I have worked, in 18.5 only because other filmmakers haven't used it. Film is like a colony and there are very few colonists. When America was wide open, with the Spanish at the Mexican border, the French in Canada, the Dutch in New York, you can be sure that the English would go to a place that was still unoccupied. It's not that I prefer the 18.5. I'm simply the only one who's explored its possibilities. I don't prefer improvisation. Quite simply, no one has worked with it for a long time. It's not a question of preference. I occupy positions that aren't occupied because, in this young medium of expression, it's a necessity. The first thing one must remember about film is that it is a young medium. And it is essential for every responsible artist to cultivate the ground that has been left fallow. If everyone worked with wide-angle lenses, I'd shoot all my films in 75mm, because I believe very

strongly in the possibilities of the 75mm. If other artists were extremely baroque, I'd be more classical than you can imagine. I don't do this out of a spirit of contradiction, I don't want to go counter to what has been done; I just want to occupy an unoccupied terrain and work there.

Since you've used the 18.5 for a long time now, you must already have explored a good portion of the terrain, and yet you persist. Isn't there some affinity between you and this lens?
No, I continue working with it because no one else has. If I kept seeing movies with shots filmed in 18.5, I'd never touch it. I'd have gotten tired of its characteristic distortion and I'd look for another language in which to express myself. But I don't see enough of these images to be weary of them, and I can look at the distortion with a fresh eye. It's not in the least a question of an affinity between me and the 18.5, but simply of the freshness of the gaze. I'd love to make a film in 100mm, and never leave the actors' faces. There are a million things that could be done! But the 18.5 is a new, important invention. Decent 18.5's have hardly been around five years, and how many people have used them? Every time I give one to the head cameraman, he's terrorized. By the end of the filming, it's his favorite lens. I may have finished with the wide-angle lens at this point. Sometimes I think that for me *Don Quixote* marks the end of the 18.5 . . . or maybe not!

Do you attribute so much importance to editing because it's somewhat neglected these days, or because, for you, it really is the very foundation of film?
I can't help but believe that editing is the essential thing for a director, the only moment when he completely controls the form of his film. When I'm filming, the sun is the determining factor in something I can't fight against; the actor brings into play something to which I must adapt myself; the story too. I simply arrange things so as to dominate whatever I can. The only place where I have absolute control is in the editing studio. Consequently, that's when the director is, potentially, a true artist, for I believe that a film is only good insofar as the director has managed to control the different materials and hasn't satisfied himself with simply keeping them intact.

Your montages take so long because you're trying out different solutions for . . .
I'm looking for a precise rhythm between one frame and the next. It's a

question of ear. Editing is the moment when film involves the sense of hearing.

So it's not problems of narration or dramatic tension that stop you?
No, it's the form, like a conductor interpreting a musical phrase with *rubato* or not. It's a question of rhythm, and, for me, that's essential—the beat.

What is your position regarding the resources offered by wide screen and color? Do you think one should turn instead to the small screen and poverty of television?
I'm convinced that when the screen is big enough, as in the case of Cinemiracle or Cinerama, there's also a poverty to it, and I adore that. I'd love to make a film with one of these methods. But between the Cinemiracle and a normal screen, there's nothing that interests me. The poverty of television is marvelous. Clearly a great classic film will be bad on a small screen, because television is an enemy to the values of classic film, but not to film itself. It's a marvelous form, the spectator is only five feet from the screen. But television isn't a dramatic form, it's a narrative form, the ideal form of expression for a storyteller. And the giant screen is also a marvelous form, because, as in television, it's a limitation, and one can't hope to elicit poetry without creating under limitations; that's clear. I also like television a lot because it gives me my only chance of working. I don't know what I'd say if I also had the chance to shoot films. But when one is working for something, one must be enthusiastic!

So working with television implies a particular conception of communication?
And also a certain richness, not visual richness, but a richness of ideas. On television one can say ten times more in ten times less time than in film, because one is only addressing two or three people. And above all, one is addressing the ear. In television, for the first time, film takes on true value, discovers its real function, because it speaks. Because the most important thing is what one says and not what one shows. Words are no longer the enemy of film; film simply supports the words, because television is merely illustrated radio.

So television might be a way of bringing film back to your beginnings in radio?
It's mostly a way of satisfying my fondness for telling stories, like Arab storytellers in a bazaar. As for me, I love all that. I never tire of hearing stories,

you know, so I make the mistake of thinking that everyone has the same passion! I prefer stories to dramas, to plays, to novels. It's an important aspect of my taste. I have a difficult time reading "great" novels. I like stories.

Isn't the public less attentive to television than to film?
They're much more attentive, because they're listening instead of watching. Television viewers listen or they don't listen, but if they listen at all, they're much more attentive than in a movie theater, because the brain is more engaged by the scene of hearing than by sight. In order to listen, you have to think. Looking is a sensual experience, more beautiful, perhaps, more poetic, but attention plays a lesser role.

So for you, television is a synthesis of film and radio?
I'm always looking for synthesis. It's work that fascinates me because I have to be sincere to what I am, and I'm merely an experimenter. My sole value in my eyes is that I don't dictate laws but am an experimenter. Experimenting is the only thing I'm enthusiastic about. I'm not interested in art works, you know, in posterity, or fame, only in the pleasure of experimentation itself. It's the only domain in which I feel that I am truly honest and sincere. I'm not at all devoted to what I do. It truly has no value in my eyes. I'm profoundly cynical about my work and about most works I see in the world. But I'm not cynical about the act of working on material. It's difficult to explain. We professional experimenters have inherited an old tradition. Some of us have been the greatest of artists, but we never made our muses into our mistresses. For example, Leonardo considered himself to be a scientist who painted rather than a painter who was a scientist. Don't think that I compare myself to Leonardo; I'm trying to explain that there's a long line of people who evaluate their work according to a different hierarchy of values, almost moral values. So I don't go into ecstasy when I'm in front of an artwork. I'm in ecstasy in front of the human function, which underlies all that we make with our hands, with our senses, etc. Our work, once it is finished, doesn't have the importance that most aesthetes give it. It's the act that interests me, not the result, and I'm only taken in by the result when it reeks of human sweat, or of a thought.

Do you have any specific directing projects?
No, I don't know. I'm seriously thinking of completely stopping all my work

in film or theater, finishing with it once and for all, because I've been too disillusioned. I've put in too much work, too much effort for what was given to me in return—not in terms of money but satisfaction. So I'm thinking of utterly abandoning film and theater, because in a sense, they've already abandoned me. I have some films to finish. I'm going to finish *Don Quixote,* but I no longer want to plunge into new endeavors. I've been thinking of leaving film for five years now, because I've spent 90% of my existence and my energy without having reached the level of an artist, and while I still have some youth left, I have to try to find another terrain where I can work, stop wasting my life trying to express myself in film. Eight films in seventeen years is not a lot. Maybe I'll make other films. Sometimes the best way of doing something one loves is to get some distance from it and then return to it. It's like a sentimental story: you can wait in front of the door of the girl to let you in, but she'll never open it. You're better off leaving and then she'll shout after you! No, it's nothing dramatic, you know. It's not that I'm bitter or anything like that, but I want to work. These days I write and I paint. I'm looking for some way of expending my energy, because I've spent the greater part of these past fifteen years in search of money, and if I were a writer, or especially a painter, I wouldn't have had to do that. I also have a serious problem regarding my personality as an actor. I have the personality of a successful actor, which encourages critics around the world to think that it's time they discourage me a bit, you know: "It would do him some good to tell him that he's not as great as all that." But they've been telling me the same thing for twenty-five years! No, I've really spent too many months, too many years looking for work, and I have but one life. So for now I'm writing and painting. I throw away everything I do, but maybe I'll finally do something good enough to keep. I have to. I can't spend my whole existence at festivals or in restaurants begging for money. I'm sure I can't make good films unless I also write the screenplay. I could make thrillers, obviously, but I have no desire to. The only film I wrote from the first to the last word is *Citizen Kane.* Well! Too many years have passed since this opportunity was given to me. Can I wait another fifteen years until someone is willing to give me his absolute confidence again? No, I have to find a more economical means of expression . . . like this microphone!

And you don't want to direct something for the stage?
In London, maybe, but I don't know. Whatever I might do in theater in the

future, I have to write it too. So, in any case, I have to stop and write, and not simply get up on stage to perform or direct, because too many talented people have displayed their virtuosity in directing plays, to their great glory. Thus I must bring my ideas and not my virtuosity to the theater. And if I make my re-entry into the theater, which I hope to do, I'll try to do it with what I have to say and not the way I have to say it, because during these past fifteen years I've quite neglected what I have to say.

And Shakespeare?
I'd love to turn towards Shakespeare, but my way of seeing Shakespeare doesn't coincide with today's taste. I'm from an entirely different school. It's a hopeless battle, because right now in the world there's a school of Shakespeare that I quite respect, but which isn't mine, and there doesn't seem to be a place for mine, or at least, when I do try to find a place for it, it's such toil! I'm not in a state anymore to accept many more defeats. I have to find a terrain on which my chances of losing don't exceed my chances of winning. And I experienced my chances of losing with Shakespeare in New York with *King Lear*. I think it was a very good show. Maybe it was bad, but if it was as bad as they said in the reviews then the only thing left for me to do is to retire, because there's no point of contact. The critic of the *New York Times* wrote, "Orson Welles is a genius without talent"! I think the scenery was really extraordinarily beautiful and no one mentioned it, neither for nor against!

Was the reception of Othello *in London better?*
Yes. Like every time I do something, there were people against it, but I nonetheless had some supporters.

And how long did you perform King Lear*?*
Four weeks, from my wheelchair. It was the maximum I could do and everyone hated my show. So why push the issue?

Interview with Orson Welles (II)

ANDRÉ BAZIN, CHARLES BITSCH, AND JEAN DOMARCHI/1958

IT SEEMS TO ME THAT THE PUBLICATION of this interview would be less than complete if I did not attempt to give the reader a sense of the extraordinary spectacle that my colleagues and I beheld. It took place in a room in the Ritz Hotel where Orson Welles received us, after a day of filming on *Roots of Heaven*. If I understood correctly, Welles was expected to attend a reception just after the interview, but instead of the hour and a half we had agreed upon, he granted us a four-hour interview, the charm of which cannot be attributed solely to whiskey. He was extraordinarily relaxed, wearing socks and a shirt wide open beneath an immense, multicolored, Othello-esque tunic re-cut as a robe. He was as god-like as Jupiter, but an affable tyrant, wielding a ten-inch cigar instead of a bolt of lightning and effortlessly intoning the melodious thunder of his voice. This time he was truly Orson the Magnificent. This needs to be noted, inasmuch as his later films might seem to indicate that he had embraced decrepitude to the point that one might imagine a certain physical deterioration. And certainly, Welles at forty-three is no longer the Welles of *Citizen Kane*, nor even of *The Third Man*, but calling him beautiful is an understatement. The seductive, doll-faced young man has come to incarnate powerful splendor. This phe-

From *Cahiers du Cinéma*, September 1958. This interview, conducted in Paris in June 1958, continues the preceding Cannes conversation. The introduction to the interview was originally written by André Bazin and translated for this collection by Alisa Hartz. The translation of the interview is from material compiled by Peter Wollen for the Film Study Center at the Museum of Modern Art, in New York City. © *Cahiers du Cinéma*. Reprinted by permission.

nomenon, indeed, is common in a certain kind of artist or, in any case, in a certain kind of director. Maturity, or at least old-age, effects a strange metamorphosis. Take a photograph of Renoir at thirty and one at age sixty: he does not seem like the same man, or, rather, he doesn't represent the same state of existence. It doesn't look as if the slim, lively and nervous gentleman who filmed *Nana* had simply plumped up with age, gradually becoming the white elephant he is today. I'm sure that if he were measured, the Jean Renoir we know would be at least half a foot taller than Jean Renoir of the thirties. Clearly he has amplified in all senses of the word; his very bones have doubled in size. Welles at forty-three, congenitally precocious, is the living illustration of this particular biology of the genius, bent on growing to the bitter end. Orson of 1958 is Welles of 1938 squared.

The other thing that this text cannot convey is the chant of his velvety voice on the recording. The laborious efforts I have to make to understand English gave me an advantage, this time, over my colleagues, allowing me to float along in the verbal music. And, truly, I must pass this on so as not to keep the memory of these images to myself alone. I've seen Welles in various circumstances over the past ten years, in private and public, but I'd never experienced this harmony of the human body and voice, the musical, spectacular state of being which blinded me in the room of the Ritz Hotel on June 27, 1958.

The day was waning. As we re-emerged out on to the Place Vendôme we were drenched and refreshed by a downpour. A photographer who had missed the whole thing was waiting outside. Our heads still echoing from the thunder of his voice, Bitsch, Domarchi and I were heading for the car, trying to work off our intellectual intoxication together, when I was suddenly struck with the image that had been hovering just out of my grasp for three hours. There was only one thing that bothered me about Welles's refined dishevelment, his multicolored tunic—something suggested by the disarray, the shirt open to his Buddha-like navel; something, or rather someone. Welles should have been nude under a greatcoat: he was Rodin's sculpture of Balzac!

I should explain to the reader that this interview was extemporized. Orson Welles had just read an article by François Truffaut in *Arts* and another by myself in the *Observateur*. Both of these articles underscored, with different nuances, the moral ambiguity of "disagreeable" characters in Welles's oeuvre, and for me, Quinlan's destiny was the crowning ambiguity of them all.

ORSON WELLES: I strongly believe that the critic always knows more about an artist's work than the artist himself; but at the same time he knows less; it's even the function of the critic to know simultaneously more and less than the artist.

——*What we would like to extract is the quintessential character who runs through all your films. Is he the one referred to by Truffaut in* Arts *when talking about* Touch of Evil: *the genius who cannot help doing wrong, or should one see in him a certain ambiguity?*
WELLES: It's a mistake to think I approve of Quinlan at all. To me, he's hateful: there is no ambiguity in his character. He's not a genius; he's a master in his own field, but as a man he's detestable. The personal element in the film is the hatred I feel for the way the police abuse their power. And that stands to reason: it's more interesting to discuss the ways in which the police abuse their power when you are dealing with a man of a certain stature—not only physically, but in terms of character—than it is with a little ordinary cop. So Quinlan is more than a little ordinary cop, but that does not stop him being hateful. There is no ambiguity about that. But it is always possible to feel sympathy for a swine, because sympathy is a natural human attribute. Hence my tenderness for people who I make no secret of considering repellent. This feeling doesn't arise from the fact that they are gifted, but from the fact of their being human beings. Quinlan is sympathetic because of his humanity, not his ideas: there is not the least spark of genius in him; if there does seem to be one, I've made a mistake. Technically he's good at his job, he's an authority. But because he has a certain breadth of ideas, because he has a heart, you can't stop yourself feeling a certain sympathy for him; in spite of everything he's human. I think Kane is a detestable man, but I have a great deal of sympathy for him as a human being.

——*What about Macbeth?*
WELLES: Same thing. I've played lots of bad characters, you know, some from choice, some not. I detest Harry Lime, he's a despicable little black marketeer, all the horrible types I've played; but they aren't "little" people, because I'm a natural for "big" characters. You know in the old French classi-

cal theatre, there were actors who played the Kings, and those who did not; I'm one of the ones who play the Kings. I have to, because of my personality. And so it results that I always do play the parts of leaders, of people who have got great breadth: I always have to be bigger than life. It's a fault in my nature. So you mustn't believe that there is anything ambiguous about the way I approach these parts. It's my personality which produces these effects, not my intentions. It's a very serious matter for a creative artist to be an actor as well; he runs a strong risk of being misunderstood; since in between what I'm saying, and what I am understood to be saying, there is my personality. And a great deal of the mystery, the confusion, and the interest, everything that can be found in the role I'm playing comes from my own personality, and not from what I'm saying. I'd be very happy never to act in a film again. I do act in them, because sometimes they allow me to be a director afterwards. If there is an ambiguity, it is because I've acted in films too much. Certainly Quinlan is a person with a world view, but it is one I detest.

——Isn't the feeling of ambiguity reinforced at the end of the film, when it is discovered that Quinlan was right all the same, since the young Mexican is guilty?
WELLES: He was wrong in spite of everything: it's pure chance. Who cares whether he's right or not?

——Isn't it important?
WELLES: That depends on your point of view. I personally believe what the Heston character says. The things said by Vargas are what I would say myself. He talks like a man brought up in the classic liberal tradition, which is absolutely my attitude. So that's the angle the film should be seen from; everything Vargas says, I say. Also is it better to see a murderer go unpunished, or the police being authorised to abuse their power? If one had to choose, I'd rather see crime going unpunished. That is my point of view. Let's consider the fact of the young Mexican being really guilty: what exactly is his guilt? That's no business of ours. The subject of the film is elsewhere. That man is only a name in a newspaper; nobody cares a damn whether he's guilty or not. It's a pure accident of the plot; the real guilty one is Quinlan. And when André Bazin writes that Quinlan is a great man etc. it's because Menzies, Quinlan's friend, says he's a great man. Nobody else says it. And Menzies says it because he sincerely believes it, but that tells you something about Menzies's personality, not Quinlan's. Quinlan is his god. And as Menzies

adores him, the real theme of the script is betrayal; the terrible necessity for Menzies to betray his friend. And that's where there is ambiguity, because I don't know whether he should have betrayed him or not. No, I really don't know. I force Menzies to betray him, but the decision does not come from him, and frankly, in his place, I would not have done it!

—*While we are talking about Menzies and Quinlan, there was one thing we did not quite understand; when Quinlan is dying, by the recording machine, he says that this is the second bullet which he got because of Menzies.*
WELLES: That's why he limps. He saved Menzies' life once in the past, and in the process got a bullet in his leg. Menzies tells Vargas's wife about it when he takes her away in the car. Perhaps they cut it?

—*Yes, they cut it.*
WELLES: Ah that's how it goes! Well . . . so, years before Quinlan had shown great courage in protecting Menzies in a gun fight, and has since walked with a stick. So when he talks about a second bullet, he is torturing his friend by sadistically reminding him of the first time he got shot on his account, but that time it was for a hero, and this time it's not.

—*And so are we to understand that your sympathy for Quinlan is purely human, and has nothing to do with his moral attitude?*
WELLES: Certainly not. My sympathy is with Menzies, and above all with Vargas. But in that case, it is not human sympathy. Vargas isn't all that human. How could he be? He's the hero of a melodrama. And in a melodrama, the human sympathy goes, of necessity, to the villain. I want to be clear about my intentions. What I want to say in the film is this: that in the modern world we have to choose between the law's morality, and the morality of simple justice, that is to say between lynching someone and letting him go free. I prefer a murderer to go free, than to have the police arrest him by mistake. Quinlan doesn't so much want to bring the guilty to justice, as to murder them in the name of the law, and that's a fascist argument, a totalitarian argument contrary to the tradition of human law and justice such as I understand it. So, for me, Quinlan is the incarnation of everything I'm fighting against, politically and morally speaking. I'm against Quinlan because he takes the right to judge into his own hands, and that's something I hate more than anything else, people who want to be the judge all on their

own. I believe one only has the right to judge if one does it according to the
principles of a religion or a law or both; otherwise if people simply decide
personally whether somebody is guilty or innocent, good or bad, the door is
open to people who lynch their fellow-men, to gangsters who walk the
streets doing what they like, it's the law of the jungle. But of course there's
one thing I gave Quinlan, which I must love him for: that is, that he did love
Marlene Dietrich, and that he did get that bullet in the place of his friend,
the fact that he has a heart. But his beliefs are detestable. The possible ambiguity is not in Quinlan's character, it is in Menzies's betrayal of Quinlan.
Kane, too, abuses the power of the popular press and challenges the authority of the law, contrary to all the liberal traditions of civilisation. He also has
very little respect for what I consider to be civilization, and tries to become
the king of his universe, a little like Quinlan in his frontier town. It's on that
level that these people resemble each other, similarly Harry Lime, who'd like
to make himself the king of a world which has no law. All these people have
this in common, and they all express, in their different ways, the things I
most detest. But I love, and I understand, I have human sympathy for these
different characters that I have created, though morally I find them detestable. Goering, for example, was a detestable man, but nevertheless one has a
certain sympathy for him; there was something so human about him, even
during the trial.

—*Himmler, on the other hand, was a complete thug.*
WELLES: Yes, so much so that it's impossible to say anything about him.
But you can look at Goering and say: Well, that man is my enemy, I hate
him, but he is human, not in his ideas but in himself.

—*From your point of view, is Othello a detestable man too?*
WELLES: Jealousy is detestable, not Othello. But insofar as he becomes so
obsessed by jealousy as to be the personification of it, he's detestable. All
these noble characters: Lear, for example, insofar as he's cruel, is hateful. One
of the very great themes in Shakespeare is that all his most interesting characters have a nineteenth-century morality; they are all villains. Hamlet is a
villain, without doubt, because he wants to kill his uncle without allowing
his soul to be saved. Think of the relish with which he describes the murder
of Rosencrantz: he's a villain. Despite everything else he may be, Renaissance
man, Shakespeare, all the things that have been written about him, he is

nonetheless a swine. All Shakespeare's great characters are swine: they are forced to be.

——*One could say the same about your characters.*
WELLES: I think one can say it about all dramatic writing which attempts to be tragic inside the framework of the melodrama. Ever since melodrama has existed, the tragic hero has a tendency to be a swine. Only the Greeks and the French classical writers were able to have heroes who were not bad men because they were tragic in the abstract. But as soon as you get mixed up with any kind of melodrama, the tragic character has to be a villain, one way or another, quite simply because a hero, in a melodrama, is nothing at all. A hero is insufferable except in a real tragedy. It is impossible to write a real tragedy for the general public; at least it has not been done since the Greeks or since the age of the classical French poetic drama. Shakespeare never wrote a pure tragedy; he couldn't. He wrote melodrama which had the stature of tragedy, but that did not stop them from having melodramatic stories. And since they are melodramas the heroes are villains. The pure heroes, the true heroes, like Brutus, are all bad parts, nobody wants to play them, nobody cares about them, nobody is interested in them. Brutus is a tremendous part, there are some wonderful speeches in it, but not one actor particularly desires to play him.

——*In* Julius Caesar, *Caesar is a swine.*
WELLES: Totally. They all are in *Julius Caesar*. It's a very interesting play because Shakespeare has feelings for and against everyone in it. And in general, it's Shakespeare's great quality never to be prejudiced one way, either morally or politically.

——*I suppose, from your point of view, Arkadin is no nicer than the rest?*
WELLES: No, Arkadin is better, because he is much rather a pure adventurer. In fact, I find him completely sympathetic.

——*What about the character played by Robert Arden?*
WELLES: Oh, he's terrible. He's the lowest of the low.

——*Which is doubtless why, when they are in conflict, Arkadin seems so noble and impressive.*

WELLES: Yes, Arkadin is not a skunk. He does, and has done, a lot of unpleasant things. Who hasn't? He's an adventurer. He's what Stalin would have been if Stalin hadn't been a Communist. The sympathetic side of Stalin—Stalin as a man, not Stalin as an historical fact—is the pity in the Russian temperament, the great sentimentality over certain things, that curious, typically Slav characteristic; I like that very much.

——If, as you say, your characters are not detestable in the human sense, this word human even if it doesn't imply approval of a world view, must imply some sort of positive value for you.
WELLES: Well, the only positive value is that it's the best I can say of my enemies. Also, when I get inside a character's skin, as actor or author, when I become that character, I draw upon the best of myself within the framework of the role, so that the character does absorb some of the best in me.

——You play the devil's advocate to yourself.
WELLES: More than the devil's advocate. More. Because, confronted with these characters, I transfigure them by giving them the best of myself, but all the same, I detest what they are.

——What do you think of Robert Browning's remark that he personally had such an elastic conscience that it would stretch to encompass the point of view of his enemies?
WELLES: Oh, he was an actor. All great writers are actors, even merely competent ones are. They have the actor's capacity for getting inside the skins of their leading characters and transfiguring them—whatever they may be, even murderers—with what they can give of themselves. They do that quite as much as actors do. And so it happens that quite often the protagonists of a story seem to be speaking for the author, whereas really all they are demonstrating is his talent, not his opinions. In other words, when Arkadin talks about cowards, he is being humorous, which is something of mine, but I'm not, for all that, Arkadin, and I don't want to have anything to do with all the real Arkadins there may be around.

——But you can't make us believe that the remarkable consistency in your choice of "detestable" characters doesn't imply more than sympathy. You are against them, but you do more than simply plead for them; you'd have difficulty in making us

believe that besides condemning them you don't in some way admire them, and want to stand surety for them, give them some sort of chance of redeeming themselves. You do give the devil a chance to redeem himself and that's surely important.
WELLES: All the characters I've played and that we've been talking about are Faustian, and I'm against the Faustian outlook, because I believe it is impossible for a man to be great unless he acknowledges something greater than himself. It can be the Law, it can be God, it can be Art, or any other idea, but it must be greater than man. I've played a whole line of egoists, and I detest egoism, the egoism of the Renaissance, the egoism of Faust, all of them. But it goes without saying that an actor is in love with the role he is playing: he is like a man embracing a woman, he gives something of himself. An actor is not the devil's advocate, he is a lover, somebody in love with someone of another sex; and Faust, for me, is another sex. I believe there are two great human types in the world and one of them is the Faust type. I belong to the others, but in playing Faust, I want to be just and loyal to him, give him the best of myself, and put forward the best arguments that I can in his favor, because after all we live in a world which was built by Faust. Our world is Faustian.

——*There are actors who will play any kind of character, but we have noticed that throughout your films, on whatever pretext, even if the scripts have nothing in common, your characters all have something in common. So one could deduce that in spite of what you say, you may indeed intend to condemn these characters, but it is a condemnation which . . .*
WELLES: I don't say I condemn them necessarily in the cinema. I only condemn them in life. In other words—and it's very important to make this distinction—I condemn them in the sense that they are against the things that I am in favour of, but I don't condemn them in my heart, only with my mind. The condemnation is cerebral. And that is complicated by the fact that I play the parts of the people I condemn. Now you are going to tell me that an actor never plays his own role; when one sets about acting a part, one begins by taking away everything that is not oneself, but one never puts in anything which isn't there already. No actor can play anything but what is in him already. And so, of course, there's Orson Welles in all these characters. I can't help it; it's he who is playing them, not only physically, but *Orson Welles*. So, I don't bring in part of my political or my moral beliefs, I put on a false nose, I do all that, but it's still Orson Welles. I believe a lot in the

blic Library
y Branch Library

ou renewed

aloged item record
74108292
day, August 26, 2019

Huck Finn

s: 1
1:15 PM
out: 4

<><><><><><><><><>
at www.sandiegolibrary.org OR by
he Mission Valley Branch Library at
3-5007. Your library card number is
d to renew borrowed items.

qualities that were involved in chivalry, and when I'm playing the part of someone I detest, I try to be very chivalrous in my interpretation.

——*Yes indeed, in all your films there is a great deal of generosity.*
WELLES: I think it's the chief virtue. I hate all the opinions which deprive humanity of the least of its privileges; if any creed demands that one should renounce something human, then I detest it. I am against all fanaticism, I hate political and religious slogans. I detest anyone who wants to cut off a note from the human scale; at every moment one ought to be able to strike any notes one desires.

——*It's a difficult position. You detest people who act in the name of religion, or politics . . .*
WELLES: No, I don't detest *them.* What I detest is that they should act that way.

——*Yes, but at the same time you say that one ought to believe in something greater than man.*
WELLES: Yes, it's a very difficult position. One has to renounce something, certainly. It would be difficult for me to explain this ambiguity. It's my pressure-point. Every artist, you know, every thinking man, has a point where he's under pressure, where he's drawn two ways by different extremes. This is just the case with me: you've put your finger on it exactly. But if I had to choose, I'd always choose respect rather than egoism, responsibility rather than adventure. And that goes against my personality, which is that of the egotistical adventurer: I'm just cut out to follow in the footsteps of the Byronic adventurer, though I detest that kind of person in everything they do.

——*You called Macbeth detestable, but he is also a poet. In one sense, wouldn't that justify him?*
WELLES: He was a detestable man until he became king, and then once he is crowned he is doomed; but once he is doomed he becomes a great man. Up to that point he is the victim of his wife and of his own ambition, and ambition is a detestable thing, a weakness; everyone who falls a victim to ambition is weak in one way or another. Shakespeare always chose great themes: Jealousy: *Othello,* Ambition: *Macbeth.* When he has made Macbeth

king, we are still only in the middle of the third act; there are still two acts
and a half where Shakespeare can relax and say: well, now we've got this
goddam ambition out of the way, I can get down to talking about a great
man, who likes good wine.

——*Do you think that Othello or Macbeth are absolutely pessimistic?*
WELLES: Shakespeare was.

——*Even in* The Tempest?
WELLES: Very much so. Do you remember the lines:

> And deeper than did ever plummet sound
> I'll drown my book.

Shakespeare was terribly pessimistic. But like a great many pessimists, he was
also an idealist. It is only optimists who are incapable of understanding what
it means to love an impossible ideal. Shakespeare was very close to the origin
of the culture he was in. The language he wrote had just been formed, the
old England of the Middle Ages was still alive in the memories of all the
people of Stratford. He was very close indeed to another age if you understand me. He was standing in the door which opened onto the modern age
and his grandparents, the old people in the village, the countryside itself,
still belonged to the Middle Ages, to the Old Europe; and actually Shakespeare still has something of it: his lyricism, his comic verve, his humanity
came from his links with the Middle Ages, which were still so close to him,
and his pessimism, his bitterness—and it's when he allows them free rein
that he touches the sublime—belong to the modern world, the world which
had just been created, not the world as it existed for eternities, but *his* world.

——*Do you think* Arden of Faversham *was written by Shakespeare?*
WELLES: No.

——*By Thomas Kyd?*
WELLES: Probably. Anyhow, not by Shakespeare.

——*Gide attributes* Arden of Faversham *to Shakespeare*
WELLES: Oh well, that doesn't surprise me. It doesn't surprise me at all
coming from him. Nobody dislikes Gide more than I do. In point of fact he

leaves me entirely cold. There are lots of writers whose ideas are the complete opposite of mine, but who I nevertheless read and enjoy; I needn't agree with them in the very least on anything but that doesn't matter. But I think Gide is a disaster; I don't want anything to do with him or his books. He's just had too much of a harmful influence on too many minds in France, young intellectuals. And he doesn't seem to me in the very least to have the mind or the imagination of a poet; he's pedestrian to say the least. It's quite obvious that he decided *Arden of Faversham* was by Shakespeare simply because it's a good play. He drew his conclusion from just one piece of evidence.

——*It's a play about the bourgeois world, which Shakespeare doesn't seem to be very interested in.*
WELLES: That's true. Shakespeare was not interested in the bourgeoisie; he always makes them into clowns. He spent the last twenty years of his life struggling to be raised into the aristocracy and have a coat of arms. One of his great obsessions, like Balzac, was with legitimacy. When you read *Richard II* you can see how horrified he was by the violence that can be done to legitimacy, you know, to the anointed king. Shakespeare had a great passion for kings, much more than for the aristocracy. I think he was rather disappointed by the Elizabethan aristocrats, but the idea of the throne and the king is one which runs throughout his work. I've always kept on telling American actors that we can never have a great Shakespearian theatre in America, because it's impossible to make a group of American actors understand what Shakespeare meant by "king": they think it means a man who one day puts on a crown and starts to sit on a throne; he may be good, he may be bad, he may be tall and thin or short and deformed; and that's the "king." They just do not understand that to Shakespeare, much more than to any other writer, a king was someone in a quite singular and separate tragic position. The crown was really one of his obsessions.

——*Would you like to direct* Richard II *on the stage?*
WELLES: I'd love that. Years ago, in Ireland, I acted in it. But I've never directed it. It's an extraordinary play. You see, Shakespeare is at his most exciting—like any other artist—when the characters he created take over and begin to live their own independent lives, leading the author against his will. Bolingbroke leads Shakespeare against his will into some marvellous scenes

which Shakespeare couldn't possibly endorse; and this gives the play a quite exceptional charge.

—*Shakespeare is obviously on Richard's side?*
WELLES: Absolutely. And yet he has to do justice to Bolingbroke, and more than that, he has to make him real, human, and he does it to such an extent that suddenly this man, Bolingbroke, comes alive, and takes over a large part of the play. You see Shakespeare trying to hold him back, but in vain, once he has got going there is no stopping him. Shakespeare often gets overwhelmed by his characters. In fact certain scholars have put forward a very interesting theory to the effect that, contrary to previous belief, Shakespeare did not only play the minor parts but the leading ones as well. He is now thought to have played Iago.

—*And he played the Ghost in* Hamlet.
WELLES: Yes, that was known. But that he should have played bigger parts, Iago, Mercutio, that's a thrilling idea. Because those are two secondary roles that can steal the play from the stars.

—*Have you ever put on* Hamlet?
WELLES: Yes, twice: in Chicago and in Dublin. It was once suggested that I should put it on with Marlon Brando, but in the end it came to nothing. I wasn't very enthusiastic about the project, though Brando could have made an interesting Hamlet. But *Hamlet* really ought one day to be put on as a play, and not simply as an opportunity for a romantic actor to show off. The play has suffered, not commercially, but in itself, from having been staged in too romantic a way.

—*Hamlet is a very strange character, because sometimes he believes in God and sometimes he does not.*
WELLES: Oh, he believes in God, I'm sure.

—*But not in his famous soliloquy*
WELLES: Oh yes. Don't you think that the world is full of people who believe in God, but don't believe in Heaven and Hell? Don't you think it's possible to believe in God without believing in Heaven and Hell? He cer-

tainly talks about Paradise a lot, all that, but not about God. He doesn't say "Is He, or is He not?" but "To be or not to be." It's very different.

——*That would suggest that the soul is not immortal?*
WELLES: Oh well, you know, there are all sorts of Christian heresies which deny the immortality of the soul; and they've been going a long time. God exists, but that does not mean that the soul is immortal. I don't think Shakespeare, who had such a legitimist attitude to the throne, the crown, God, had ever consciously questioned the existence of God. But as for God's court, His palace, His courtiers, His Heaven and Hell, he might have wondered whether they existed. But he did believe that the temporal crown and throne existed, as his way of speaking about royalty bears witness and you can't feel like that about a king without affirming the existence of God. A king without God? That does not make sense, because the king is God's representative.

——*But Shakespeare is also a man of the Renaissance, and criticism of religion began at that time.*
WELLES: No, excuse me. It began before. Here, in Paris.

——*Yes, but in England.*
WELLES: No, it began there before, too. Think of Thomas Wyckham! No, excuse me, but I don't believe the English Renaissance was interested in criticising religion. The real time for that was the 14th century

——*People were prudent in the 14th century. In the Renaissance they began to be less so.*
WELLES: Yes, but what happened in the Renaissance was that man became the central theme in the tragedy of life. That was what happened; the new importance of man. Faust first makes his appearance during the Renaissance. But there was no criticizing of religion; it was simply relegated to a secondary role in the tragedy of life. Shakespeare was not interested in religion, no more than the Renaissance writers were, Italian or otherwise.

——*I said that because Shakespeare had doubtless read Montaigne*
WELLES: Montaigne? Did you mention Montaigne? He's my favorite writer, you know.

——Shakespeare will have read Montaigne in Johannes Florio's translation.
WELLES: The famous Florio. Yes, possibly.

——And Montaigne's scepticism, his fundamental irreligiousness perhaps had . . .
WELLES: No, that I can't accept, because really for me, Montaigne is the greatest writer of any time, anywhere. I literally read him every week like some people read the Bible, not very much at a time; I open my Montaigne, I read a page or two, at least once a week, just because I like it so much. There is nothing I like more.

——In French, or . . .
WELLES: In French, for the pleasure of his company. Not so much for what he says, but it's a bit like meeting a friend, you know. It's something very dear to me, something marvellous. Montaigne is a friend for whom I have a great affection. And he has some things in common with Shakespeare, too. Not the violence of course.

——Would you agree that Shakespeare is the greatest Italian?
WELLES: As well as being the greatest Englishman. But not the greatest Frenchman. He wasn't in the least French. But Italian, yes, and Italy at that time had so much influence on England. So it's not surprising.

——The Ancient World also had a great influence.
WELLES: Yes, but Italy most of all. You know, England dreaming of Italy, just like Rome dreaming of Greece; it's a very particular kind of dream. It lasted three hundred years.

——Plutarch was bad for Shakespeare in Julius Caesar; *it's not one of his better plays.*
WELLES: No, but it's one of his most effective, like *Richard III*. It's one of those that come across to the audience with the most impact.

——To get back to your own work. It has always seemed to me that there is a profound unity discernible in it, which I would have said derived from a Nietzschean view of life. Is this so?
WELLES: I don't know what it derives from, but I hope there is a unity to my work, because if your work doesn't belong to you like your own flesh and

blood, then it can't be of any interest, I believe, and I feel sure you would agree with me, that a work of art is good to the degree in which it expresses the mind of the person who created it. I always feel very involved with my scripts, ideologically. I'm not interested in them as scripts; it's their ideological basis that I'm interested in. I hate rhetoric in a play, or moralizing speeches, but nonetheless the moral basis of a play is the essential thing, in my view.

——*But your ideology is not the normal one, it's one of superiority.*
WELLES: Well, I certainly can't deny that I'm more interested in character than virtue. You could call that a Nietzschean viewpoint; but I think I'd call it aristocratic, as opposed to bourgeois. Sentimental bourgeois morality makes me sick; I prefer courage to all the other virtues.

——*That's what we were meaning to say when we talked about a different kind of morality, a morality of superiority.*
WELLES: Oh, I don't believe it's all that different. It's only different from the morality of the nineteenth or twentieth century.

——*The leading character of* The Lady from Shanghai, *for example, doesn't fit at all into the present-day way of life.*
WELLES: No, certainly he doesn't. He is both a poet and a victim. But once again, he represents—I don't want to seem to be using this word like a snob—he represents an aristocratic point of view. I don't mean something baronial, but more connected to the old ideas of chivalry, with very ancient European roots. There is nothing specifically Nietzschean about that, Nietzsche's ideology is only another expression, another form of this very old ideology which has nothing to do with the industrial revolution, the bourgeoisie and all those ideas I don't like. I'm a man who loves to do satire, but we live in an age where it is impossible to find work as a satirist. I've never been able to do a film or a play on a satirical subject: nobody is interested in it. And it is very difficult to attack vulgar morality without having recourse to satire: I've been obliged to do it in the cinema by having resource to melodrama, which is much less effective. Take a story like *Touch of Evil:* it's about a superior being, because Heston is a superior man, not because he is handsome, or because he has an imposing manner, but because he is civilized, and cultured in a deeper way. It's not only that he is good, and incapable of doing anything low, but he understands what it is to be good. Thus you have

in him a man who is capable of standing up to a scoundrel without preaching, and the arguments that he makes against police power are such as could only be made by a cultivated man.

——*In* Citizen Kane *and* Lady from Shanghai, *were you intending to criticize American civilization?*
WELLES: I certainly was. I think every artist has an obligation to criticize his own civilization, his contemporaries. It's clearly and obviously the task of an artist of any ambition. Every French person ought to criticize the present French civilization. It's a responsibility.

——*But was it your intention to criticize a capitalistic viewpoint?*
WELLES: The capitalistic viewpoint as opposed to the materialistic viewpoint? If I admitted that I was criticizing capitalism, it would look as if I were adopting a Marxist attitude, and that's not so. It's no accident that *Citizen Kane* is banned in Russia. They don't like it at all, any more than the capitalists like it. I am an anti-materialist. I don't like money or power, or the harm they do to people. It's a very simple old idea. And I am specially opposed to plutocracy; it's American plutocracy that I am attacking, from different angles in several films: *The Magnificent Ambersons, Lady from Shanghai,* and *Citizen Kane.*

——*And in* Touch of Evil?
WELLES: There too, but from now on I'm more interested in the abuse of power by the police and the State, because today the State is more powerful than money. So I'm looking for a way of saying that.

——*A lot of French critics have said that* Citizen Kane *was very influenced by Dos Passos.*
WELLES: I've never read Dos Passos. I read an essay of his once, and that's all. But that wasn't out of the famous *42nd Parallel.* I don't think I have been influenced by Dos Passos; if I have been, it's pure chance. For instance, American critics say that my film was influenced by Proust, and that's manifestly wrong.

——*Wouldn't you say that the greatest influence discernible in your work was Shakespeare?*

WELLES: Yes, without any doubt.

——*For instance, in* Touch of Evil *the nightwatchman character.*
WELLES: Yes, the complete Shakespearian clown, and like the Shakespearian clowns, somewhat marginal to the story. And you know, that part was
improvised; no dialogue was written for it. I hired the actor, and built up the
part impromptu. A famous American critic saw the film and detested it
chiefly because of this character, he was just astonished; why have such a
character at all? But why not? Also, such people didn't exist in real life. Well,
they can in a film! This critic was really shocked by that nightwatchman, as
were a lot of other Americans. I am very American myself; my tastes don't
shock the average American so much, simply the American intellectual. It's
very odd; I don't intend it, that's how it turns out. American intellectuals are
a different breed from me, I don't manage to communicate with them at all.
I try, but if by chance they do like one of my films it's always for the wrong
reasons. I know they were very shocked by that nightwatchman, because he
was a real clown, a real Pierrot Lunaire, and it seems to me as though the
horrific atmosphere by which he is surrounded could not of necessity bring
forth anything but a fantastic creature of this kind, an Elizabethan figure, as
you say. And the fellow is marvelous in the role; he's somewhat related to
those sketched-in characters that turn up in old ghost stories.

——*There's a strange thing in* Touch of Evil; *the way you direct the scene where
Heston is listening to the conversation between Quinlan and Menzies makes it seem
like the scene where Othello is listening to the conversation between Iago and
Bianca.*
WELLES: I hadn't thought of it, but yes, it's true!

——*While Quinlan is walking straight along the road, Heston goes along a very
devious, difficult way. Why should the person who is listening-in be doing that?*
WELLES: He has to go through this labyrinth, among the derricks, because
he is the intruder; it's a scene where there is no place for him. Two old friends
are talking; if they saw Heston, nothing would happen. I therefore thought
he ought to look as though he was having a hard time of it, laboring, as one
labors to dig up gold, climbing, like one climbs a mountain. This kind of job
doesn't suit him and he detests it, as he says to Menzies; at this moment
Vargas loses his integrity. He is therefore thrown into a world in which he

does not morally belong; he becomes the low kind of person who listens at doors and he isn't able to do it. I've therefore tried to make it as though the machine were leading him, so that he is the victim of that, rather than of his own curiosity. He isn't very familiar with how to use this recording machine, and he just follows it and obeys it, because this thing doesn't belong to him: he's not a spy, he isn't even a cop.

——*There is a mystery that we'd like to clear up: are you the director of* Journey into Fear?
WELLES: No; for the first five sequences I was on the set, I decided the camera angles. And after that I often said where the camera should be. In other words I came on to the set with the camera, determined the composition of the shots, did light-tests, decided where the camera should be at what point in the dialogue, etc. So I to a certain extent "designed" the film, but I can't say I directed it; the director was Norman Foster. And it was he who made that film about the poor little boy and his bull, of which there's just a new version showing now on the Champs Elysées, you know, with a Cocteau drawing on the posters.

——*And what about* Les Clameurs Se Sont Tues?
WELLES: Yes. It was originally an episode of *It's All True,* from a script by Robert Flaherty. They took all the ideas and remade it according to their lights. And when it got an Oscar for the best original screenplay, no one turned up to receive it. People were saying the author must be a Communist! Not at all: nobody came because Flaherty was dead, and RKO didn't want to hear my name mentioned. I'd been shooting on it for three months, but RKO didn't let me finish and sacked me. Several years later the King Brothers took up the story again, and got RKO to distribute it, and so there were no more rights to pay. They worked hand in hand with RKO and acted as though it was an original story: *those are the facts.* The little boy we found is now a strapping twenty-five-year-old Mexican.

——*Is there no hope of ever seeing* It's All True *one day?*
WELLES: Not that episode anyway, because there has now been this remake. The rest perhaps, but it's impossible to tell. It's a very tough problem, because at RKO the film has already been through their profits and loss account which has allowed them to have a reduction in their tax; and it's

very difficult to get the thing going again because the government has given RKO a rebate on their excess tax, which they immediately spent. So it would be complicated now, even if RKO were in agreement. Perhaps one day it will be possible to do something. I've spent endless time, you know, months, years, trying to save this film. But the most interesting bit, the story I did about the "jangadeiros," those people who went down the Amazon to see the President of Brazil, is lost: it was a pure documentary. But RKO burnt it all: I saw nothing, except the color tests.

——*There was said to be 400,000 feet of film.*
WELLES: That's untrue. When RKO changed hands they said I had shot that much in order to justify my dismissal.

——*How much did you really shoot?*
WELLES: The normal footage for a film. I can't remember exactly: about 100,000 feet.

——*Was your share in making* The Third Man *about equivalent to your share in* Journey into Fear?
WELLES: It was more. I would prefer not to be asked about that, it's a delicate matter, because I wasn't the producer; I've a right to tell you about what I did on *Journey into Fear* though.

——*We feel there are sequences that you directed yourself completely, like for instance the one in front of the Great Wheel.*
WELLES: "Direct" is a word I must explain. The whole question is who takes the initiative. First of all I don't want to look as though I'm upstaging Carol Reed; secondly, he is incontestably a very competent director; thirdly, he has in common with me that if someone has a good idea, he lets them get on with it; he likes to see something inspired happening, and doesn't try to put it down because it's not his, as too many little film directors do. But it's tricky to say anything about this film, because I've been very discreet, and I don't want now . . . All I can tell you is that I entirely wrote the role of Harry Lime, because I got thinking about that cast of mind which sees everything in terms of a joke. I'm not the originator of the cuckoo gag; I got it from a Hungarian play, and as every Hungarian play is plagiarized from another Hungarian play it's a moot point where that gag comes from. I heard

it in my childhood, not exactly the same, but very similar. You know it's very old. And the real joke is that actually cuckoo clocks are made in the Black Forest, not in Switzerland.

——*There is such a close link between Harry Lime and your other characters . . .*
WELLES: As I said, I wrote everything to do with his character, I created him all round; it was more than just a part for me. Harry Lime is without doubt a part of my creative work; and he's a Shakespearian character too; he's very close to the Bastard in *King John*.

——*The character of Harry Lime is the one which, of all the parts you've played, seems the most closely attached to you, if not you as a private personality, you as an aesthetic personality.*
WELLES: Now that's interesting: it's the only part I've played without make-up!

——*Were you made up in* Lady from Shanghai?
WELLES: Yes, just a little on the bridge of my nose. Psychologically, I need to disguise myself.

——*And for Harry Lime you weren't made up?*
WELLES: No. It's an essential thing for an actor. For anyone who isn't an actor, it would be difficult to appreciate how important it is. But for an actor for whom the role itself is important and not just his own personality, the part you play without make-up is something quite extraordinary.

——*So make-up is something of great importance to you?*
WELLES: Because I like to hide myself. Seriously, it's camouflage. I don't like to see myself on the screen, and when I direct a film, I have to see the rushes: therefore, the more I am made up the less I recognize myself, and the more capable I am of making an objective judgment. I hide from my own image, which I don't enjoy seeing at all.

——*From what you say, it seems as though you belong more to Europe than America?*
WELLES: No, I belong to those whose company I appreciate, whose books I've read, whose conversation I enjoy, whose paintings delight my eyes. I

belong to the fellowship whose sympathies go back to ancient Greek roots, a few members of which are contemporaries of mine. It's a particular fellowship and there are some Americans in it and some Europeans, ancient and modern.

—*Is it a very restricted fellowship?*
WELLES: Not as restricted as all that. But what I love is not what I am. Some people just love themselves exactly as they are, and always find reasons to justify themselves. But because I am not in love with myself does not mean I'm neurotic. When I look at it in cold blood, I don't like the Fausts, the adventurers, the egoists, any of that bunch. In my view, it is their world we are living in. But nevertheless I can't detest them; I can't stop myself from finding them very attractive: they have a great deal of charm.

—*You are in a decidedly uncomfortable position.*
WELLES: But every artist is. The greatest danger for any artist is to find himself in a comfortable position; it is his duty to look for and remain in the most uncomfortable position possible.

—*Is the kind of uneasiness which one sees in the actors when you are directing part of this policy of being uncomfortable? They always seem not to be balanced quite right, to be in a precarious attitude.*
WELLES: Their attitude is very important. You will never see an actor imitating me in one of my films. If they look uncomfortable, I've let them get like that themselves. I've never shown them how. Ask any of the actors I've directed if they have ever felt uneasy personally when working for me, and they will tell you not. I don't terrorize actors. You know, there are two great schools of lion-taming, the French and the German. In the one, the French method, the animals are strictly kept in precise positions. In the other, the German method, the animals always look as though they were about to attack the trainer; one would have thought the former method would have been the German one, and the latter the French, but it's exactly the opposite. Likewise, there are two great schools of filmmakers; one where the director dominates the actor and terrifies him into becoming his creature entirely, and the other, to which I belong; I do not attempt to dominate my actors, all my actors will tell you that. Therefore, if they do seem to look uneasy, it's that I've seen them get into that precise attitude one evening, and I've real-

ized it was good, but I've never imposed it on them; I haven't said: watch, and do it after me! All the great German directors, Reinhardt, Körter (I'm talking about stage directors), employed the method of getting people to do exactly as they were shown. I don't indicate the kind of emphasis I want in the words either; if an actor has to say the line "Good morning Mr. Welles," I don't tell him to say it in such and such a way; I always let him say it his way. If my actors tend to look uneasy, it's because I think in most films actors have it too easy; they are allowed to act in the most lackadaisical manner, they don't even have to go to the trouble of appearing even a bit like beings of flesh and blood. In any case, my actors are not uneasy with their profession itself. You understand the difference?

——Yes, certainly. But you don't so much like having them sitting down, discussing endlessly, etc. You prefer them to keep moving?
WELLES: In *Arkadin*, Akim Tamiroff sits down on a chair and doesn't move from it for eight minutes. Katina Paxinou is also seated, and she doesn't move either, except the gestures required for a game of cards. In *Touch of Evil* it was different; I had a lot of young actors, I was very pleased and I had them move about a lot.

——You said that Arkadin was not an especially detestable man. What's your conception of the character? Is he like Kane?
WELLES: No, Arkadin is closer to Harry Lime, because he is a profiteer, an opportunist, a person who lives off the decay of the world, a parasite which feeds off the universal corruption of things, but he doesn't attempt to justify himself, like Harry Lime, by thinking himself a sort of "superman." Arkadin is a Russian adventurer, a corsair.

——Basil Zaharoff?
WELLES: Better. Zaharoff was a shabby character. Arkadin is a person who has made his way largely in a corrupt world; he doesn't try to be more than that world, he's trapped in it and is the best he could be within that frame of reference. He is the best possible "expression" of that universe.

——So seen in that way, Arkadin is the hero of a world . . .
WELLES: No, he's a character, not a hero—I've never played a hero in the cinema. I have in the theatre. I'd like one day to play a great heroic role in a

film, but it's difficult to find—Arkadin is the expression of a certain European world. He could have been Greek, Russian, Georgian. It's as if he had come from some wild area to settle in an old European civilization, and were using the energy and the intelligence natural to the Barbarian to make a good living from it. He's the Hun, the Goth, the Savage, who succeeds in conquering Rome. That's what he is: the Barbarian out to conquer European civilization, or Genghis Khan attacking the civilization of China. And this kind of character is admirable; it's only Arkadin's ideology which is detestable, but not his mind, because he's courageous, passionate, and I think it's really impossible to detest a passionate man. That is why I detest Harry Lime: he has no passion, he is cold; he is Lucifer, the fallen angel.

——*It seems to us as though you are divided between two conceptions of the world: a Renaissance conception and a Puritan conception.*
WELLES: Certainly not. Neither Renaissance, nor Puritan. I'm a man of the Middle Ages, with certain implications due to the barbarity of America. I am Arkadin to the degree that I belong to a wild nation which is also a new nation and ambitious to get ahead. But Puritan, certainly not.

——*You are shocked by that because in America the word Puritan has stronger connotations than it does here.*
WELLES: A Puritan is someone who refuses one permission to do something. The essential definition of Puritanism—I've made a study of it—is that it assumes the right to forbid someone to do something. For me that's the perfect definition of everything I'm opposed to. A moralist is not a Puritan.

——*Well, let's put it another way: that you are divided between the moral judgment made by your head and the moral judgment made by your heart.*
WELLES: No. I believe that I am divided between my personality and my beliefs, not between my heart and my mind. Have you the least idea, gentleman, what I'd be like if I just followed my personality?

——*We've been very struck in your work, from* Lady from Shanghai *to* Arkadin *and a little less explicitly perhaps in* Touch of Evil, *by the theme of character. Doesn't the scorpion say, "It's my character"? Is it an excuse that the scorpion makes to the frog? We would like to know how your own ideas relate to the story of*

the scorpion, because basically what we have been talking about does pose, does it not, the problem of the frog and the scorpion?
WELLES: Oh yes, well, there's a lot to say about that. Point number one. The frog was an idiot.

——So you think there was culpable stupidity on the part of the frog?
WELLES: Yes indeed!

——And do you consider that the scorpion was evil?
WELLES: Neither of them was any good. But seriously. I must insist that I was very serious when I said that I not only put forward the best possible arguments for my enemies being as they are, but I put into their mouths the best possible justifications I can find for their point of view. Nevertheless I do not feel that one can justify one's acts by saying it is one's character, although I admit that it is very tempting to do so. There is nothing more attractive than a bastard admitting he's a bastard. A man can be anything, a swine, a murderer, can admit to me that he's killed three people—the moment he admits it he's my brother, because he is frank. I believe that frankness does not excuse crime, but it makes it very seductive, gives it attraction. It is nothing to do with morality; it's a question of what is and is not attractive.

——That's a feminine view of life.
WELLES: The only good artists are feminine. I don't believe an artist exists whose dominant characteristic is not feminine. It's nothing to do with homosexuality; but intellectually an artist must be a man with feminine aptitudes. It's even more difficult for a woman because she must have masculine and feminine aptitudes . . . and then it gets very complicated. For a man it's quite simple.

——And so the scorpion is half forgiven?
WELLES: The point of the story is that the man who declares to the world "I am as I am, take me or leave me as such" has a kind of tragic dignity. It is a question of dignity, of stature, of attractiveness, of breadth of personality, but that doesn't justify him. In other words this story ought to be understood as a part of the drama, but not as a justification of Arkadin or of murder in general. And it's not puritanism that makes me against crime. Don't forget

I'm against the police too. As I see them, my ideas are more anarchic and aristocratic. Whatever judgment you may pass on the morality of my position, you should see its anarchic and aristocratic sides.

——*You are against evil, yet you believe that character . . .*
WELLES: Is the essential thing. That is the traditional aristocratic viewpoint.

——*Would you go so far as to say that it is better to have character than to do good?*
WELLES: No. No. "Character" has two meanings in English. If I talk about my character, that means that I am made like that, it is the equivalent of the Italian *"sono fatto cosi."* But in the story of the frog, it's the other meaning of the word which is not only the way one is made, but how one has decided to be. It's above all the way you behave in the face of death, because one can only judge people by their attitude to death. It's a very important distinction of meaning, because the term, used in this sense, can only be explained by the use of anecdotes.

——*Could it be translated by* personnalité?
WELLES: No.

——*Or* tempérament?
WELLES: Not exactly. I don't think there is an exact equivalent in French. It's not "the character" but just "character." Your character, my character: we understand what that means. But "character" can only be properly understood in an aristocratic context; I don't mean that only the nobility, people with titles and houses and lands, can understand the meaning. I don't want to look like a snob. "Character" is an aristocratic concept, just as "virtue" is a bourgeois concept. We don't care about virtue. What is character? For example: when the Germans came at six in the morning to take away and deport Colette's husband, who she loved desperately, instead of a dramatic farewell all she did was to give him a little pat and say "Go along with them at once!" That's character! I don't mean specially Colette herself, not anything general about her, but just what she did at that moment, it need only be a second. That scorpion story is Russian in origin.

——*In* Lady from Shanghai *O'Hara says that when he does something stupid he does it all the way. It's therefore his character too: isn't he the scorpion of the story?*

WELLES: Him? He's the frog. Oh yes, but completely! And more: he's a poetic frog, but a frog all the same! "Character" is the way one behaves when one denies the laws one should obey, and refuses to act in accordance with the emotions one feels; it's the way one behaves in the face of life and death. And the worst criminals, the most hateful, can have "character."

——Macbeth, for example?
WELLES: Not to that degree. *Macbeth* is much more a great play than the study of a great man. Othello has "character" but not Macbeth. The great moment, you know, the great flash of "character" in Shakespeare is in one of the least good of his plays, *Romeo and Juliet*: it is when Romeo learns Juliet is dead. He says then, "Is it e'en so? Then I defy you, stars." At that moment, it's Shakespeare talking, not Romeo.

——Have you seen Castellani's film?
WELLES: No.

——There is one of your films we haven't talked about, which was the least well-received by the French critics, and that's The Stranger.
WELLES: Good, well, I'm pleased we haven't, because it's the worst. There is nothing of me in that film. John Huston did the script, without being in the credits; I did it to show I could be just as good a director of other people's stories as anyone else, and in addition I did it in ten days less than the scheduled shooting time. But I didn't write a word of the script. No, I'm wrong; I did write one or two scenes that I liked well enough, but they were cut; they took place in South America and had nothing to do with the story. No, that film had absolutely no interest for me. But I didn't do it with a completely cynical attitude, I didn't deliberately make a mess of it; quite the contrary, I tried to do it as well as I could. But it's the one of my films of which I am least the author. I don't know if it is good or bad. The few little things that I really like are the small observations on the town, the chemist, details of that type.

——Would you tell us the film directors you admire most.
WELLES: You won't like what I am going to say, because the people who I admire are the least highly-valued by cinema intellectuals; it seems like a tragic misunderstanding to me. My favorite filmmaker is De Sica: I know I'm upsetting you. And John Ford. But the Ford of twenty years ago, the De Sica of twelve years ago. Ah *Sciusa*; it's the best film I ever saw.

——*What about the young American directors?*

WELLES: Detestable. Nothing to say about them. I despise them.

——*And Eisenstein? His name is sometimes brought up when your films are discussed.*

WELLES: I've never seen a film by Eisenstein. Oh, yes I have. Once; but I had a very long correspondence with him. Do you know why? Because I had violently attacked *Ivan the Terrible* in an American paper. And in Russia, one day, he heard about this article and wrote me an immense letter. I replied. He replied, I replied, etc. For years, we exchanged letters on cinema aesthetics. I know I don't hold the same opinions as you on the cinema. You like my films, thank heaven, but I don't like at all what you like. Also I don't see many films; the last masterpiece I saw was *Sciusa*. I'm very sorry. But that's my taste.

——*Some American directors have been seen as your disciples: Robert Aldrich, Nicholas Ray.*

WELLES: I haven't seen anything of Aldrich's. I have seen some things by Nicholas Ray but I didn't find them interesting. I left the cinema after four reels of *Rebel Without a Cause*: I get angry just thinking about that film.

——*What do you think about Vincente Minnelli?*

WELLES: Hey, we're meant to be having a serious conversation. We're talking about real filmmakers.

——*And what about the German directors?*

WELLES: Oh, the famous French theory about my having been influenced by the Germans? I've never seen a German film in my life. It's always been claimed that I'd seen *The Nibelungen* by . . . I've forgotten his name; that it had influenced my *Macbeth*. That's wrong. I've never seen that film. On the other hand, the German theatre had a very great influence on me. Among the young directors, the only one who seems any good to me is Kubrick: *The Killing* wasn't too bad, but *Paths of Glory* is disgusting; but there again I left after the second reel.

——*Did you see a lot of German stage productions?*

WELLES: An enormous number, when I was young, a kid, before Hitler's day. I went to see masses of German plays, also Russian and French plays. In my films I've been more influenced by the theatre than the cinema, because at the age when I was readily influenced, I went to see plays and not films. In reality there are not many filmmakers who have made much of an impression on me, or rather a few isolated ones, who aren't very highly esteemed by intellectuals. De Sica for example. You ought to be ashamed of not liking De Sica. If we could discuss it again in two hundred years you might have changed your tune.

——What about Rossellini?
WELLES: Now him, I have seen all his films: he's an amateur. Rossellini's films simply prove that the Italians are born actors, and that all you need to do in Italy to pass as a film director is get a camera and put a few people in front of it.

——So you're a self-made cameraman, if one can put it like that?
WELLES: I've only been influenced by somebody once: prior to making *Citizen Kane* I saw *Stagecoach* forty times. I didn't need to learn from somebody who had something to say, but from somebody who would show me how to say what I had in mind; and John Ford is perfect for that. I took Gregg Toland as cameraman because he came and said he would like to work with me. In the first ten days I did the lighting myself, because I thought the director should do everything, even the lights. Gregg Toland said nothing but discreetly put things right behind my back. I finally realized, and apologized. At the time, apart from John Ford, I admired Eisenstein—but not the other Russians—and Griffith, Chaplin, Clair and Pagnol, especially *La Femme du Boulanger*. Today I admire the Japanese cinema, Mizoguchi and Kurosawa, *Ugetsu Monogatari* and *Living*. I liked the cinema better before I began to do it. Now I can't stop myself hearing the clappers at the beginning of each shot; all the magic is destroyed. This is how I'd classify the arts, in order of the pleasure they give me: literature first, then music, then painting, then the theatre. In the theatre there is an unpleasant impression that one gets; the people are there looking at you, and for two hours, you're a prisoner of the stage. But I am going to tell you a much more terrible confidence; I don't like the cinema, except when I'm shooting; then you have to know how not to be afraid of the camera, force it to deliver everything it has to give, because it's nothing but a machine. It's the poetry that counts.

The BBC *Monitor* Interview

HUW WHELDON/1960

HUW WHELDON: *Orson, I know it's true that you've never, oddly enough, curiously enough, perhaps, ever in all your life talked about the actual making of* Citizen Kane *and* The Magnificent Ambersons, *although there have, naturally, been promotional interviews and publicity interviews and so on and so forth, but I know that you never have—why?*
WELLES: Well first of all as a matter of principle, Huw, because I think artists should talk on any subject in the world except their own work and that should speak for the artist. I do find it pompous and boring the things that my colleagues say about their best work and I have tried to avoid that up until tonight.

HW: *Tonight you are prepared to answer a question or two . . .*
WELLES: I'm resigned . . . I'm happy to, because . . . now *Citizen Kane* and *The Magnificent Ambersons* are going to be seen on television, by a lot of people who haven't seen these films and there are some things they might be interested in knowing that I would be happy to tell, which is quite another thing than carrying on about your art.

HW: *Of course it is. All right, let me start straight away by not carrying on at all about art: Is it true that when* Citizen Kane *was being made people actually tried to stop it being made, and is it true that Randolph Hearst, the newspaper tycoon,*

This interview was telecast on the BBC's *Monitor* program, 13 March 1960. Published by permission of the BBC.

took it as being an attack on himself and tried to stop it, when it was *made, from being shown?*

WELLES: To the first part of your question there was indeed a very definite effort to stop the film during shooting by those elements in the studio who were attempting to seize power, because in those days studio politics, particularly RKO and indeed many of the big studios in Hollywood, were very much like Central American Republics and there were revolutions and counterrevolutions and every sort of palace intrigue, and there was a big effort to overthrow the then head of the studio, who was taken to be out of his mind because he had given me this contract, which made the making of these films possible; and stopping me or proving my incompetence would have won their cause, so it wasn't malice toward me, it was a cold-blooded political manoeuvre—having nothing to do with Mr. Hearst. That came later. You asked me, did Mr. Hearst try to stop it—that's quite another story—he didn't—he, Mr. Hearst, was quite a bit like Kane, although Kane isn't really founded on Hearst in particular, there are many people who sat for it so to speak—but he was like Kane in that he wouldn't have stooped to such a thing, but he had many hatchet men, editors and representatives of this great network of newspapers all over the country and to get in good with the Chief there was a good deal of very strong intimidation, including an effort to frame me on a criminal charge, which a policeman was good enough to tell me about. It's sensational and silly and dangerous and gangsterish as that—it really can't be exaggerated—but Mr. Hearst must be absolved.

HW: *Was Mr. Hearst's staff absolutely wrong? I mean when you say that it was based on that kind of man—was he really stronger in your mind than just being that kind of man?*

WELLES: Well let me ask you if you think he was libelled?

HW: *Well I don't know* him, *you see.*

WELLES: I see, yes, well do you think that the figure of Kane himself is a deeply unsympathetic figure (H.W.: No.)? In the Soviet Union, for example, the film has been forbidden general distribution because this important capitalist and newspaper tycoon and anti-social and crypto-fascist figure, etc. etc., to quote all the slogans, is too sympathetic. For that reason it is not shown, never has been.

HW: *No, I wouldn't take it as being too sympathetic. Now that takes me on to another point I would like to bring up. When you read about* Citizen Kane, *a lot of the things you read suggest that it was a very big social document, a massive attack on big American institutions of the day. Now I've always seen it rather as a story, to be honest. Naturally any story has got its implications, but I have seen it as a story. I would like to know what your intentions were. Did you mean it as a social document or as a story?*

WELLES: I must confess to having to—I trust—answer this in a way that I loathe. I must admit that it was intended, consciously, as a sort of social document—as an attack on the acquisitive society and indeed on acquisition in general, but I didn't think that up and then try to find a story to match the idea. Of course I think the storyteller's first duty is always to the story.

HW: *It makes it all the more ironic, doesn't it, that it should have been stopped in the Soviet Union.*

WELLES: Yes, but of course it wasn't at all a Communist picture or a Marxist picture—it was an attack on property and the acquisition of property and the corruption . . . and of the acquisitive society of the man of real gifts and real charm and real humanity who destroys himself and everything near him—because, you know, tired old words, Mammon and all that; he really was, you know.

HW: *Now, when you made this film you were only 25, weren't you?*

(Film Clip from *Citizen Kane:* Kane as young newspaper editor)

WELLES: I think I should explain that I never looked as young as all that—the idea was to look very young indeed, indeed younger than anybody ever could look. And my whole face was yanked up with pieces of fish-skin in the way old ladies are fixed up nowadays.

HW: *Yes, in that way, I can't help feeling you must have been young sometime, Orson.*

WELLES: I was certainly 25 years old but there's a sort of untouched look about that face you may have noticed, which is impossible in real life.

HW: *Now the thing I noticed in particular about that scene—I mean everybody knows that you had the most astonishing contract that Hollywood has ever provided, ever, ever . . .*

WELLES: Not financially speaking—in terms of authority and rights— financially it wasn't extraordinary in any way at all; it was extraordinary in the control it gave me over my own material.

HW: *You had total control?*
WELLES: Total control—so much so that the rushes, which perhaps I should explain are the pieces of film that are shown at the end of the day's work and are always checked by everybody in the studio, department heads, the bankers, distributors and everything, long before there's a rough-cut— but according to the terms of my contract the rushes couldn't be seen by anyone, and indeed the film couldn't be seen until it was ready for release.

HW: *Except yourself . . .*
WELLES: Yes, and my own FAMILY—and it was a family, we were a little closed group.

HW: *Now, seeing that you had never in all your life ever made a film before* Kane, *and had never, so far as I am aware, been in a studio before* Kane *(WELLES: It's true . . .) quite apart from how you landed this contract, which was a result of enormous notoriety at the time and other gifts, what I would like to know is, how did you . . .*
WELLES: No, really, I must interrupt you, I got that good contract because I didn't really want to make a film.

HW: *Well, you had better develop that.*
WELLES: And you know, when you don't really want to go up to Holly- wood, at least this was true in the old days, the golden days of Hollywood, when you honestly didn't want to go, then the deals got better and better. In my case I didn't want money, I wanted authority, so I asked the impossi- ble, hoping to be left alone; and at the end of a year's negotiations I got it, simply because there was no real vocation there—my love for films began only when we started work.

HW: *Now, what I would like to know is, where did you get the confidence from to make a . . .*
WELLES: Ignorance, ignorance, sheer ignorance—you know there's no con- fidence to equal it. It's only when you know something about a profession, I think, that you're timid or careful.

HW: *How did this ignorance show itself?*

WELLES: I thought you could do anything with a camera, you know, that the eye could do and the imagination could do and if you come up from the bottom in the film business you're taught all the things that the cameraman doesn't want to attempt for fear he will be criticized for having failed. And in this case I had a cameraman who didn't care if he was criticized if he failed, and I didn't know there were things you couldn't do, so anything I could think up in my dreams I attempted to photograph.

HW: *You got away with enormous technical advances, didn't you?*

WELLES: Simply by not knowing that they were impossible, or theoretically impossible. And of course, again, I had a great advantage not only in the real genius of my cameraman but in the fact that he, like all great men, I think, who are masters of a craft, told me right at the outset that there was nothing about the camera work that I couldn't learn in half a day, that any intelligent person couldn't learn in half a day. And he was right.

HW: *It's true of an awful lot of things.*

WELLES: You know, the great mystery that requires 20 years doesn't exist in any field. Certainly not in a camera—it's the most overrated mystery on earth, you know. And I was lucky enough to be told by the absolute best living cameraman. Like a doctor—you know very good doctors often tell you, "You know we really don't know anything much about medicine"—I've noticed an awful lot of good doctors do talk that way, but only the very good ones.

HW: *You don't believe them, of course.*

WELLES: I do, implicitly—I don't think they know much. It doesn't seem to be the topic under discussion.

HW: *Now, in* Kane *there were these technical advances which everybody has talked about until they're blue in the face. And then I think if you see* Kane *again today, you can see have been largely digested by the film industry. I mean you see the ceilings are now in the shots, the lighting of* Kane *is now in all kinds of films— they've been digested. The thing that I noticed when I saw it the other day, before talking to you today, which I don't think has been digested at all, is the notion of making a film with a team of actors who've been brought from one theatre.*

WELLES: It's very interesting you should say that, because nobody's ever pointed it out as far as I know. The whole cast of that play, the entire cast, were a team from a theatre; we worked together for years. There was nobody who didn't belong to it except the second girl and the wife, but I mean the great body of the people were, and all of them were new to films—nobody had ever been in front of a camera before in the entire picture . . .

HW: *No, so I believe.*
WELLES: . . . at once, so. And that was deliberate; we didn't want anybody who knew anything, because we thought they would both show us up and change the dimension of the film, but it is true that that gives a kind of style, automatic style, to anything, just as a theatre in which players live and work together for a certain length of time begins to make its effect.

HW: *Yes, I don't ever recollect seeing a film, ever, except* Kane *and the* Ambersons—
WELLES: It's never happened, because nobody's ever had such a contract, just as I could never make *Kane* again until I got such a contract; nobody else will make *that* sort of picture under those ideal circumstances until another man will give a studio and its facilities to an artist to make the film he wants to make. It sounds terribly simple, but it literally never happens.

HW: *Why not? I mean, why never, if a film can be made with a team of actors of this kind and it does provide it with a style, it seems to stand to reason that it should—why shouldn't it ever happen?*
WELLES: Oh, coming back to the team of actors, of course, there aren't teams of actors anymore. There were two teams of actors in America in our time. One was the Group Theatre and the other was the Mercury, which was mine. Mercury came to Hollywood with Mercury productions, and the Group Theatre regarded pictures as rather a come-down from their lofty aspirations, and took it for money in separate ways, so that you had Garfield and Kazan and all these brilliant people moving off in different directions and only gathering together years afterwards and getting their strength together again, but they regarded films as a commercial adventure of which they weren't entirely persuaded in terms of merit, you see. And if they had gone as a unit, as a group—they were even more tightly knit than we were because

they made rather a thing of that—and they would have made extraordinary films. (H.W.: Yes, no doubt.) Oh no question, really no question.

H W : *When eventually* Kane *was made it was an enormous success as all the world knows, and it has gone on being a success, and it's a long time ago now. Have you ever regretted that so great a success came so early?*
WELLES: Well, I've regretted early successes in many fields, but I don't regret that in *Kane* because it was the only chance I ever had of that kind. I'm glad I had it at any time in my life—I wish I had it more often. I wish I had, you know, a chance like that every year; there would be 18 pictures, not just one.

H W : *Two,* Ambersons.
WELLES: Two, except *Ambersons.* At the end of it there's a very serious piece of surgery involved there, a change.

H W : *Which wasn't done by you.*
WELLES: No. There are two short scenes in it I didn't write or direct and over 3 reels were taken out in their entirety, and they were, in my view, the reason for making the film, not simply good reels, but the whole film was a preparation for those reels which were too tough and too . . . er—in those days, too hard-boiled for the exhibitors' tastes, and by the time I returned from South America—that's a long story I won't go into—to supervise the release of *Ambersons,* RKO had fallen into the hands of the counterrevolutionary forces. And I no longer was invited into the cutting-room.

H W : *You have been denied the cutting-room before?* (WELLES: Several times, yes)—*just recently in* Touch of Evil?
WELLES: That's happened really quite often to extremely individual filmmakers; I'm not saying it's a qualitative thing—it's a style, and there's a certain kind of filmmaker who really wants to make the film entirely on his own and that sort of fellow is the sworn enemy of the system . . . and the system is at great pains to denigrate such a person—not only myself but many people like myself—and that's happened in Russia as well as here . . . in America, it's happened in England, it happens everywhere in varying degrees. They rightly regard the artist as the enemy of their profession.

HW: *What do you think of Hollywood, Orson?*

WELLES: I'm not at all against Hollywood, not at all. It's, I think, a remarkable community with a great history and a very entertaining place to work in. The obvious things against it are so obvious that there's really no need to list them over again; anything you can say about Hollywood is true, good and bad; there's no extreme statement that doesn't apply.

HW: *Before we leave* Kane, *I would just like to look for a moment at one other excerpt . . .*

(Film Clip: Welles standing in front of gigantic fireplace)

I would like to ask you about that rather a technical question in a way; when you were making that sort of scene, that sort of shot, did you ever feel nervous that maybe you had gone too far? I put myself in your shoes, you see. If I had made that I would be terrified that I was just on the point of toppling over into farce, that I had made the fire too big, that I had made the room too large. Did you have this sort of anxiety?

WELLES: No, because the room is that big.

HW: *What room is that big?*

WELLES: Awfully pompous answer—his room.

HW: *Pompous question, perhaps.*

WELLES: No, not at all, you're quite right and I should have had that fear, but I do feel that a man like Kane is very close to farce and very close to parody—very close to burlesque, and that's why I tried every sort of thing from sentimental tricks to an attempt at genuine humanity—to keep him always counterbalanced; but of course anybody who could build a place of that kind, you know, is very close to low comedy.

HW: *Of course he is, that's quite right, good . . .*

WELLES: . . . and there's something terribly sad about it too. He's cut off from his newspapers, you know, he's talking about when the Bull-Dog edition is coming out, I think, if I remember.

HW: *Yes, yes he is. I'd like to turn now to something quite different. I know that Bernard Braden was witty and penetrating enough at one time to put a very simple question to you, which seemed to me a very good one, and that was "What does the word HOME mean to you"?*

WELLES: America. I didn't reply in those terms to Braden because, being a Canadian, and that is in our terms an American, because we don't make really all that distinction.

HW: *In our terms, of course, not American because we do . . .*

WELLES: I know you do, you see, it's very interesting. Of course, the real answer to home for me is America itself and I never feel anything except I've lived all my life as a cosmopolitan, but I have never considered myself as a man without a country. I'm very much an American and I deeply regret my inability to make films on American subjects, because they're the ones that interest me most.

HW: *Is it true that as a boy of 10 or 12 or 13 or whatever it was, that in fact you went rollicking around the world with your father?*

WELLES: Well, all of my childhood—my father lived part of every year in Peking and we travelled around—I rollicked round my whole childhood.

HW: *But what school?*

WELLES: Oh, very little school—about 3¹/₂ years.

HW: *What was your father?*

WELLES: He retired! . . . early in his life, having been an automobile manufacturer as in *Magnificent Ambersons*. He was one of the first in the world, the first in America, and one of the first automobile racers, and he gave it up, however, taking the view that automobiles were a passing phase, just as they were becoming very big, and went into the manufacture of bicycle lamps—on which he made a fortune. I don't know what that proves but you asked me what my father was. He was also a playboy, bon viveur, he was a great friend of Mr. Hearst's—among other things—and of Booth Tarkington, who wrote the novel on which *Magnificent Ambersons* was based. So there's a very close connection in both films to my father.

HW: *All right, that brings us back; I wasn't going to come back to* Kane, *but it brings us back to something I was going to ask you and forgot. I have heard it suggested that* Citizen Kane *is in some sort of sense autobiographical. Now you've*

just said that The Magnificent Ambersons *was in some sort of way autobiographical or at least about your own family* . . .
WELLES: Yes, in those chapters in an autobiography which have to do with
one's family, there's certainly truth because both have their sources in that
kind of thing, but the notion that Kane himself is some sort of version of
myself—I really fail to recognise; it may be out of blindness, but it seems to
me that Kane is everything that I'm not—good and bad.

HW: *Yes. Why do you choose, seeing that you are American, to live so much of
your life in Europe?*
WELLES: Because I don't get very much work in America.

HW: *As simple as that, is it?*
WELLES: Yes.

HW: *Where do you think good films are being made nowadays, if anywhere?*
WELLES: Those that are of any interest at all are being made all over. This
is not a period in which a country has any particular monopoly, unless it be
Japan and the young people in France just for a moment. These cycles come
and go—it's a very bad period now for films.

HW: *I would like to come back to* The Magnificent Ambersons *for a minute and
look at this clip where Agnes Moorehead is acting with Tim Holt.*
    (Film clip from *Magnificent Ambersons* of Agnes Moorehead on the stairs
with Tim Holt)
    *What I would like to ask you about, that is as a director, did you find that Agnes
Moorehead was a total actress in her own right as it were before she started on
films; that is to say as an actress did she take like a duck to water to films? Or did
she have to be directed into this sort of performance, which is a startling performance?*
WELLES: Well, every really fine actor has to be directed. It's only second
rate ones that don't need to be directed at all, because there's nothing a
director can do with them, except turn them on and let them do their turn,
you know? It's really fine ones that a director can do most with, and fine
ones who welcome directing, and that applies equally in the theatre and
films. The differences in the mediums are very small in the point of view of
acting in my view.

HW: *Do you prefer acting on films or acting in the theatre yourself?*

WELLES: I prefer acting in the theatre, but I really much prefer directing in all mediums, and *Ambersons* was a very happy experience for me because it's the only film I have ever made in which I didn't have to appear. It was a joy not to have to stand in front of a camera. And also to build a film around my own personality, which is very special and imposes certain limitations on any story that I'm in.

HW: *A lot of people of course say very often that one of the faults with you as an artist is that you direct yourself too much.*

WELLES: Well, I don't get to direct very often anybody so I don't know how much justice there is in that. I average one picture in four years, so you can't really say that I'm running myself into the ground as an auto-director.

HW: *Mind you, you have been in some of your own films, haven't you?*

WELLES: Yes, but they aren't all that numerous. In a period of 20 years, there haven't been all that many films for it to be possible to say that directing myself has had an effect on me as an actor; the experience hasn't occurred often enough, the directing of myself has been in the theatre and that is much more difficult than in films; it's very much easier to direct yourself in a film.

HW: *Is it? Why?*

WELLES: Well of course . . . shorter pieces . . . and of course you're making it for a machine, not for a public you know.

HW: *How do you choose a subject? What is the background to the choice of a subject? If the world was free to you and America was free and everyone was free and you could get contracts where you could make films as you wanted them, what sort of subjects would you tend to go for?*

WELLES: Well, they would be mainly contemporary subjects in the main or near our own periods, and they would be American more than anything.

HW: *Though, mind you, in the theatre you've very often gone for Shakespeare, haven't you?*

WELLES: Because that is my equipment as an actor.

HW: *You've directed Shakespeare too?*

WELLES: Yes, but I've also directed a great many contemporary things. When I'm thinking of films, I think of directing in the sense of writing-directing. I don't recognize a film as being completely a man's work unless he's also its author. So I answered your question assuming that you also meant I would be the author of the script as I was in the case of *Kane* and *Ambersons*. My only award in my entire career in films from America is for *Kane* as writer, you know? Toland didn't even get it as cameraman.

HW: Didn't *he?*

WELLES: No, no . . . they hissed every time our names were mentioned at the Academy Awards that year. Poor Toland had to wait for two years until he made *How Green Was My Valley* to get back into the good graces of everybody.

HW: *You said that your equipment allowed you to be a Shakespearean actor. Do you think that any actor . . .*

WELLES: Any actor who can do Shakespeare, or even thinks he can, does because it's such a joy—let me put it that way. Shakespeare wrote the best parts for anybody. Even people who have no right to do it—myself probably included; it's such a joy to play these parts.

HW: *Do you really think there is such a thing as a Shakespeare actor or just good actors?*

WELLES: No, but there are actors who imagine themselves in Shakespeare And I suppose that's what a Shakespearean actor is, you know. There are other actors more modest or more realistic or more humane in their regard for the sensibilities of an audience who don't make such presumptions.

HW: *Why are so many English actors on Broadway?*

WELLES: Because we like English actors, always have, there always have been—it isn't a new thing. As long as I can remember, since a baby, English actors have been immensely successful in America.

HW: *All right, let's come back to you. You said that if you direct a film you want to be its author as well, and it's known that you're an actor in films.*

WELLES: Not necessarily want to be. I prefer to be and those are the films I respect most. I was simply replying. You were saying what would I want most, and I want most to be the author of my films. But I have read film scripts or known films that I would like to direct. The films I am offered in America are invariably those I don't even want to go to see, you know. I do get jobs offered me but they really are very bad, and I do accept films as an actor that I don't respect very much. Minimum respect, minimum hopes go into the making of them. But as a director I don't feel I can do an honest job with the money investment on something I really hold in contempt. An actor's job is limited enough, so you can try to make that one thing as good as you can and be a good craftsman and take your money, and rush home with it and make a film as I have now, a new one coming up, but as a director, if you take something that is really contemptible, I think you are prostituting yourself, seriously, to do that.

HW: *Are you ever afraid that you have, in a sense, attempted too much? I mean you've done radio and you've written films . . .*

WELLES: I don't think I've attempted enough. I don't think anybody does. I think it's an age of terrible specialization—I think everybody has many more capacities than they have the gall to try out. And I regret how little adventuring I've done, not how much.

HW: *Is this really so?*

WELLES: Everybody of any gift or of any sort of authority or any capacity to communicate is, in my view, potentially good at any job that you could think of, that he or she could conceivably do. It has always been my joy in the few times when I have had a position where I could give jobs to people to try to put them into new jobs to show them they could do other things. It gives me a great deal of pleasure to see other people, you know, breaking out of specialization. It isn't really an exercise in my own ego.

HW: *There is another view, isn't there, that by putting shackles round yourself, by going into a prison, that you can produce works of memorable glory. A lot of the greatest artists the world has ever known have been, have forced themselves, into tremendous limitations, haven't they?*

WELLES: I don't think so, I think some of them have these limitations. I don't know of a great artist who has deliberately . . .

HW: *But he has used his limitations . . .*

WELLES: Ah . . . then he's using the maximum, including the limitations. I think an artist always uses the maximum, and if that includes starvation he uses starvation. If it involved the threat of deafness or blindness or madness he uses that, but he doesn't seek it.

HW: *At this stage I would like to take you once more back to* The Magnificent Ambersons—*to this excerpt.*
  (Film clip: *Ambersons*)
WELLES: May I tell you how it was made?

HW: *Please do.*
WELLES: We built a set. You may notice that the camera never moves—there's a very slight pan—that is a slight look from one direction to another on its own axis, the camera itself never moves. The actors were rehearsed for five weeks before we started the film. And on this scene at least four days, except that this scene was never written. No word of it was written—and we discussed everybody's life, each character's, their background, their position at this moment in the story, what they would think about everything and then sat down and cranked the camera, and every actor made up his lines as he went along. The scene lasts 3½ minutes or something in its entirety and was written by the actors as we went along. I'm very proud of them for it. It has an extraordinary effect, entirely due to their work and their preparation for doing it.

HW: *Which makes the question I was going to put unnecessary in fact—*(WELLES: What was that?) *This sounds like the Method.*
WELLES: It sounds terribly like it except that it's close in my view to the pure Stanislavsky than to Strasberg; but that's a very specialist reply to your question. It isn't Method really, because I didn't use The Method in preparing the actors. I believe in preparing actors by telling them about the entire society in which they live rather than emphasizing the psychological and psychiatric and Freudian aspects of characterization. That was never discussed. It was what the town was like they lived in, and what sort of schools they went to, and what they would think in this situation. Then out of their own experience they made it real or not, so it is certainly a method and certainly a close relative of the Method, but not The Method. All those actors would roar with indignation if they heard themselves accused of it.

H W : *When you hear yourself described as a showman, Orson, does that hurt you?*
W E L L E S : I think it hurts me in the opinion of a great many, very serious
and rather sober-sided egg-heads, particularly in the cinema world or everywhere; they regard that as a sort of lamentable failing on my part which they
must forgive. I think being a showman is a perfectly splendid thing to be and
I hope I am. I do know it interferes with me on a certain level of criticism. I
regret that, but I regard it as a weakness on the part of my critics. It sounds
arrogant, but I don't mean that they haven't a right to criticize me. l mean
that showmanship is not, in my view, a very bad thing. It's a very good thing,
it's our duty to try to get to the public isn't it, or ought to be, and showmanship is just that. And I—I—I am very cranky and in many ways timid and
very much against publicity, and always have bad, awful word, public relations because I hate all that and my only way of getting to the public is
through a certain flair for showmanship because I have none for public relations. I hate newspaper men, I hate interviews, except with Huw Wheldon,
and do everything I can to ruin the, another awful word, image of myself,
you know. But showmanship is my only way of getting to them at all.

H W : *Now you regard yourself not only as a showman, but as an artist too? I mean
these things aren't exclusive, that's the point.*
W E L L E S : Certainly not, certainly not. I think any theatre artist, as opposed
to a purely literary artist, I think to some extent I am a literary man, you
know. If we were speaking in French, artist wouldn't be such a pompous
word, but perhaps in English it is, without our meaning it to be. But as a
literary man you don't have to be some kind of showman, although most of
them are too.

H W : Some *are.*
W E L L E S : Most of them. That's another discussion. It's very few that really
aren't some kind. You know, there's almost no such thing as a theatre artist
who isn't a showman. It's, you know, by definition—what are you doing?
Performing in front of the public, or addressing them with your work if
you're not?

H W : *Let me ask you another question, the same kind. Do you regard the phrase
"actor-manager" as derogatory?*

WELLES: No, not at all, I think it's a marvelous one, I wish there were more and I think it's a splendid title.

HW: *You've in a way tried to make yourself an actor-manager in films, and succeeded.*
WELLES: Yes, as Chaplin has, as von Stroheim. There have been actor-managers and I think many of the most interesting films are actor-manager films, strangely enough.

HW: *Yes, the actor-manager tradition, of course, goes a long way back. Now you'd say that this must persist, this is part of our whole set-up.*
WELLES: Oh, I don't think anything must persist. I don't think films will persist. I don't think the theatre necessarily must. I don't think any art is eternal. I don't think anything is eternal that man makes in the real world.

HW: *Orson, I . . .*
WELLES: I know it's a very sweeping gesture, but finally everything disappears under the sands, even if nothing blows up, and we really don't know what the painting was like in Greece—or much about the music, you know.

HW: *There is such a thing as posterity, you know.*
WELLES: Yes, it's a limited idea. Behan's brother wrote a play called *Posterity be Damned.* I don't know if it's a good play or not, but it entirely expresses my feelings on the subject.

HW: *In the long run, like Kane said, we're all dead.*
WELLES: Yes, posterity is just another version of success, which is always rightly suspect.

HW: Citizen Kane *has been seen largely, I believe, recently—you must know this much better than I do—in France, and I know that some of the French critics have said that what ought to be done now is to forget all the technical advances and so on that* Citizen Kane *made and it should now be regarded as* Madame Bovary *is regarded. I don't know whether you have ever heard this, but even if you only hear it now from me for the first time . . .*
WELLES: It's true they have been saying that and it pleased me very much, not only because it's a great compliment, and we love compliments, and live

on them. It's silly for people to criticize us for liking compliments because what else are we—we need them to live, and we get fewer of them than anybody realizes, and that was a great compliment. Apart from that, I am very bored by the aesthetics of the cinema. I regard the whole bag of tricks of the cinema as being so petty and so simple and so uninteresting essentially. It's what a film says rather than a question of cinematic style and plastic shrinery, you know all this kind of special language that these people talk about in the cinema clubs; and I feel myself tremendously at odds with cinema clubs as much as with Hollywood, so I was very pleased finally to get from serious people in one country consideration for one of my films on the grounds that I think a film should be considered if it's considered seriously at all. It's not just all this business about the cinema. It isn't even an art form any more than prose is just a word: "prose," you know. What matters is what you're saying in it. The reality of the people or the world you create in it, not how you're doing it and all that.

H W : *However, it brings us back a little bit; it suggests that there is after all some kind of posterity—I mean you get this purring feeling . . .*
WELLES: Yes, of a limited kind. And of course we all enjoy, we try to find out anything that's good that's said because people of my kind really aren't, as I said, praised very often, so you do purr when something like that is said. Most of the praise that I get is harder to take than the criticisms, because I regard it as misplaced, you know. It's hateful to be applauded for what one considers to be the wrong thing—much worse than a terrible scalding attack, you know, that's never hurt anybody.

H W : *Orson, you're forever appearing in films even bigger than you yourself are— padded, clothed up . . .*
WELLES: Yes, anything to hide me, hoping not to be recognized when I'm in the street.

H W : *Oh, you'll be recognized.*
WELLES: Not as an actor, but as the fellow who had an interview with Huw Wheldon. I don't mind, you see, being recognized as that.

H W : *Have you ever, like the clown who wanted to play Hamlet, have you ever in your heart of hearts wanted, really passionately, to play a little tiny man, a slender little figure?*

WELLES: Yes, yes, and almost did it—Cyrano—who should be, I think, tiny, not necessarily slender, but tiny. He should be a little bantam rooster, I think, he should come to about here on me, you know. When I was going to do it with Alex Korda we were going to make the doorknobs higher on the doors, and the chairs bigger and everything to make him look tiny.

HW: *And hire very very tall actors . . .*

WELLES: Well, no, you can trick all that, you know. We're always standing around on what we call amble boxes, anyway, you know. There's one Western cowboy star who makes a weekly series. He's so tall that all the actors come to about here on him, you know—so they spend their lives walking around on platforms. That part of it's easy. There's one other small part I wanted to play once. I've always wanted to make a short, a one-reel farce about an infant prodigy, symphonic conductor, aged seven, with myself in a bobbed wig and a Fauntleroy collar and short trousers, clambering up onto the podium with a great long baton. With an enormous excitable Neapolitan family in the wings, you know, trembling at my frowns, you know, and conducting the *Messiah* or something, you know, aged 7. Myself, my eyes all made up and everything like that. I think it might be terribly funny.

HW: *I sincerely hope you never make it, that's all I can say.*

WELLES: You do? It frightens you?

HW: *It does, it frightens me. (Laughter)*

   Lastly, Orson, let me ask you this: In the end, what would you like people to remember you by when, after all, the time has come for you, like everybody else, to shuffle off this mortal coil?

WELLES: Well, I wish they would forget the things that are written in the serious American books, the kind of books that my children would find about me, which are written about the cinema, which are *very* derogatory; almost every American book on the cinema pricks the bubble and proves that what is said about me is a lie and I am no good. There is no book that says I am good in American literature; and I must say that talking about posterity . . . all I care about is, er, really my children, my grandchildren, if they ever say as I do, wondering about my grandfather who was a politician and a cabinet minister in America; and I would like to know more about him, and if somebody should ever want to know about me, which is the only posterity, I cannot take the rest of it seriously. I really wish there was something nicer that they could read about me . . .

HW: *I hope, Orson, somebody writes it for you pretty soon.*
WELLES: Thank you.

HW: *Thank you very much.*

A Trip to Don Quixoteland:
Conversations with Orson Welles

JUAN COBOS, MIGUEL RUBIO, AND
J. A. PRUNEDA/1964

CAHIERS: *In* The Trial, *it seems that you were making a severe criticism of the abuse of power; unless it concerns something more profound. Perkins appeared as a sort of Prometheus.*
WELLES: He is also a little bureaucrat. I consider him guilty.

CAHIERS: *Why do you say he is guilty?*
WELLES: Who knows? He belongs to something that represents evil and that, at the same time, is part of him. He is not guilty as accused, but he is guilty all the same. He belongs to a guilty society, he collaborates with it. In any case, I am not a Kafka analyst.

CAHIERS: *A version of the scenario exists with a different ending. The executioners stab K to death.*
WELLES: That ending didn't please me. I believe that in that case it is a question of a "ballet" written by a pre-Hitler Jewish intellectual. After the death of six million Jews, Kafka would not have written that. It seemed to me to be pre-Auschwitz. I don't want to say that my ending was good, but it was the only solution. I had to move into high gear, even if it was only for several instants.

From *Cahiers du Cinéma in English,* number 5, 1966. This interview was conducted in Madrid over a three-month period, May–July 1964. Reprinted by permission of the British Film Institute.

CAHIERS: *One of the constants of your work is the struggle for liberty and the defense of the individual.*
WELLES: A struggle for dignity. I absolutely disagree with those works of art, those novels, those films that, these days, speak about despair. I do not think that an artist may take total despair as a subject; we are too close to it in daily life. This genre of subject can be utilized only when life is less dangerous and more clearly affirmative.

CAHIERS: *In the transposition of* The Trial *to the cinema, there is a fundamental change; in Kafka's book, K's character is more passive than in the film.*
WELLES: I made him more active, properly speaking. I do not believe that passive characters are appropriate to drama. I have nothing against Antonioni, for example, but, in order to interest me, the characters must do something, from a dramatic point of view, you understand.

CAHIERS: *Was* The Trial *an old project?*
WELLES: I once said that a good film could be drawn from the novel, but I, myself, didn't think of doing it. A man came to see me and told me he believed he could find money so that I could make a film in France. He gave me a list of films and asked that I choose. And from that list of fifteen films I chose the one that, I believe, was the best: *The Trial*. Since I couldn't do a film written by myself, I chose Kafka.

CAHIERS: *What films do you really want to do?*
WELLES: Mine. I have drawers full of scenarios written by me.

CAHIERS: *In* The Trial, *was the long travelling shot of Katina Paxinou dragging the trunk while Anthony Perkins talks to her an homage to Brecht?*
WELLES: I did not see it that way. There was a long scene with her, that lasted ten minutes and that, moreover, I cut on the eve of the Paris premiere. I did not see the film as a whole except for one time. We were still in the process of doing the mixing, and here the premiere fell on us. At the last moment I abridged the ten minute scene. It should have been the best scene in the film and it wasn't. Something went wrong, I guess. I don't know why, but it didn't succeed. The subject of that scene was free will. It was stained with *comedie noir;* that was a fad with me. As you know, it is always directed against the machine and favorable to liberty.

CAHIERS: *When Joseph K sees the transparencies at the end, with the story of the guard, the door etc., does this concern your own reflections on the cinema?*

WELLES: It concerns a technical problem posed by the story to be told. If it were told at that precise moment, the public would go to sleep; that is why I tell it at the beginning and only recall it at the end. The effect then is equivalent to telling the story at that moment and I was able in this way to tell it in a few seconds. But, in any case, I am not the judge.

CAHIERS: *A critic who admires your work very much said that, in* The Trial, *you were repeating yourself . . .*

WELLES: Exactly, I repeated myself. I believe we do it all the time. We always take up certain elements again. How can it be avoided? An actor's voice always has the same timbre and, consequently, he repeats himself. It is the same for a singer, a painter . . . There are always certain things that come back, for they are part of one's personality, of one's style. If these things didn't come into play, a personality would be so complex that it would become impossible to identify it.

It is not my intention to repeat myself but in my work there should certainly be references to what I have done in the past. Say what you will, but *The Trial* is the best film I have ever made. One repeats oneself only when one is fatigued. Well, I wasn't fatigued. I have never been so happy as when I made this film.

CAHIERS: *How did you shoot Anthony Perkins' long running scene?*

WELLES: We built a very long platform and the camera was placed on a rolling chair.

CAHIERS: *But it's enormously fast!*

WELLES: Yes, but I had a Yugoslavian runner to push my camera.

CAHIERS: *What is astonishing in your work in this continual effort to bring solutions to the problems posed by direction . . .*

WELLES: The cinema is still very young and it would be completely ridiculous to not succeed in finding new things for it. If only I could make more films! Do you know what happened with *The Trial?* Two weeks before our departure from Paris for Yugoslavia, we were told that there would be no possibility of having a single set built there because the producer had already made another film in Yugoslavia and hadn't paid his debts. That's why it was necessary to utilize that abandoned station. I had planned a completely different film. Everything was invented at the last minute because physically my film had an entirely different conception. It was based on an absence of sets. And this gigantism I have been reproached for is, in part, due to the fact that the only set I possessed was that old abandoned station. An empty railroad station is immense! The production, as I had sketched it, comprised sets that gradually disappear. The number of realistic elements were to become fewer and fewer and the public would become aware of it, to the point where the scene would be reduced to free space as if everything had dissolved.

CAHIERS: *The movement of the actors and the camera in relation to each other in your films is very beautiful.*
WELLES: That is a visual obsession. I believe, thinking about my films, that they are based not so much on pursuit as on a search. If we are looking for something, the labyrinth is the most favorable location for the search. I do not know why, but my films are all for the most part a physical search.

CAHIERS: *You reflect about your art a great deal.*
WELLES: Never *a posteriori*. I think about each of my films when I am preparing for them. I do an enormous amount of preparation for each film and I set aside the clearest sketch when starting. What is marvelous about the cinema, what makes it superior to the theatre, is that it has many elements that may conquer us but may also enrich us, offer us a life impossible anywhere else. The cinema should always be the discovery of something. I believe that the cinema should be essentially poetic; that is why, during the shooting and not during the preparation, I try to plunge myself into a poetic development, which differs from narrative development and dramatic development. But, in reality, I am a man of ideas; yes, above all else—I am even more a man of ideas than a moralist, I suppose.

CAHIERS: *Do you believe it is possible to have a form of tragedy without melodrama?*
WELLES: Yes, but that is very difficult. For any *auteur* who comes out of the Anglo-Saxon tradition, it is very difficult. Shakespeare never arrived at it. It is possible but up to the present, no one has succeeded. In my cultural tradition, tragedy cannot escape from melodrama. We may always draw from

tragic elements and perhaps even the grandeur of tragedy but melodrama is always inherent to the Anglo-Saxon cultural universe. There's no doubt about it.

CAHIERS: *Is it correct that your films never correspond to what you were thinking of doing before starting them? Because of producers, etc.*

WELLES: No, in reality, in what concerns me, creation, I must say that I am constantly changing. At the beginning, I have a basic notion of what the final aspect of the film will be, more or less. But, each day, at every moment one deviates or modifies because of the expression in an actress's eyes or the position of the sun. I am not in the habit of preparing a film and then setting myself to make it. I prepare a film but I have no intention of making *this* film. The preparation serves to liberate me, so that I may work in my fashion; thinking of bits of film and of the result they will give; and there are parts that deceive me because I haven't conceived them in a complete enough way. I do not know what word to use because I am afraid of pompous words when I talk about making a film. The degree of concentration I utilize in a world that I create, whether this be for thirty seconds or for two hours, is very high; that is why, when I am shooting, I have a lot of trouble sleeping. This is not because I am preoccupied but because, for me, this world has so much reality that closing my eyes is not sufficient to make it disappear. It represents a terrible intensity of feeling. If I shoot in a royal location I sense and I see this site in so violent a way that, now, when I see these places again, they are similar to tombs, completely dead. There are spots in the world that are, to my eyes, cadavers; that is because I have already shot there—for me, they are completely finished. Jean Renoir said something that seems to be related to that: "We should remind people that a field of wheat painted by Van Gogh can arouse a stronger emotion than a field of wheat in nature." It is important to recall that art surpasses reality. Film becomes another reality. Apropos, I admire Renoir's work very much even though mine doesn't please him at all. We are good friends and, truthfully, one of the things I regret is that he doesn't like his films for the same reason I do. His films appear marvelous to me because what I admire most in an *auteur* is authentic sensitivity. I attach no importance to whether or not a film is a technical SUCCESS: moreover, films that lack this genre of sensitivity may not be judged on the same level with technical or aesthetic knowingness. But the cinema, the true cinema, is a poetic expression and Renoir is one of the rare poets. Like Ford, it is in his style. Ford is a poet. A comedian. Not for women, of course, but for men.

CAHIERS: *Apart from Ford and Renoir, who are the* cinéastes *you admire?*
WELLES: Always the same ones; I believe that on this point I am not very original. The one who pleases me most of all is Griffith. I think he is the best director in the history of the cinema. The best, much better than Eisenstein. And, for all that, I admire Eisenstein very much.

CAHIERS: *What about that letter Eisenstein sent you when you had not yet started in the cinema?*
WELLES: It was apropos *Ivan the Terrible.*

CAHIERS: *It appears that you said his film was like something by Michael Curtiz . . .*
WELLES: No. What happened is that I wrote a criticism of *Ivan the Terrible* for a newspaper and, one day, I received a letter from Eisenstein, a letter that came from Russia and ran to forty pages. Well, I answered him and in this fashion an exchange began that made us friends by correspondence. But I said nothing that could be seen as drawing a parallel between him and Curtiz. That would not be just. *Ivan the Terrible* is the worst film of a great *cinéaste.*

It's that I judged Eisenstein on his own level and not in a way that would be appropriate to a minor *cinéaste.* His drama was, before all else, political. It had nothing to do with his having to tell a story that he didn't want to tell. It was because, in my opinion, he was not suited to make period films. I think the Russians have a tendency to be more academic when they treat another period. They become rhetoricians, and academicians, in the worst sense of the word.

CAHIERS: *In your films, one has the sensation that real space is never respected: it seems not to interest you . . .*
WELLES: The fact that I make no use of it doesn't in the least signify that it doesn't please me. In other terms, there are many elements of the cinematographic language that I do not utilize, but that is not because I have something against them. It seems to me that the field of action in which I have my experience is one that is least known, and my duty is to explore it. But

that does not mean to say that it is, for me, the best and only—or that I deviate from a normal conception of space, in relation to the camera. I believe that the artist should explore his means of expression.

In reality, the cinema, with the exception of a few little tricks that don't go very far, has not advanced for more than thirty years. The only changes are with respect to the subjects of films. I see that there are directors, full of future, sensitive, who explore new themes but I see no one who attacks form, the manner of saying things. That seems to interest no one. They resemble each other very much in terms of style.

CAHIERS: *You must work very quickly. In twenty-five years of cinema, you have made ten films, you have acted in thirty, you have made a series of very long programs for television, you have acted and directed in the theatre, you have done narrations for other films and, in addition, you have written thirty scenarios. Each of them must have taken you more than six months.*
WELLES: Several of them even longer. There are those that took me two years but that is because I set them aside from time to time in order to do something else and picked them up again afterwards. But it is also true that I write very rapidly.

CAHIERS: *You write them completely, with dialogue?*
WELLES: I always begin with the dialogue. And I do not understand how one dares to write action before dialogue. It's a very strange conception. I know that in theory the word is secondary in cinema but the secret of my work is that everything is based on the word. I do not make silent films. I must begin with what the characters say. I must know what they say before seeing them do what they do.

CAHIERS: *However, in your films the visual part is essential.*
WELLES: Yes, but I couldn't arrive at it without the solidity of the word taken as a basic for constructing the images. What happens is that when the visual components are shot the words are obscured. The most classical example is *Lady From Shanghai*. The scene in the aquarium was so gripping visually that no one heard what was being said. And what was said was, for all that, the marrow of the film. The subject was so tedious that I said to myself, "this calls for something beautiful to look at." Assuredly, the scene was very beautiful. The first ten minutes of the film did not please me at all. When I think

of them I have the impression it wasn't me that made them. They resemble any Hollywood film.

I believe you know the story of *Lady From Shanghai.* I was working on that spectacular theatre idea *Around the World in 80 Days,* which was originally to be produced by Mike Todd. But, overnight, he went bankrupt and I found myself in Boston on the day of the premiere, unable to take my costumes from the station because 50,000 dollars was due. Without that money we couldn't open. At that time I was already separated from Rita; we were no longer even speaking. I did not intend to do a film with her. From Boston I got in touch with Harry Cohn, then director of Columbia, who was in Hollywood and I said to him, "I have an extraordinary story for you if you send me 50,000 dollars, by telegram in one hour, on account, and I will sign a contract to make it." Cohn asked, "What story?" I was telephoning from the theatre box-office; beside it was a display of pocket books and I gave him the title of one of them: *Lady From Shanghai.* I said to him, "Buy the novel and I'll make the film." An hour later we received the money. Later I read the book and it was horrible so I set myself, top speed, to write a story. I arrived in Hollywood to make the film with a very small budget and in six weeks of shooting. But I wanted more money for my theatre. Cohn asked me why I didn't use Rita. She said she would be very pleased. I gave her to understand that the character was not a sympathetic one, that she was a woman who killed and this might hurt her image as a star in the public eye. Rita was set on making this film and it, instead of costing 350,000 dollars, became a two million dollar film. Rita was very cooperative. The one who was horrified on seeing the film was Cohn.

CAHIERS: *How do you work with actors?*
WELLES: I give them a great deal of freedom and, at the same time, the feeling of precision. It's a strange combination. In other words, physically, and in the way they develop, I demand the precision of ballet. But their way of acting comes directly from their own ideas as much as from mine. When the camera begins to roll, I do not improvise visually. In this realm, everything is prepared. But I work very freely with the actors. I try to make their life pleasant.

CAHIERS: *Your cinema is essentially dynamic . . .*

WELLES: I believe that the cinema should be dynamic although I suppose any artist will defend his own style. For me, the cinema is a slice of life in movement that is projected on a screen; it is not a frame. I do not believe in the cinema unless there is movement on the screen. This is why I am not in agreement with certain directors who content themselves with a static cinema. For me, these are dead images. I hear the noise of the projector behind me and, when I see these long, long walks along streets, I am always waiting to hear the director's voice saying, "Cut!"

The only director who does not move either his camera or his actors very much, and in whom I believe, is John Ford. He succeeds in making me believe in his films even though there is little movement in them. But with the others I have the impression that they are desperately trying to make Art. However, they should be making drama and drama should be full of life. The cinema, for me, is essentially a dramatic medium, not a literary one.

CAHIERS: *That is why your* mise en scène *is lively: it is the meeting of two movements, that of the actors and that of the camera. Out of this flows an anguish that reflects modern life very well . . .*

WELLES: I believe that that corresponds to my vision of the world; it reflects that sort of vertigo, uncertainty, lack of stability, that *mélange* of movement and tension that is our universe. And the cinema should express that. Since cinema pretends to be an art it should be, above all, film and not the sequel to another, more literary, medium of expression.

CAHIERS: *Herman G. Weinberg said, while speaking of* Mr. Arkadin, *"In Orson Welles' films, the spectator may not sit back in his seat and relax; on the contrary, he must meet the film at least half-way in order to decipher what is happening, practically every second; if not, everything is lost."*

WELLES: All my films are like that. There are certain *cinéastes,* excellent ones, who present everything so explicitly, so clearly, that in spite of the great visual power contained in their films one follows them effortlessly—I refer only to the narrative thread. I am fully aware that, in my films, I demand a very specific interest on the part of the public. Without that attention, it is lost.

CAHIERS: Lady From Shanghai *is a story that, filmed by another director, would more likely have been based on sexual questions . . .*

WELLES: You mean that another director would have made it more obvious. I do not like to show sex crudely on the screen. Not because of morality or puritanism; my objection is of a purely aesthetic order. In my opinion, there are two things that can absolutely not be carried to the screen: the realistic presentation of the sexual act and praying to God. I never believe an actor or actress who pretends to be completely involved in the sexual act if it is too literal, just as I can never believe an actor who wants to make me believe he is praying. These are two things that, for me, immediately evoke the presence of a projector and a white screen, the existence of a series of technicians and a director who is saying, "Good. Cut." And I imagine them in the process of preparing for the next shot. As for those who adopt a mystical stance and look fervently at the spotlights . . .

For all that, my illusion almost never ends when I see a film. While filming, I think of someone like myself: I utilize all of my knowledge in order to force this person to want to see the film with the greatest interest. I want him to believe what is there on the screen; this means that one should create a real world there. I place my dramatic vision of a character in the world . . . if not, the film is something dead. What there is on the screen is nothing but shadows. Something even more dead than words.

CAHIERS: *Do you like comedy?*
WELLES: I have written at least five scenarios for comedy and in the theatre I have done more comedies than dramas. Comedy fills me with enthusiasm but I have never succeeded in getting a film producer to let me make one. One of the best things I did for television was a program in the genre of comedy. For example, I like Hawks' comedies very much. I even wrote about twenty-five minutes of one of them. It was called *I Was a Male War Bride.* The scenarist fell ill and I wrote almost a third of the film.

CAHIERS: *Have you written scenarios of comedies with the intention of making them?*
WELLES: I believe the best of my comedies is *Operation Cinderella.* It tells of the occupation of a small Italian town (which was previously occupied by the Saracens, the Moors, the Normans and, during the last war, by the English and, finally, the Americans) by a Hollywood film company . . . and this new occupation unfolds exactly like a military operation. The lives of all

the inhabitants of the town are changed during the shooting of the film. It's a gross farce. I want very much to do a comedy for the cinema.

In a certain sense, *Quixote* is a comedy, and I put a lot of comedy in all of my films but it is a genre of comedy that—and I regret to tell you this because it is a weakness—is understood only by Americans, to the exclusion of spectators in other countries, whatever they may be. There are scenes that, seen in other countries, awake not the slightest smile and that, seen by Americans, immediately appear in a comic vein. *The Trial* is full of humor, but the Americans are the only ones to understand its amusing side. This is where my nationality comes through: my farces are not universal enough. Many are the arguments I've had with actors due to the fact that scenes are posed in absolute forms of comedy and only at the last five minutes do I change them into drama. This is my method of working: showing the amusing side of things and not showing the sad side until the last possible second.

CAHIERS: *What happened when you sold the subject of* Monsieur Verdoux *to Chaplin?*

WELLES: I never argued with Chaplin because of *Monsieur Verdoux*. What annoys me is that now he pretends that he did not buy this subject from me. As an actor, Chaplin is very good, sensational. But in the comic cinema I prefer Buster Keaton to him. *There* is a man of the cinema who is not only an excellent actor but an excellent director, which Chaplin is not. And Keaton always has fabulous ideas. In *Limelight,* there was a scene between the two of them that was ten minutes long. Chaplin was excellent and Keaton sensational. It was the most successful thing he had done in the course of his career. Chaplin cut almost the entire scene, because he understood who, of the two, had completely dominated it.

CAHIERS: *There is a kinship between your work and the works of certain authors of the modern theatre, like Beckett, Ionesco and others . . . what is called the theatre of the absurd.*

WELLES: Perhaps, but I would eliminate Ionesco because I do not admire him. When I directed *Rhinoceros* in London, with Laurence Olivier in the principal role, as we repeated the work from day to day it pleased me less. I believe that there is nothing inside it. Nothing at all. This kind of theatre comes out of all types of expression, all types of art of a certain epoch, is thus forged by the same world as my films. The things this theatre is composed of are the same composed in my films, without this theatre's being in my cinema or without my cinema's being in this theatre. It is a trait of our times. There is where the coincidence comes from.

CAHIERS: *There are two types of artists: for example, Velázquez and Goya; one disappears from the picture, the other is present in it; on the other hand you have Van Gogh and Cézanne . . .*
WELLES: I see what you mean. It's very clear.

CAHIERS: *It seems to me that you are on the Goya side.*
WELLES: Doubtless. But I very much prefer Velázquez. There's no comparison between one and the other, as far as being artists is concerned. As I prefer Cézanne to Van Gogh.

CAHIERS: *And between Tolstoy and Dostoievsky?*
WELLES: I prefer Tolstoy.

CAHIERS: *But as an artist . . .*
WELLES: Yes, as an artist. But I deny that, for I do not correspond to my tastes. I know what I'm doing and when I recognize it in other works my interest is diminished. The things that resemble me the least are the things that interest me the most. For me Velázquez is the Shakespeare of painters and, for all that, he has nothing in common with my way of working.

CAHIERS: *What do you think of what is called modern cinema?*
WELLES: I like certain young French cineastes, much more than the Italians.

CAHIERS: *Did you like* L'Année dernière à Marienbad?
WELLES: No. I know that this film pleased you; not me. I held on up to the fourth reel and after that I left at a run. It reminded me too much of *Vogue* magazine.

CAHIERS: *How do you see the development of the cinema?*
WELLES: I don't see it. I rarely go to the movies. There are two kinds of writers, the writer who reads everything of interest that is published, exchanges letters with other writers, and others who absolutely do not read

their contemporaries. I am among the latter. I go to the movies very rarely and this is not because I don't like it, it is because it gives me no enjoyment at all. I do not think I am very intelligent about films. There are works that I know to be good but which I cannot stand.

CAHIERS: *It was said that you were going to make* Crime and Punishment; *what became of this project?*
WELLES: Someone wanted me to do it. I thought about it, but I like the book too much. In the end, I decided that I could do nothing and the idea of being content to illustrate it did not please me at all. I don't mean to say by that that the subject was beneath me, what I mean is that I could bring nothing to it. I could only give it actors and images and, when I can only do that, the cinema does not interest me. I believe you must say something new about a book; otherwise it is better not to touch it.

Aside from that, I consider it to be a very difficult work, because, in my opinion, it is not completely comprehensible outside of its own time and country. The psychology of this man and this constable are so Russian, so nineteenth-century Russian, that one could never find them elsewhere; I believe that the public would not be able to follow it all the way.

CAHIERS: *There is, in Dostoievsky, an analysis of justice, of the world, that is very close to yours.*
WELLES: Perhaps too close. My contribution would most likely be limited. The only thing I could do is to direct. I like to make films in which I can express myself as *auteur* rather than as interpreter. I do not share Kafka's point of view in *The Trial*. I believe that he is a good writer, but Kafka is not the extraordinary genius that people see him as today. That is why I was not concerned about excessive fidelity and could make a film by Welles. If I could make four films a year, I would surely do *Crime and Punishment*. But as it costs me a great deal to convince producers I try to choose what I film very carefully.

CAHIERS: *With you, one seems to find, at the same time, the Brechtian tendency and the Stanislavski tendency.*
WELLES: All I can say is that I did my apprenticeship in Stanislavski's orbit; I worked with his actors and found them very easy to direct. I do not allude to "Method" actors; that's something else altogether. But Stanislavski was

marvelous. As for Brecht, he was a great friend of mine. We worked together on *Galileo Galilei.* In reality he wrote it for me. Not for me to act in, but in order for me to direct it.

CAHIERS: *How was Brecht?*
WELLES: Terribly nice. He had an extraordinary brain. One could see very well that he had been educated by the Jesuits. He had the type of disciplined brain characterized by Jesuit education. Instinctively, he was more of an anarchist than a Marxist, but he believed himself a perfect Marxist. When I said to him one day, while we were talking about *Galileo,* that he had written a perfectly anti-communist work, he became nearly aggressive. I answered him, "But this Church you describe has to be Stalin and not the Pope, at this time. You have made something resolutely anti-Soviet!"

CAHIERS: *What relationship do you see between your work as a film director and as a theatre director?*
WELLES: My relationships with these two milieux are very different. I believe that they are not in intimate rapport, one with the other. Perhaps in me, as a man, that relationship exists, but technical solutions are so different for each of them that, in my spirit, I establish absolutely no relationship between these two mediums.

In the theatre, I do not belong to what has succeeded in becoming the Brechtian idea of theatre; that particularly withdrawn form has never been appropriate to my character. But I have always made a terrible effort to recall to the public, at each instant, that it is in a theatre. I have never tried to bring the scene to it. And that is the opposite of the cinema.

CAHIERS: *Perhaps there is a relationship in the way the actors are handled.*
WELLES: In the theatre there are 1,500 cameras rolling at the same time—in the cinema there is only one. That changes the whole aesthetic for the director.

CAHIERS: *Did Huston's* Moby Dick, *on which you worked, please you?*
WELLES: The novel pleases me very much but it doesn't please me as a novel so much as a drama. There are two very different things in the novel: that sort of pseudo-biblical element that is not very good, and also that curi-

ous 19th-century American element, of the apocalyptical genre, that can be rendered very well in the cinema.

CAHIERS: *In the scene you acted in the film—did you make any suggestions as to the way of handling it?*
WELLES: All we did was discuss the way in which it would be shot. You know that my sermon is very long. It goes on throughout a full reel, and we never repeated it. I arrived on the set already made-up and dressed. I got up on the platform and we shot it in one take. We did it using only one camera angle. And that is one of Huston's merits, because another director would have said, "Let's do it from another angle and see what we get." He said, "Good," and my role in the film ended right there!

CAHIERS: *You are in the process of preparing for a film on bullfighting.*
WELLES: Yes, but a film about the amateurs of bullfighting, the following . . . I think that the true event in the *corrida* is the arena itself—but one cannot do a film about it. From the cinematographic point of view the most exciting thing about it is the atmosphere. The *corrida* is something that already possesses a well defined personality. The cinema can do nothing to render it dramatic. All one may do is photograph it. Actually, my biggest preoccupation is knowing that Rosi is already in the process of shooting while I have put in four years, off and on, writing my scenario. Because of him, finding the necessary money will be more difficult: they'll say to me, "We already have a film about bullfighting, made by a serious *cineaste;* who wants one more?" However, I hope I will succeed in making this film, but I still don't know how I'm going to find the money. Rosi shot something last year at Pamplona, in 16mm. He showed it to Rizzoli, and said, "Look at this beautiful thing," and Rizzoli gave him carte blanche. Now it's only a matter of knowing whether it will be a good film or a bad film. It is better for me that the film be good. If it fails, I will have even more trouble raising the funds.

CAHIERS: *There is talk from time to time of your first sojourn in Spain, before the Civil War . . .*
WELLES: When I arrived in Spain, for the first time, I was seventeen years old and had already worked in Ireland as an actor. I only stayed in the south, in Andalusia. In Seville, I lived in the Triana section. I was writing detective

stories; I spent only two days a week on this and it brought in three hundred dollars. With this money I was a *grand seigneur* in Seville. There were so many people thrilled by the *corrida* and I caught the virus myself. I paid the novice fee at several *corridas* and thus was able to debut—on the posters I was called "The American." My greatest thrill was being able to practice the *métier* of *torero* three or four times without having to pay. I came to the realization that I was not good as a *torero* and decided to apply myself to writing. At that time I hardly thought of the theatre and still less of the cinema.

CAHIERS: *You said one day that you have a great deal of difficulty finding the money to make your films, that you have spent more time struggling to get this money than working as an artist. How is this battle at this time?*

WELLES: More bitter than ever. Worse than ever. Very difficult. I have already said that I do not work enough. I am frustrated, do you understand? And I believe that my work shows that I do not do enough filming. My cinema is perhaps too explosive; because I wait too long before I speak. It's terrible. I have bought little cameras in order to film if I can find the money. I will shoot it in 16mm. The cinema is a *métier* . . . nothing can compare to the cinema. The cinema belongs to our times. It is "the thing" to do. During the shooting of *The Trial,* I spent marvelous days. It was an amusement, happiness. You cannot imagine what I felt.

When I make a film or at the time of my theatrical premieres, the critics habitually say, "This work is not as good as the one of three years ago." And if I look for the criticism of that one, three years back, I find an unfavorable review that says that that isn't as good as what I did three years earlier. And so it goes. I admit that experiences can be false but I believe that it is also false to want to be fashionable. If one is fashionable for the greatest part of one's career, one will produce second-class work. Perhaps by chance one will arrive at being a success but this means that one is a follower and not an innovator. An artist should lead, blaze trails.

What is serious is that in countries where English is spoken, the role played by criticism concerning serious works of cinema is very important. Given the fact that one cannot make films in competition with Doris Day, what is said by reviews such as *Sight and Sound* is the only reference.

Things are going particularly badly in my own country. *Touch of Evil* never had a first-run, never had the usual presentation to the press and was not the object of any critical writing in either the weeklies, the reviews or the daily papers. It was considered to be too bad. When the representative from Universal wanted to exhibit it at the Brussels Fair in 1958, he was told that it wasn't a good enough film for a festival. He answered that, in any case, it must be put on the program. It went unnoticed and was sent back. The film took the *grand prix*, but it was no less sent back.

CAHIERS: *Do you consider yourself a moralist?*
WELLES: Yes, but against morality. Most of the time, that may appear paradoxical but the things I love in painting, in music, in literature, represent only my penchant for what is my opposite. And moralists bore me very much. However, I'm afraid I am one of them!

CAHIERS: *In what concerns you, it is not so much a question of a moralist's attitude but rather an ethic that you adopt in the face of the world.*
WELLES: My two Shakesperean films are made from an ethical point of view. I believe I have never made a film without having a solid ethical point of view about its story. Morally speaking, there is no ambiguity in what I do.

CAHIERS: *But an ambiguous point of view is necessary. These days, the world is made that way.*
WELLES: But that is the way the world appears to us. It is not a true ambiguity: it's like a larger screen. A kind of a moral cinemascope. I believe it is necessary to give all the characters their best arguments, in order that they may defend themselves, including those I disagree with. To them as well, I give the best defensive arguments I can imagine. I offer them the same possibility for expression as I would a sympathetic character.

That's what gives this impression of ambiguity: my being chivalrous to people whose behavior I do not approve of. The characters are ambiguous but the significance of the work is not. I do not want to resemble the majority of Americans, who are demagogues and rhetoricians. This is one of America's great weaknesses, and rhetoric is one of the greatest weaknesses of American artists; above all, those of my generation. Miller, for example, is terribly rhetorical.

CAHIERS: *What is the problem in America?*
WELLES: If I speak to you of the things that are wrong it won't be the obvious ones; those are similar to what is wrong in France, in Italy or in Spain;

we know them all. In American art the problem, or better, one of the problems, is the betrayal of the Left by the Left, self-betrayal. In one sense, by stupidity, by orthodoxy and because of slogans; in another, by simple betrayal. We are very few in our generation who have not betrayed our position, who have not given other people's names . . .

That is terrible. It can never be undone. I don't know how one starts over after a similar betrayal; that differs enormously, however, from this, for example, a Frenchman who collaborated with the Gestapo in order to save his wife's life; that is another genre of collaboration. What is so sad about the American Left is that it betrayed in order to save its swimming pools. There was no American Right in my generation. Intellectually it didn't exist. There were only Leftists and they mutually betrayed each other. The Left was not destroyed by McCarthy: it demolished itself, ceding to a new generation of Nihilists. That's what happened.

You can't call it "Fascism." I believe that the term "Fascism" should only be utilized in order to define a quite precise political attitude. It would be necessary to find a new word in order to define what is happening in America. Fascism must be born out of chaos. And America is not, as I know it, in chaos. The social structure is not in a state of dissolution. No, it doesn't correspond at all to the true definition of Fascism. I believe it is two simple, obvious things: the technological society is not accustomed to living with its own tools. That's what counts. We speak of them, we use them but we don't know how to live with them. The other thing is the prestige of the people responsible for the technological society. In this society the men who direct and the savants who represent technique do not leave room for the artist who favors the human being. In reality, they utilize him only for decoration.

Hemingway says, in *The Green Hills of Africa,* that America is a country of adventure and, if the adventure disappears there, any American who possesses this primitive spirit must go elsewhere to seek adventure: Africa, Europe, etc. . . . It is an intensely romantic point of view. There is some truth in it, but if it is so intensely romantic it is because there is still an enormous quantity of adventure in America. In the cinema, you cannot imagine all that one may do in it. All I need is a job in cinema, is for someone to give me a camera. There is nothing dishonorable about working in America. The country is full of possibilities for expressing what is happening all over the world. What really exists is an enormous compromise. The ideal American type is perfectly expressed by the Protestant, individualist, anti-conformist and this is the type that is in the process of disappearing. In reality, a very few of him remain.

CAHIERS: *What was your relationship with Hemingway?*

WELLES: My relationship with Hemingway has always been very droll. The first time we met was when I had been called to read the narration for a film that he and Joris Ivens had made about the war in Spain; it was called *Spanish Earth*. Arriving, I came upon Hemingway, who was in the process of drinking a bottle of whiskey; I had been handed a set of lines that were too long, dull, had nothing to do with his style, which is always so concise and so economical. There were lines as pompous and complicated as this: "Here are the faces of men who are close to death," and this was to be read at a moment when one saw faces on the screen that were so much more eloquent. I said to him, "Mr. Hemingway, it would be better if one saw the faces all alone, without commentary."

This didn't please him at all and, since I had, a short time before, just directed the Mercury Theatre, which was a sort of avant-garde theatre, he thought I was some kind of faggot and said, "You—effeminate boys of the theatre, what do you know about real war?"

Taking the bull by the horns, I began to make effeminate gestures and I said to him, "Mister Hemingway, how strong you are and how big you are!" That enraged him and he picked up a chair; I picked up another and, right there, in front of the images of the Spanish Civil War, as they marched across the screen, we had a terrible scuffle. It was something marvelous: two guys like us in front of these images representing people in the act of struggling and dying . . . we ended by toasting each other over a bottle of whiskey. We have spent our lives having long periods of friendship and others during which we barely spoke. I have never been able to avoid gently making fun of him, and this no one ever did; everyone treated him with the greatest respect.

CAHIERS: *As an artist and as a member of a certain generation, do you feel isolated?*

WELLES: I have always felt isolated. I believe that any good artist feels isolated. And I must think that I am a good artist, for otherwise I would not be able to work and I beg your pardon for taking the liberty of believing this; if someone wants to direct a film, he must think that he is good. A good artist should be isolated. If he isn't isolated, something is wrong.

CAHIERS: *These days, it would be impossible to present the Mercury Theatre.*
WELLES: Completely impossible for financial reasons. The Mercury Theatre was possible only because I was earning three thousand dollars a week on the radio and spending two thousand to sustain the theatre. At that time, it was still cheap to sustain a theatre. Plus I had formidable actors. And what was most exciting about this Mercury Theatre was that it was a theatre on Broadway, not "off." Today, one might have a theatre off-Broadway, but that's another thing.

What characterized the Mercury Theatre was that it was next door to another where they were doing a musical comedy, near a commercial theatre, it was in the theatre center. Part of the neighboring bill of fare was the Group Theatre which was the official theatre of the Left: we were in contact without having an official relationship; we were of the same generation, although not on the same path. The whole thing gave the New York of that time an extraordinary vitality. The quality of actors and audiences is no longer what it was in those marvelous years. The best theatre should be in the center of everything.

CAHIERS: *Does that explain your permanent battle to remain in the milieu of the cinema and not outside of the industry?*
WELLES: I may be rejected but, as for me, I always want to be right in the center. If I am isolated, it is because I am obliged to be, for such is not my intention. I am always aiming for the center. I fail, but that is what I try to attain.

CAHIERS: *Are you thinking of returning to Hollywood?*
WELLES: Not at the moment. But who knows what may change at the next instant? I am dying to work there because of the technicians, who are marvelous. They truly represent a director's dream.

CAHIERS: *A certain anti-Fascist attitude can be found in your films . . .*
WELLES: There is more than one French intellectual who believes that I am a Fascist . . . it's idiotic, but that's what they write. What happens with these French intellectuals is that they take my physical aspect as an actor for my

ideas as an *auteur*. As an actor I always play a certain type of role: Kings, great men, etc. This is not because I think them to be the only persons in the world who are worth the trouble. My physical aspect does not permit me to play other roles. No one would believe a defenseless, humble person played by me. But they take this to be a projection of my own personality. I hope that the great majority at least considers it obvious that I am anti-Fascist . . .

True Fascism is always confused with Futurism's early Fascistic mystique. By this I make allusion to the first generation of Italian Fascism, which was a way of speaking that disappeared as soon as the true Fascism imposed itself, because it was an idiotic romanticism, like that of d'Annunzio and others. That is what disappeared. And that is what the French critics are talking about.

True Fascism is gangsterism of the low-born middle class, lamentably organized by . . . good, we all know what Fascism is. It is very clear. It is amusing to see how the Russians have been mistaken about the subject of *Touch of Evil*. They have attacked it pitilessly, as if it were a question of the veritable decadence of Western civilization. They were not content to attack what I showed: they attacked me too.

I believe that the Russians didn't understand the words, or some other thing. What is disastrous in Russia is that they are fully in the middle ages, the middle ages in its most rigid aspect. No one thinks for himself. It is very sad. The orthodoxy has something terrible about it. They live only by slogans they have inherited. No one any longer knows what these slogans signify.

CAHIERS: *What will your* Falstaff *be like?*
WELLES: I don't know . . . I hope it will be good. All I can say is that from the visual point of view it will be very modest and, I hope, at the same time satisfying and correct. But as I see it, it is essentially a human story and I hope that a good number of stupid cinema people will feel deceived. That is because, as I just said, I consider that this film should be very modest from the visual point of view. Which doesn't mean it will be visually non-existent but rather that it will not be loud on this level. It concerns a story about 3 or 4 people and these should, therefore, dominate completely. I believe I shall use more close-ups. This will really be film completely in the service of the actors.

CAHIERS: *You are often accused of being egocentric. When you appear as an*

actor in your films, it is said that the camera is, above all, in the service of your
personal exhibition . . . For example, in Touch of Evil *the shooting angle moves*
from a general shot to a close-up in order to catch your first appearance on getting
out of the car.

WELLES: Yes, but that is the story, the subject. I wouldn't act a role if it was
not felt as dominating the whole story. I do not think it is just to say that I
utilize the camera to my profit and not to the profit of the other actors. It's
not true. Although they will say it even more about *Falstaff:* but it is precisely
because in the film I am playing Falstaff, not Hotspur.

At this time I think and rethink, above all, of the world in which the story
unfolds, of the appearance of the film. The number of sets I will be able to
build will be so restrained that the film will have to be resolutely anti-
Baroque. It will have to have numerous rather formal general shots, like what
one may see at eye level, wall frescoes. It is a big problem creating a world in
period costumes. In this genre, it is difficult to get a feeling of real life, few
films arrive at it. I believe this is due to the fact that one has not concretized,
in all its details, before starting to work, the universe presupposed by such a
film.

Falstaff should be very plain on the visual level because above all it is a
very real human story, very comprehensible and very adaptable to modern
tragedy. And nothing should come between the story and the dialogue. The
visual part of this story should exist as a background, as something secondary. Everything of importance in the film should be found on the faces; on
these faces that whole universe I was speaking of should be found. I imagine
that it will be "the" film of my life in terms of close-ups. Theoretically, I am
against close-ups of all types, although I consider few theories as given and
am for remaining very free. I am resolutely against close-ups, but I am convinced that this story requires them.

CAHIERS: *Why this objection to close-ups?*
WELLES: I find it marvelous that the public may choose, with its eyes, what
it wants to see of a shot. I don't like to force it and the use of the close-up
amounts to forcing it: you can see nothing else. In *Kane* for example, you
must have seen that there were very few close-ups, hardly any. There are
perhaps six in the whole film. But a story like *Falstaff* demands them, because
the moment we step back and separate ourselves from the faces, we see the
people in period costumes and many actors in the foreground. The closer we

are to the face the more universal it becomes; *Falstaff* is a somber comedy, the story of the betrayal of friendship.

What pleases me in *Falstaff* is that the project has interested me as an actor although I am rarely interested in something for the cinema in terms of being an actor. I am happy when I do not perform. And *Falstaff* is one of the rare things that I wish to achieve as an actor. There are only two stories I wish to do as an actor that I have written. In *The Trial* I absolutely did not want to perform and, if I did it, it is because of not having found an actor who could take the part. All those we asked refused.

CAHIERS: *At the beginning you said you would play the part of the priest . . .*
WELLES: I shot it, but, as we hadn't found an actor for the role of the lawyer, I cut the sequences in which I appeared as a priest and started shooting again. *Falstaff* is an actor's film. Not only my role but all the others are favorable for showing a good actor's worth. My *Othello* is more successful in the theatre than on film. We shall see what happens with *Falstaff,* which is the best role that Shakespeare ever wrote. It is a character as great as Don Quixote. If Shakespeare had done nothing but that magnificent creation, it would suffice to make him immortal. I wrote the scenario under the inspiration of three works in which he appears, one other in which he is spoken of, and complete it with things found in still another. Thus, I worked with five Shakespeare works. But, naturally, I wrote a story about *Falstaff,* about his friendship with the prince and his repugnance when the prince becomes King. I have great hopes for this film.

CAHIERS: *There is a line spoken by Charles Foster Kane to his banker, which we would like very much to hear you explain: "I could have been a great man, if I hadn't been so rich."*
WELLES: Good, the whole story is in that. Anything at all may destroy greatness: a woman, illness, riches. My hatred at richness in itself is not an obsession. I do not believe that richness is the only enemy of greatness. If he had been poor, Kane would not have been a great man but one thing is sure and that is that he would have been a successful one. He thinks that success brings greatness. As for that, it is the character that says it, not I. Kane arrives at having a certain class but never greatness.

It isn't because everything seems easy to him. That is an excuse he gives himself. But the film doesn't say that. Obviously, since he is the head of one of the biggest fortunes in the world, things become easier, but his greatest error was that of the American plutocrats of those years, who believed that money automatically conferred a certain stature to a man. Kane is a man who truly belongs to his time. This type of man hardly exists anymore. These were the plutocrats who believed they could be President of the United States, if they wanted to. They also believed they could buy anything. It wasn't even necessary to be intelligent to see that it isn't always like that.

CAHIERS: *Are they more realistic?*
WELLES: It's not a question of realism. This type of plutocrat no longer exists. Things have changed a great deal, above all economic structures. Very few rich men today succeed in retaining absolute control of their own money: their money is controlled by others. It is, like many other things, a question of organization. They are prisoners of their money. And I don't say this from a sentimental point of view; there is no longer anything but boards of directors and the participation of diverse opinions . . . they are no longer free to commit the sort of follies that used to be possible. The moment has passed for this type of egocentric plutocrat, in the same way that this type of newspaper owner has disappeared.

What is very specific about Kane's personality is that he never earned money; he passed his life doing nothing but spending it. He did not belong to that category of rich men who made fortunes: he only spent it. Kane didn't even have the responsibility of the true capitalist.

CAHIERS: *Did* Citizen Kane *bring in a lot of money?*
WELLES: No, it's not a question of that. The film went well. But my problems with Hollywood started before I got there. The real problem was that contract, which gave me, free and clear, carte blanche and which had been signed before I went out there. I had too much power. At that time I was faced with a machination from which I have never recovered, because I have never had an enormous box office success. If you have such success, from that instant on you are given everything!

I had luck as no one had; afterwards, I had the worst bad luck in the history of the cinema, but that is in the order of things: I had to pay for having had the best luck in the history of cinema. Never has a man been given so much power in the Hollywood system. An absolute power. And artistic control.

CAHIERS: *There are* cinéastes, *in Europe, who possess this power.*
WELLES: But they don't possess the American technical arsenal, which is a grandiose thing. The man who pushes the camera, those who change the lights, the one who handles the crane—they have children at the University. You are side by side with men who don't feel themselves to be workers but who think of themselves as very capable and very well paid artisans. That makes an enormous difference; enormous.

I could never have done all that I did in *Touch of Evil* elsewhere. And it is not only a question of technique, it essentially concerns the human competence of the men with whom I worked. All this stems from the economic security they enjoy, from the fact that they are well paid, from the fact that they do not think of themselves as belonging to another class.

Throughout the entire European cinema industry, to a greater or lesser degree, one feels that there is a greater barrier posed by educational differences. In all European countries one is called "Doctor," "Professor," etc., if one has gone to a university; the great advantage in America is that there, at times, you find directors who are less learned than the man who pushes the camera. There is no "professor." Classes do not exist in the American cinema world. The pleasure one experiences working with an American crew is something that has no equivalent on earth. But you pay a price for that. There are the producers, and that group is as bad as the technicians are good.

CAHIERS: *How did you shoot that very long sequence in Marcia's living room during the interrogation of Sanchez?*
WELLES: In Europe, there are three cameramen as good as the American cameramen. The one who made *The Trial* with me is sensational. But what there isn't is someone capable of handling the crane. In America, this man has an enormous auto, he is instructed, and considers himself as important to the film as the cameraman himself. In that scene in Marcia's house there were about sixty chalk marks on the ground: that tells you how knowledgeable and intelligent the man who guides the camera must be in order to do well. At that moment, I am at his mercy, at the mercy of his precision. If he can't do it with assurance, the scene is impossible.

CAHIERS: *Was it really Charlton Heston who proposed you as director of* Touch of Evil?

WELLES: What happened is even more amusing. The scenario was proposed to Charlton Heston who was told that it was by Orson Welles; at the
other end of the line, Heston understood that I was to direct the film, in
which case he was ready to shoot anything at all, no matter what, with me.
Those at Universal did not clear up his misunderstanding; they hung up and
automatically telephoned me and asked me to direct it. The truth is that
Heston said, textually, this: "I will work in any film at all directed by Orson
Welles." When they proposed that I direct the film I set only one condition:
to write my own scenario! And I directed and wrote the film without getting
a penny for it, since I was being paid as an actor.

CAHIERS: *In relation to the original novel, you made many changes . . .*
WELLES: My God! I never read the novel; I only read Universal's scenario.
Perhaps the novel made sense, but the scenario was ridiculous. It all took
place in San Diego, not on the Mexican border, which completely changes
the situation. I made Vargas a Mexican for political reasons, I wanted to show
how Tiajuana and the border towns are corrupted by all sorts of mish-mash,
publicity more or less about American relations; that's the only reason.

CAHIERS: *What do you think of the American Cinema, as seen from Europe?*
WELLES: I am surprised by the tendency of the serious critics to find elements of value only among the American directors of action films, while
they find none in the American directors of historical films. Lubitsch, for
example, is a giant. But he doesn't correspond to the taste of cinema aesthetes. Why? I know nothing about it. Besides, it doesn't interest me. But
Lubitsch's talent and originality are stupefying.

CAHIERS: *And von Sternberg?*
WELLES: Admirable! He is the greatest exotic director of all time and one of
the great lights.

CAHIERS: *Let's talk about other directors. What do you think of Arthur Penn?
Have you seen* The Left-Handed Gun?
WELLES: I saw it first on television and then as cinema. It was better on
television, more brutal, and beyond that I believe that at that time Penn had
more experience directing for television and so handled it better, but for
cinema this experience went against him. I believe him to be a good theatre

director, an admirable director of actresses—a very rare thing: very few *ciné-astes* possess that quality.

I have seen nothing by the most recent generation, except for a sampling of the avante-garde. Among those whom I would call "younger generation" Kubrick appears to me to be a giant.

CAHIERS: *But, for example,* The Killing *was more or less a copy of* The Asphalt Jungle?

WELLES: Yes, but *The Killing* was better. The problem of imitation leaves me indifferent, above all if the imitator succeeds in surpassing the model. For me, Kubrick is a better director than Huston. I haven't seen *Lolita* but I believe that Kubrick can do everything. He is a great director who has not yet made his great film. What I see in him is a talent not possessed by the great directors of the generation immediately preceding his, I mean Ray, Aldrich, etc. Perhaps this is because his temperament comes closer to mine.

CAHIERS: *And those of the older generation? Wyler, for example? and Hitch-cock?*

WELLES: Hitchcock is an extraordinary director; William Wyler a brilliant producer.

CAHIERS: *How do you make this distinction between two men who are both called directors?*

WELLES: A producer doesn't make anything. He chooses the story, works on it with the scenarist, has a say in the distribution and, in the old sense of the term American producer, even decides on the camera angles, what sequences will be used. What is more, he defines the final form of the film. In reality, he is a sort of director's boss.

Wyler is this man. Only he's his own boss. His work, however, is better as boss than as director, given the fact that in that role he spends his clearest moments waiting, with the camera, for something to happen. He says nothing. He waits, as the producer waits in his office. He looks at twenty impeccable shots, seeking the one that has something and, usually, he knows how to choose the best one. As a director he is good but as a producer he is extraordinary.

CAHIERS: *According to you, the role of director consists in making something happen?*

WELLES: I do not like to set up very strict rules but, in the Hollywood system, the director has one job. In other systems he has another job. I am against absolute rules because even in the case of America we find marvelous films achieved under the absolute tyranny of the production system. There are even films much respected by film societies that weren't made by directors but by producers and scenarists . . . under the American system, no one is capable of saying whether a film was or was not directed by a director.

CAHIERS: *In an interview, John Houseman said that you got all of the credit for* Citizen Kane *and that this was unfair because it should have gone to Herman J. Mankiewicz, who wrote the scenario.*

WELLES: He wrote several important scenes. (Houseman is an old enemy of mine.) I was very lucky to work with Mankiewicz: everything concerning Rosebud belongs to him. As for me, sincerely, he doesn't please me very much; he functions, it is true, but I have never had complete confidence in him. He serves as a hyphen between all the elements. I had, in return, the good fortune to have Gregg Toland who is the best director of photography that ever existed and I also had the luck to hit upon actors who had never worked in films before; not a single one of them had ever found himself in front of a camera until then. They all came from my theatre. I could never have made *Citizen Kane* with actors who were old hands at cinema, because they would have said right off, "Just what do you think we're doing?" My being a newcomer would have put them on guard and, with the same blow, would have made a mess of the film. It was possible because I had my own family, so to speak.

CAHIERS: *How did you arrive at* Citizen Kane's *cinematic innovations?*

WELLES: I owe it to my ignorance. If this word seems inadequate to you, replace it with innocence. I said to myself: this is what the camera should be really capable of doing, in a normal fashion. When we were on the point of shooting the first sequence, I said, "Let's do that!" Gregg Toland answered that it was impossible. I came back with, "We can always try; we'll soon see. Why not?" We had to have special lenses made because at that time there weren't any like those that exist today.

CAHIERS: *During the shooting, did you have the sensation of making such an important film?*

WELLES: I never doubted it for a single instant.

CAHIERS: *What is happening with your* Don Quixote? *It was announced so long ago.*
WELLES: It's really finished; it only needs about three weeks' work, in order to shoot several little things. What makes me nervous is launching it: I know that this film will please no one. This will be an execrated film. I need a big success before putting it in circulation. If *The Trial* had been a complete critical success, then I would have had the courage to bring out my *Don Quixote*. Things being what they are I don't know what to do: everyone will be enraged by this film.

CAHIERS: *How do you see the central character?*
WELLES: Exactly as Cervantes did, I believe. My film takes place in modern times but the characters of Don Quixote and Sancho are exactly as they were, at least, I repeat, to my way of thinking. This wasn't the case with Kafka; I utilize these two characters freely but I do it in the same spirit as Cervantes. They are not my characters, they are the Spanish writer's.

CAHIERS: *Why did you choose to film* Don Quixote?
WELLES: I started by making a half hour television show out of it; I had just enough money to do it. But I fell so completely in love with my subject that I gradually made it longer and continued to shoot depending on how much money I had. You might say that it grew as I made it. What happened to me is more or less what happened to Cervantes, who started to write a novella and ended up writing *Don Quixote*. It's a subject you can't let go of once you've started.

CAHIERS: *Will the film have the same scepticism as the novel?*
WELLES: Certainly! I believe that what happened to the book will happen to my film of chivalry and he ended up creating the most beautiful apology for them that can be found in literature. However, touching on the defense of that idea of chivalry, the film will be more sincere than the novel, even though today it is more anachronistic than when Cervantes was writing.

I myself appear in the character of Orson Welles, but Sancho and Don Quixote say only the lines given them by Cervantes; I have put no words in their mouths.

I do not think the film is less sceptical because I believe that, if we push the analysis to the end, Cervantes' scepticism was in part an attitude. His scepticism was an intellectual attitude: I believe that, under the scepticism, there was a man who loved the knights as much as Don Quixote himself. Above all, he was Spanish.

It is truly a difficult film. I should also say that it is too long; what I am going to shoot will not serve to complete the footage—I could make three films out of the material that already exists. The film, in its first form, was too commercial; it was conceived for television and I had to change certain things in order to make it more substantial. The drollest thing about it is that it was shot with a crew of six people. My wife was script-girl, the chauffeur moved the lights around, I did the lighting and was second cameraman. It is only with the camera that one can have his eye on everything in such a way.

Playboy Interview: Orson Welles

KENNETH TYNAN/1967

THE PERFORMING ARTS HAVE NOW ENJOYED the professional services of George Orson Welles for 35 years—ever since 1931, when he arrived at the Gate Theatre in Dublin, passed himself off as a well-known actor from the New York Theatre Guild and began playing leads at the age of 16. . . . During the past 20 years, living mainly in Europe, Welles has been a rogue elephant at large in most of the performing media. . . . You can never tell how or where he will manifest himself next. In the course of his career— apart from writing and directing films and plays, and acting in both—he has been a novelist, a painter, a ballet scenarist, a conjurer, a columnist, a television pundit and an amateur bullfighter. There's symbolic if not literal truth in the story about how he once addressed a thinly attended meeting of admirers with the words: "Isn't it a shame that there are so many of me and so few of you?"

He has grown fat spreading himself thin. A passive figure sculpted in foam rubber, he is preceded wherever he goes by his belly and an oversized cigar; and his presence is immediately signaled, even to the blind, by the Bacchic earthquake of his laughter. His first European base was a villa near Rome, but nowadays he lives with his Italian wife and their daughter Beatrice in an expensive suburb of Madrid. "I used to be an American émigré in Italy," he says. "Now I'm an Italian émigré in Spain." At 51, he has long since joined the select group of international celebrities whose fame is self-sustaining, no

This interview originally appeared in *Playboy* magazine, March 1967. Reprinted by permission of Matthew Tynan.

matter how widely opinions of their work may vary, and no matter how much the work itself may fluctuate in quality. (Other members of the club in recent times have been Chaplin, Ellington, Cocteau, Picasso and Hemingway.)

My interview with him took place last spring in London. Welles was appearing with Peter Sellers and David Niven in *Casino Royale,* the James Bond film that has everything but Sean Connery. Characteristically, Welles had insisted on living in a furnished apartment directly over the Mirabelle, one of the most expensive and arguably the best restaurant in London. Thus, he could be sure of gourmet room service. Empty caviar pots adorned every table. Imposingly swathed in the robes of a Buddhist priest, he sipped Dom Pérignon champagne and talked far into the night.

Shortly afterward, Welles took his Falstaff film, *Chimes at Midnight* [released in the U.S. as *Falstaff*], to the Cannes Festival. Not all the critics were ecstatic; one said that Welles was the only actor who ever had to slim down to play Falstaff. But the jury reacted warmly; and so did the audience at the prize-giving ceremony, which began with the announcement of a special award to "M. Orson Welles, for his contribution to world cinema." Jeers and whistles greeted many of the other prizes; but for this one, everybody rose—avant-garde critics and commercial producers alike—and clapped with their hands held over their heads. The ovation lasted for minutes. Welles beamed and sweated on the stage of the Festival Palace, looking like a melting iceberg and occasionally tilting forward in something that approximated a bow.

Later, at his hotel, he talked with me about his next production—*Treasure Island,* in which he would play Long John Silver. Then he would complete *Don Quixote* and make a film of *King Lear.* After that, there were plenty of other projects in hand. "The bee,' he said happily, 'is always making honey."

PLAYBOY: *You've been a celebrity now for 30 years. In all that time, what's the most accurate description anyone has given of you?*
WELLES: I don't want *any* description of me to be accurate: I want it to be flattering. I don't think people who have to sing for their supper ever like to be described truthfully—not in print, anyway. We need to sell tickets, so we need good reviews.

PLAYBOY: *In private conversation, what's the pleasantest thing you ever heard about yourself?*

WELLES: Roosevelt saying that I would have been a great politician. Barrymore saying that Chaplin and myself were the two finest living actors. I don't mean that I *believe* those things, but you used the word "pleasant." What I really enjoy is flattery in the suburbs of my work—about things I'm not mainly or even professionally occupied with. When an old bullfighter tells me I'm one of the few people who understand the bulls, or when a magician says I'm a good magician, that tickles the ego without having anything to do with the box office.

PLAYBOY: *Of all the comments, written or spoken, that have been made about you, which has displeased you the most?*
WELLES: Nothing spoken. It's only written things I mind—for example, everything Walter Kerr ever wrote about me. It takes a big effort for me to persuade myself that anything bad I read about myself isn't true. I have a primitive respect for the printed word as it applies to me, especially if it's negative. I can remember being described in Denver, when I was playing Marchbanks in *Candida* at the age of 18, as "a sea cow whining in a basso profundo." That was more than 30 years ago, and I can still quote the review verbatim. I can never remember the good ones. Probably the bad ones hurt so much and so morbidly because I've run the store so long. I've been an actor-manager in radio, films and the theater; and in a very immediate way, I've been economically dependent on what's written about me, so that I worry about how much it's going to affect the gross. Or maybe that's just a justification for hypersensitivity.

PLAYBOY: *Talking about critics, you once complained: "They don't review my work, they review* me.*" Do you feel that's still true?*
WELLES: Yes—but I suppose I shouldn't kick about it. I earn a good living and get a lot of work because of this ridiculous myth about me. But the price of it is that when I try to do something serious, something I care about, a great many critics don't review that particular work, but me in general. They write their standard Welles piece. It's either the good piece or the bad piece, but they're both fairly standard.

PLAYBOY: *In an era of increasing specialization, you've expressed yourself in almost every artistic medium. Have you never wanted to specialize?*

WELLES: No. I can't imagine limiting myself. It's a great shame that we live in an age of specialists, and I think we give them too much respect. I've known four or five great doctors in my life, and they have always told me that medicine is still in a primitive state and that they know hardly anything about it. I've known only one great cameraman—Gregg Toland, who photographed *Citizen Kane.* He said he could teach me everything about the camera in four hours—and he did. I don't believe the specialist is all that our epoch cracks him up to be.

PLAYBOY: *Is it possible nowadays to be a Renaissance man—someone who's equally at home in the arts and the sciences?*
WELLES: It's possible and it's also necessary, because the big problem ahead of us today is synthesis. We have to get all these scattered things together and make sense of them. The wildest kind of lunacy is to go wandering up some single street. It's better not only for the individual but for society that our personal horizons should be as wide as possible. What a normally intelligent person can't learn—if he's genuinely alive and honestly curious—isn't really worth learning. For instance, besides knowing something about Elizabethan drama, I think I could also make a stab at explaining the basic principles of nuclear fission—a fair enough stab to be living in the world today. I don't just say: "That's a mystery that ought to be left to the scientists." Of course, I don't mean that I'm ready to accept a key post in national defense.

PLAYBOY: *Since World War Two, you've lived and worked mostly outside the United States. Would you call yourself an expatriate?*
WELLES: I don't like that word. Since childhood, I've always regarded myself as an American who happens to live all over the place. "Expatriate" is a dated word that relates to a particular 1920ish generation and to a romantic attitude about living abroad. I'm prejudiced against the word rather than the fact. I might very well cease to be an American citizen someday, but simply because, if you're forming a production company in Europe, it's economically helpful to be a European. I'm not young enough to bear arms for my country, so why shouldn't I live where I like and where I get the most work? After all, London is full of Hungarians and Germans and Frenchmen, and America is full of *everybody*—and *they* aren't called expatriates.

PLAYBOY: *Isn't it true that you chose to live in Europe because the U.S. Govern-*

ment refused to allow you tax deductions on the losses you suffered in your 1946
Broadway production of Around the World in Eighty Days?
WELLES: My tax problems began at that time, but that wasn't why I went
to Europe. I spent many of these years in Europe paying the Government
back all that money I lost, which they wouldn't let me write off as a loss
because of some bad bookkeeping. I like living in Europe: I'm not a refugee.

PLAYBOY: *You aren't a Catholic, yet you decided to live in two intensely Catho-*
lic countries—first Italy and now Spain. Why?
WELLES: This has nothing to do with religion. The Mediterranean culture
is more generous, less guilt-ridden. Any society that exists without natural
gaiety, without some sense of ease in the presence of death, is one in which
I am not immensely comfortable. I don't condemn that very northern, very
Protestant world of artists like Ingmar Bergman; it's just not where I live. The
Sweden I like to visit is a lot of fun. But Bergman's Sweden always reminds
me of something Henry James said about Ibsen's Norway—that it was full of
"the odor of spiritual paraffin." How I sympathize with that!

PLAYBOY: *If you could have picked any country and period in which to be born,*
would you have chosen America in 1915?
WELLES: It wouldn't have been all that low on my list, but anyone in their
senses would have wanted to live in the golden age of Greece, in 15th Century Italy or Elizabethan England. And there were other golden ages. Persia
had one and China had four or five. Ours is an extraordinary age, but it
doesn't even look very silver to me. I think I might have been happier and
more fulfilled in other periods and places—including America at about the
time when we started putting up roofs instead of tents.

PLAYBOY: *Are there any figures in American history you identify with?*
WELLES: Like most Americans, I wish I had some Lincoln in me; but I
don't. I can't imagine myself being capable of any such goodness or compas-
sion. I guess the only great American whose role I might conceivably have
occupied is Tom Paine. He was a radical, a true independent—not in the
comfortable, present-day liberal sense, but in the good, tough sense that he
was prepared to go to jail for it. It's been my luck, good or bad, not to have
been faced with that choice.

PLAYBOY: *Your parents separated when you were six, but you traveled widely with your mother, who died two years later. You then went around the world with your father, who died when you were fifteen. What places do you remember most vividly from this early globe-trotting period?*

WELLES: Berlin had about three good years, from 1926 onward, and so did Chicago about the same time. But the best cities were certainly Budapest and Peking. They had the best talk and the most action right up to the end. But I can't forget a party I attended somewhere in the Tyrol some time in the mid-Twenties. I was on a walking tour with several other little boys, and our tutor took us to eat at a big open-air beer garden. We sat at a long table with a lot of Nazis, who were then a little-known bunch of cranks, and I was placed next to a small man with a very dim personality. He made no impression on me at the time, but later, when I saw his pictures, I realized that I had lunched with Adolf Hitler.

PLAYBOY: *In many of the films you've written and directed, the hero has no father. We know nothing about Citizen Kane's father; and George, in* The Magnificent Ambersons, *ruins the life of his widowed mother by forbidding her to remarry. In your latest film,* Falstaff, *the hero is Prince Hal, whose legitimate father, Henry IV of England, is a murderous usurper: but his spiritual father, whom you play yourself—*

WELLES: Is Falstaff.

PLAYBOY: *Right. Does this attitude toward fathers reflect anything in your own life?*

WELLES: I don't think so. I had a father whom I remember as enormously likable and attractive. He was a gambler, and a playboy who may have been getting a bit old for it when I knew him, but he was a marvelous fellow, and it was a great sorrow to me when he died. No, a story interests me on its own merits, not because it's autobiographical. The Falstaff story is the best in Shakespeare—not the best play, but the best story. The richness of the triangle between the father and Falstaff and the son is without parallel; it's a complete Shakespearean creation. The other plays are good stories borrowed from other sources and made great because of what Shakespeare breathed into them. But there's nothing in the medieval chronicles that even hints at the Falstaff-Hal-King story. That's Shakespeare's story, and Falstaff is entirely his creation. He's the only great character in dramatic literature who is also good.

PLAYBOY: *Do you agree with W. H. Auden, who once likened him to a Christ figure?*
WELLES: I won't argue with that, although my flesh always creeps when people use the word "Christ." I think Falstaff is like a Christmas tree decorated with vices. The tree itself is total innocence and love. By contrast, the king is decorated only with kingliness. He's a pure Machiavellian. And there's something beady-eyed and self-regarding about his son—even when he reaches his apotheosis as Henry V.

PLAYBOY: *Do you think* Falstaff *is likely to outrage Shakespeare lovers?*
WELLES: Well, I've always edited Shakespeare, and my other Shakespearean films have suffered critically for just that reason. God knows what will happen with this one. In the case of *Macbeth* or *Othello,* I tried to make a single play into a filmscript. In *Falstaff,* I've taken five plays—*Richard II,* the two parts of *Henry IV, Henry V* and *The Merry Wives of Windsor*—and turned them into an entertainment lasting less than two hours. Naturally, I'm going to offend the kind of Shakespeare lover whose main concern is the sacredness of the text. But with people who are willing to concede that movies are a separate art form, I have some hopes of success. After all, when Verdi wrote *Falstaff* and *Otello,* nobody criticized *him* for radically changing Shakespeare. Larry Olivier has made fine Shakespearean movies that are essentially filmed Shakespearean plays; I use Shakespeare's words and characters to make motion pictures. They are variations on his themes. In *Falstaff,* I've gone much further than ever before, but not willfully, not for the fun of chopping and dabbling. If you see the history plays night after night in the theater, you discover a continuing story about a delinquent prince who turns into a great military captain, a usurping king, and Falstaff, the prince's spiritual father, who is a kind of secular saint. It finally culminates in the rejection of Falstaff by the prince. My film is entirely true to that story, although it sacrifices great parts of the plays from which the story is mined.

PLAYBOY: *Does the film have a "message"?*
WELLES: It laments the death of chivalry and the rejection of merry England. Even in Shakespeare's day, the old England of the greenwood and

Maytime was already a myth, but a very real one. The rejection of Falstaff by the prince means the rejection of that England by a new kind of England that Shakespeare deplored—an England that ended up as the British Empire. The main change is no excuse for the betrayal of a friendship. It's the liberation of that story that justifies my surgical approach to the text.

PLAYBOY: *May we check on a few of the popular rumors about you? It's been said that your pictures always go over the budget. True or false?*

WELLES: False. I'm not an overspender, though I've sometimes been a delayed earner. *Citizen Kane,* for instance, cost about $850,000. I've no idea how much profit it's made by now, but it must be plenty. That profit took time, and it didn't go to me. All the pictures I've directed have been made within their budgets. The only exception was a documentary about South America that I started in 1942, just after I finished shooting *The Magnificent Ambersons.* I was asked to do it by the Government for no salary but with $1,000,000 to spend. But it was the studio's money, not the Government's, and the studio fired me when I'd spent $600,000, on the basis that I was throwing money away. This is when the legend started. The studio spent a lot of dough and a lot of manpower putting it into circulation.

PLAYBOY: *Another prevalent rumor is that you have the power of clairvoyance. Is that true?*

WELLES: Well, if it exists, I sure as hell have it; if it doesn't exist, I have the thing that's mistaken for it. I've told people their futures in a terrifying way sometimes—and please understand that I hate fortunetelling. It's meddlesome, dangerous and a mockery of free will—the most important doctrine man has invented. But I was a fortuneteller once in Kansas City, when I was playing a week's stand there in the theater. As a part-time magician, I'd met a lot of semi-magician racketeers and learned the tricks of the professional seers. I took an apartment in a cheap district and put up a sign—$2 READINGS—and every day I went there, put on a turban and told fortunes. At first I used what are called "cold readings"; that's a technical term for things you say to people that are bound to impress them and put them off their guard so that they start telling you things about themselves. A typical cold reading is to say that you have a scar on your knee. Everybody has a scar on their knee, because everybody fell down as a child. Another one is to say that a big change took place in your attitude toward life between the ages of 12 and 14.

But in the last two or three days, I stopped doing the tricks and just talked. A woman came in wearing a bright dress. As soon as she sat down, I said, "You've just lost your husband"; and she burst into tears. I believe that I saw and deduced things that my conscious mind did not record. But consciously, I just said the first thing that came into my head, and it was true. So I was well on the way to contracting the fortuneteller's occupational disease, which is to start believing in yourself; to become what they call a "shut-eye." And that's dangerous.

PLAYBOY: *A third charge often leveled against you is that you dissipate too much energy in talk. The English critic Cyril Connolly once said that conversation, for an artist, was "a ceremony of self-wastage." Does that phrase give you a pang?*
WELLES: No, but it reminds me of Thornton Wilder and his theory of "capsule conversations." He used to say to me: "You must stop wasting your energy, Orson. You must do what I do—have capsule conversations." Just as a comic can do three minutes on his mother-in-law, Thornton could do three minutes on Gertrude Stein or Lope de Vega. That's how he saved his energy. But I don't believe that you have more energy if you save it. It isn't a priceless juice that has to be kept in a secret bottle. We're social animals, and good conversation—not just parroting slogans and vogue words—is an essential part of good living. It doesn't behoove any artist to regard what he has to offer as something so valuable that not a second of it should be frittered away in talking to his chums.

PLAYBOY: *It's also been said that you spend too much time in the company of ski bums and pretenders to Middle European thrones. Do you agree?*
WELLES: I don't know many people in either of those categories. Those that I do know are all right, but they're certainly not my constant companions. However, I have nothing against being known as a friend of *any* sort of person.

PLAYBOY: *A good deal of space and veneration is lavished on you in such avant-garde movie magazines as* Cahiers du Cinéma. *What do you think of the New Wave French directors so admired by these journals?*
WELLES: I'm longing to see their work! I've missed most of it because I'm afraid it might inhibit my own. When I make a picture, I don't like it to refer to other pictures; I like to think I'm inventing everything for the first time. I

talk to *Cahiers du Cinéma* about movies in general because I'm so pleased that they like mine. When they want long highbrow interviews, I haven't the heart to refuse them. But it's a complete act. I'm a fraud: I even talk about "the art of the cinema." I wouldn't talk to my friends about the art of the cinema—I'd rather be caught without my pants in the middle of Times Square.

PLAYBOY: *How do you feel about the films of Antonioni?*
WELLES: According to a young American critic, one of the great discoveries of our age is the value of boredom as an artistic subject. If that is so, Antonioni deserves to be counted as a pioneer and founding father. His movies are perfect backgrounds for fashion models. Maybe there aren't backgrounds that good in *Vogue,* but there ought to be. They ought to get Antonioni to design them.

PLAYBOY: *And what about Fellini?*
WELLES: He's as gifted as anyone making pictures today. His limitation—which is also the source of his charm—is that he's fundamentally very provincial. His films are a small-town boy's dream of the big city. His sophistication works because it's the creation of someone who doesn't have it. But he shows dangerous signs of being a superlative artist with little to say.

PLAYBOY: *Ingmar Bergman?*
WELLES: As I suggested a while ago, I share neither his interests nor his obsessions. He's far more foreign to me than the Japanese.

PLAYBOY: *How about contemporary American directors?*
WELLES: Stanley Kubrick and Richard Lester are the only ones that appeal to me—except for the old masters. By which I mean John Ford, John Ford and John Ford. I don't regard Alfred Hitchcock as an American director, though he's worked in Hollywood for all these years. He seems to me tremendously English in the best Edgar Wallace tradition, and no more. There's always something anecdotal about his work; his contrivances remain contrivances, no matter how marvelously they're conceived and executed. I don't honestly believe that Hitchcock is a director whose pictures will be of any interest a hundred years from now. With Ford at his best, you feel that

the movie has lived and breathed in a real world, even though it may have been written by Mother Machree. With Hitchcock, it's a world of spooks.

PLAYBOY: *When you first went to Hollywood in 1940, the big studios were still omnipotent. Do you think you'd have fared better if you'd arrived 20 years later, in the era of independent productions?*

WELLES: The very opposite. Hollywood died on me as soon as I got there. I wish to God I'd gone there sooner. It was the rise of the independents that was my ruin as a director. The old studio bosses—Jack Warner, Sam Goldwyn, Darryl Zanuck, Harry Cohn—were all friends, or friendly enemies I knew how to deal with. They all offered me work. Louis B. Mayer even wanted me to be the production chief of his studio—the job Dore Schary took. I was in great shape with those boys. The minute the independents got in, I never directed another American picture except by accident. If I'd gone to Hollywood in the last five years, virgin and unknown, I could have written my own ticket. But I'm not a virgin; I drag my myth around with me, and I've had much more trouble with the independents than I ever had with the big studios. I was a maverick, but the studios understood what that meant, and if there was a fight, we both enjoyed it. With an annual output of 40 pictures per studio, there would probably be room for one Orson Welles picture. But an independent is a fellow whose work is centered around his own particular gifts. In that setup, there's no place for me.

PLAYBOY: *Is it possible to learn how to direct movies?*

WELLES: Oh, the various technical jobs can be taught, just as you can teach the principles of grammar and rhetoric. But you can't teach writing, and directing a picture is very much like writing, except that it involves 300 people and a great many more skills. A director has to function like a commander in the field in time of battle. You need the same ability to inspire, terrify, encourage, reinforce and generally dominate. So it's partly a question of personality, which isn't so easy to acquire as a skill.

PLAYBOY: *Do you think it would help if there were a Federally subsidized film school in the United States?*

WELLES: If they *made* movies instead of *talking* about making movies, and if all classes on theory were rigorously forbidden, I could imagine a film school being very valuable, indeed.

PLAYBOY: *Do you think movie production ought to be aided by public money, as it is in many European countries?*
WELLES: If it is true—and I believe it is—that the theater and opera and music should be subsidized by the state, then it's equally true of the cinema, only more so. Films are more potent socially and have more to do with this particular moment in world history. The biggest money should go to the cinema. It needs more and has more to say.

PLAYBOY: *What do you see as the next development in the cinema?*
WELLES: I hope it *does* develop, that's all. There hasn't been any major revolution in films in more than 20 years, and without a revolution, stagnation sets in and decay is just around the corner. I hope some brand-new kind of moviemaking will arise. But before that happens, some form of making films more cheaply and showing them more cheaply will have to be evolved. Otherwise, the big revolution won't take place and the film artist will never be free.

PLAYBOY: *Given world-wide distribution, do you think any film could change the course of history?*
WELLES: Yes. And it might be a very bad film.

PLAYBOY: *Let's turn to the theater. Five years ago you said, "London is the actor's city, Paris is the playwright's city and New York is the director's city." Do you still agree with that judgment?*
WELLES: Today, I'd say that New York is David Merrick's city. Paris has ceased to be interesting at all as far as theater is concerned. London is still the great place for actors—but not for actresses. The English theater is a man's world. "London is a man's town, there's power in the air; And Paris is a woman's town, with flowers in her hair." I don't know who wrote that terrible old poem, but it continues to be true. Nobody in England writes great parts for women.

PLAYBOY: *Have you any unfulfilled theatrical ambitions?*
WELLES: I'd like to run a theater school, but not—and it makes me very sad to say this—not in America. Especially not in New York. Two generations of American actors have been so besotted by the Method that they have a built-in resistance to any other approach to theater. I don't want to drive the

Method out of New York, but I wish it would move over and leave room for a few other ideas about acting. The last time I tried to work in New York, I found no one who wasn't touched by it.

PLAYBOY: *Do you think American actors are equipped to play the classics?*
WELLES: They should be, but they're less able to than they were when we were running the Mercury Theatre around a quarter of a century ago. Part of the reason is that New York was a much more cosmopolitan city in those days. We were still within speaking distance of the age when it was called the melting pot. People were still first- and second-generation Europeans, and there was a genuine internationalism that did not come from the mass media. It just came from Uncle Joe having been born in a Warsaw suburb, and there were foreign-language theaters and I don't know how many foreign-language newspapers. All this gave a fertilizing richness to the earth that has now gone. New York has become much more standardized. Nowadays it's a sort of premixed manhattan cocktail, with a jigger of Irishness, Jewishness, WASP, and so forth. And that's your modern New Yorker, no matter where his grandfather came from. He may be just as nice a guy, but he isn't as various.

PLAYBOY: *Have you any predictions about the future of the theater in general?*
WELLES: I believe that the theater, like ballet and grand opera, is already an anachronism. It still gives us joy and stimulation: it still offers the artist a chance to do important work—qualitatively, perhaps, work as good as has ever been done. But it isn't an institution that belongs to our times, and it cannot expect a long future. It's not true that we've always had the theater. That's a dream. We've had it for only a few periods of history, no matter what its partisans say to the contrary. And the theater as we know it is now in its last stages.

PLAYBOY: *Looking back on your career in the performing arts, do you ever regret that you didn't go into politics?*
WELLES: Sometimes very bitterly. There was a time when I considered running as a junior Senator from Wisconsin; my opponent would have been a fellow called Joe McCarthy. If you feel that you might have been useful and effective in public office, you can't help being disappointed in yourself for never having tried it. And I flatter myself that I might have been. I think I

Orson Welles, *Citizen Kane*, 1941

Agnes Moorehead and Tim Holt, *The Magnificent Ambersons*, 1942

Joseph Cotten and Orson Welles, *Journey into Fear*, 1943

Edward G. Robinson, Loretta Young, and Orson Welles, *The Stranger*, 1946

Orson Welles and Jeanette Nolan (center right), *Macbeth*, 1948

Orson Welles and Suzanne Cloutier, *Othello*, 1952

Orson Welles, *Mr. Arkadin*, 1955

Charlton Heston and Orson Welles, *Touch of Evil*, 1958

Orson Welles, *Chimes at Midnight*, 1966

Orson Welles and Roger Coggio, *The Immortal Story*, 1968

am—at least potentially—a better public speaker than an actor, and I might have been able to reach people, to move and convince them. Oratory today is an almost nonexistent art, but if we lived in a society where rhetoric was seriously considered as an art—as it has been at many periods in world history—then I would have been an orator.

PLAYBOY: *What are your politics—and have they changed in the last 25 years?*
WELLES: Everyone's politics have changed in the last 25 years. You can't have a political opinion in a vacuum; it has to be a reaction to a situation. I've always been an independent radical, but with wide streaks of emotional and cultural old-fashionedness. I have enormous respect for many human institutions that are now in serious decay and likely never to be revived. Although I'm what is called a progressive, it isn't out of dislike for the past. I don't reject our yesterdays. I wish that parts of our dead past were more alive. If I'm capable of originality, it's not because I want to knock down idols or be ahead of the times. If there's anything rigid about me, it's a distaste for being in vogue. I would much rather be thought old-fashioned than "with it." But in general, I still belong to the liberal leftist world as it exists in the West. I vote that way and stand with those people. We may disagree on one issue or another, but that is where I belong.

PLAYBOY: *Where do you stand on the Vietnam war?*
WELLES: There's a newspaper in front of me right now that says that, according to a poll, popular support for Johnson's Vietnam program is going down. By the time this appears in print, anything I say will probably be shared by many more people. America doesn't have a history of losing wars and it has only a few bad wars on its conscience: this is one of them.

PLAYBOY: *You've met many of the great men and women of your time. Is there any living person you'd still like to meet?*
WELLES: Mrs. Sukarno, for obvious reasons, and Chou En-lai, mostly out of curiosity—I don't know if he'd be as interesting now as I always heard he used to be. He might be old and stiff and sad. I wish I'd known George Marshall, Winston Churchill and Wilson Mizner [an early 20th-century American playwright] better than I did. I never knew Pope John and that's a real regret. And although it may sound a little demagogic, I'd love to talk to an old lady named Elizabeth Allen: she's English, she's been living in a tin hut

in a forest for about 80 years and she makes the most beautiful pictures you ever saw out of rags. She's just had her first exhibition in London and she is superlative. But above everybody else, I'd like to meet Robert Graves. Not only because I think he's the greatest living poet, but because he has given me through the years the kind of pleasure that you get from close friends. I'd like to have some more of that stuff, only firsthand.

PLAYBOY: *Is there anyone, living or dead, with whom you'd like to change places?*
WELLES: If you've had as much luck as I have, it would be a sort of treachery to want to be anyone but yourself.

PLAYBOY: *What is your major vice?*
WELLES: *Accidia*—the medieval Latin word for melancholy, and sloth. I don't give way to it for long, but it still comes lurching at me out of the shadows. I have most of the accepted sins—envy, perhaps, the least of all. And pride. I'm not sure that is a sin; it's the only place where I quarrel with the Christian list. If it's a virtue, I don't recognize much of it in myself: the same is true if it's a vice.

PLAYBOY: *Do you consider gluttony a bad vice?*
WELLES: All vice is bad. A lot of vices are secret, but not gluttony—it shows. It certainly shows on me. But I feel that gluttony must be a good deal less deadly than some of the other sins. Because it's affirmative, isn't it? At least it celebrates some of the good things of life. Gluttony may be a sin, but an awful lot of fun goes into committing it. On the other hand, it's wrong for a man to make a mess of himself. I'm fat, and people shouldn't be fat.

PLAYBOY: *What is your attitude toward pornography and the literary use of four-letter words?*
WELLES: Four-letter words are useful tools, but when they cease to be more or less forbidden, they lose their cutting edge. When we wish to shock, we must have something left in our verbal quiver that will actually do the job. As for pornography, I don't agree with the present permissiveness in publishing it. By this I don't mean *Lady Chatterley's Lover*—the sort of book about physical love that used to be banned. I mean hard-core pornography—the blue novel and the blue movie. The difference is quite clear; it becomes

blurred only when you have to testify in a court. We all know perfectly well what we mean by what the French call *cochon*. It's not only piggish but lonely. Hard-core pornography may begin as a fairly benign sexual stimulant, but it ends up pretty vicious and sick. Then it isn't a harmless release for that which is sick in us; it excites and encourages the sickness, particularly in young people who have yet to learn about sex in terms of love and shared joy. The sexual habits of consenting adults are their own business. It's the secondhandedness of the printed thing that I don't like; not the fact that people *do* it, but that other people sit alone and read about it.

PLAYBOY: *If the decision were yours, would you censor anything in films or the theater?*

WELLES: I am so opposed to censorship that I must answer no—nothing. But if there were no censorship, I have a little list of the things I would prefer not to have shown. Not too often, anyway. Heavy spice isn't good for the palate; and in the theater and films, when there's too much license, what is merely raw tends to crowd out almost everything else, and our dramatic vocabulary is impoverished. If you show the act of copulation every time you do a love scene, both the producers and the public get to feel that no other kind of love scene is worth doing, and that the only variations on the theme are variations of physical position. No, artists should not be censored, but I do think they should restrain themselves, in order not to weaken the language of their art. Take the old Roman comedies: Once you bring out those great leather phalluses, you get so there isn't any other sort of joke you can do. It's the same with violence, or any theatrical extreme. If it's pushed too far, it tends to erode the middle register of human feeling. However, propaganda against any kind of loving human relationship is despicable and probably ought to be censored.

PLAYBOY: *But how do you reconcile that with—*

WELLES: For 30 years people have been asking me how I reconcile X with Y! The truthful answer is that I don't. Everything about me is a contradiction, and so is everything about everybody I know. We are made out of oppositions; we live between two poles. There's a Philistine and an aesthete in all of us, and a murderer and a saint. You don't reconcile the poles. You just recognize them.

PLAYBOY: *Did you have a religious upbringing?*

WELLES: Quite the contrary. My mother was born a Catholic but then became a student of Oriental religions, in which she later lost interest. She taught me to read the Bible as a wonderful piece of literature. My father was a total agnostic, and Dr. Bernstein—the guardian who looked after me when my parents died—always made fun of the Bible stories. That shocked me as a child. I have a natural sense of veneration for what man has aspired to beyond himself, in East or West. It comes easily and instinctively to me to feel reverence rather than a gleeful skepticism. I read the mystics, though I'm not a mystic myself.

PLAYBOY: *Do you believe in God?*

WELLES: My feelings on that subject are a constant interior dialogue that I haven't sufficiently resolved to be sure that I have anything worth communicating to people I don't know. I may not be a believer, but I'm certainly religious. In a strange way, I even accept the divinity of Christ. The accumulation of faith creates its own veracity. It does this in a sort of Jungian sense, because it's been made true in a way that's almost as real as life. If you ask me whether the rabbi who was crucified was God, the answer is no. But the great, irresistible thing about the Judaeo-Christian idea is that man—no matter what his ancestry, no matter how close he is to any murderous ape—really is unique. If we are capable of unselfishly loving one another, we are absolutely alone, as a species, on this planet. There isn't another animal that remotely resembles us. The notion of Christ's divinity is a way of saying that. That's why the myth is true. In the highest tragic sense, it dramatizes the idea that man is divine.

PLAYBOY: *Does your idealization of man apply equally to woman? Are there any limitations on what a woman can achieve?*

WELLES: No. There's a limitation on what she is *likely* to do, but not on what she *can* do. Women have managed to do everything; but the likelihood that they're going to do it often is statistically small. It's improbable that they will ever be as numerous as men in the arts. I believe that if there had never been men, there would never have been art—but if there had never been women, men would never have made art.

PLAYBOY: *Whom would you choose as a model of the way men ought to behave toward women?*

WELLES: Robert Graves. In other words, total adoration. Mine is less total than it ought to be. I'm crazy about the girls, but I do like to sit around the port with the boys. I recognize in myself that old-fashioned Edwardian tendency—shared by many other societies in other epochs—to let the ladies leave us for a while after dinner, so the men can talk. We'll join them later. I've talked endlessly to women for sexual purposes—years of my life have been given up to it. But women usually depress or dominate a conversation to its detriment—though, of course, there are brilliant and unnerving exceptions. In a sense, every woman is an exception. It's the generality that makes a male chauvinist like me.

PLAYBOY: *In the opinion of some, the frontiers of art—and reality—may soon be pushed back by the use of hallucinogenic drugs. What do you think about these so-called aids to perception?*
WELLES: The use of drugs is a perverse expression of individualism, antisocial and life-denying. It's all part of a great reaction—especially in the West—against the inevitably collective nature of society in the future. Let me put it discursively. European women are painting their eyelids to look Chinese. Japanese women are having operations to look American; white people are getting sun-tanned and Negroes are having their hair dekinked. We are trying to become as much like one another as possible. And with this great mass movement—which is both good and bad, both a denial of cultural heritage and an affirmation of human solidarity—there goes a retreat from the crowd into one's lonely self. And that's what this drug business is all about. It isn't an assertion of individuality; it's a substitute for it. It's not an attempt to be different when everyone else is becoming more alike; it's a way of copping out. And that's the worst thing you can do. I much prefer people who rock the boat to people who jump out.

PLAYBOY: *If art is an expression of protest, as some philosophers have felt, do you think it's possible that in an automated world of abundance, devoid of frustrations and pressures, nobody would feel compelled to create art?*
WELLES: I don't believe that, even in a perfect oyster shell, there will never be another grain of sand, and therefore never another pearl. And I don't accept that art is necessarily based on unhappiness. It's often serene and joyous and a kind of celebration. That isn't to deny the vast body of work that has been created in conditions of spiritual and economic wretchedness and

even torment, but I see no reason to think that culture will be poorer because people are happier.

PLAYBOY: *Some critics assert that modern art can be produced by accident—as in action painting, aleatory music and theatrical Happenings. Do you think it's possible to create a work of art without intending to?*

WELLES: Categorically no. You may create something that will give some of the pleasures and emotions that a work of art may give, just as a microscopic study of a snowflake or a tapeworm or a cancer cell may be a beautiful object. But a work of art is a conscious human effort that has to do with communication. It is that or it is nothing. When an accident is applauded as a work of art, when a cult grows up around the deliciousness of inadvertent beauty, we are in the presence of the greatest decadence the West has known in its history.

PLAYBOY: *Do you agree with those modern artists who say: "I don't care what happens to my work tomorrow—it's only meant for today"?*

WELLES: No, because an artist shouldn't care what happens today either. To care about today to the exclusion of any other time, to be self-consciously contemporary, is to be absurdly parochial. That's what is wrong about the artist's association with the huckster. Today has been canonized, beatified. But today is just one day in the history of our planet. It's the be-all and the end-all only for somebody who is selling something.

PLAYBOY: *What effect do you feel the advertising industry is having on artists—on writers as well as painters and designers?*

WELLES: The advertisers are having a disastrous effect on every art they touch. They are not only seducing the artist, they are drafting him. They are not only drawing on him, they are sucking the soul out of him. And the artist has gone over to the advertiser far more than he ever did to the merchant. The classic enemy of art has always been the market place. There you find the merchant and the charlatan—the man with goods to sell and the man with the snake oil. In the old days you had merchant princes, ex-pushcart peddlers turned into Hollywood moguls, but by and large honest salesmen, trying to give the public what they believed was good—even if it wasn't—and not seriously invading the artist's life unless the artist was willing to make that concession. But now we're in the hands of the snake-oil boys. Among the advertisers, you find artists who have betrayed their kind and are busy getting their brethren hooked on the same drug. The advertising profession is largely made up of unfrocked poets, disappointed novelists, frustrated actors and unsuccessful producers with split-level homes. They've somehow managed to pervade the whole universe of art, so that the artist himself now thinks and functions as an advertising man. He makes expendable objects, deals in the immediate gut kick, revels in the lack of true content. He paints a soup can and calls it art. A can of soup, well enough designed, could be a work of art: but a painting of it, never.

PLAYBOY: *Have you any theories about what will happen to you after death?*
WELLES: I don't know about my soul, but my body will be sent to the White House. American passports ask you to state the name and address of the person to whom your remains should be delivered in the event of your death. I discovered many years ago that there is no law against putting down the name and address of the President. This has a powerful effect on the borders of many countries and acts as a sort of diplomatic visa. During the long Eisenhower years, I would almost have been willing to die in order to have my coffin turn up some evening in front of his television set.

PLAYBOY: *How would you like the world to remember you?*
WELLES: I've set myself against being concerned with any more worldly success than I need to function with. That's an honest statement and not a piece of attitudinizing. Up to a point, I have to be successful in order to operate. But I think it's corrupting to care about success; and nothing could be more vulgar than to worry about posterity.

Orson Welles: Shakespeare, Welles, and Moles

RICHARD MARIENSTRAS/1974

RICHARD MARIENSTRAS: *Mr. Welles, of all film directors you are not only the most flamboyant and the most controversial . . .*

ORSON WELLES: I am not in the least an ostentatious director.

RM: *It seems that among the modern directors you are . . .*

OW: I don't think so. Fellini is much more flamboyant than I am.

RM: *But you started before he did.*

OW: Yes, and now I'm much less flamboyant than he is. I hope so, because for me, flamboyance . . . I don't know if this is the case in French, but in English "flamboyant" is pejorative. And I don't feel that my Shakespearean films are at all flamboyant.

RM: Macbeth *isn't flamboyant, but it is a baroque film.*

OW: Yes, but baroque is not rococo. It's hard for me to imagine a Shakespearean film that wouldn't be visually baroque: his plays are works from the Renaissance, not from Brecht's era.

This two-hour interview was filmed in Paris in December 1974 for a French television series featuring major stage and screen "mediators" of Shakespeare. Only two films of fifty-five minutes each were produced, one with Welles telecast in 1975, the other with Peter Brook. The full text of the Welles interview was eventually published in *Positif,* July–August 1998. Translated for this collection by Alisa Hartz. Reprinted by permission of Richard Marienstras. Bracketed annotations are the author's.

R M : *Peter Brook doesn't direct Shakespeare in quite this manner. He presents a much more tense and controlled Shakespeare.*

O W : I think all directors who make Shakespearean films make controlled films. Excuse me for insisting: in the case of Peter Brook, it's not control. Maybe you're thinking of his rather dry aesthetic, but that's not control. In the end, there's control in Bernini, too.

R M : *Peter Brook avoids using images that are too dazzling. He controls their flamboyance.*

O W : Yes, perhaps. I've never seen a Shakespearean film directed by Peter Brook. I've only seen his productions on stage. I saw one very flamboyant, very rococo work, but it was magnificent.

R M : Titus Andronicus, *for example?*

O W : Yes. But also *Measure for Measure*: this was a remarkable production by Peter Brook.

R M : *Recently [1970] he directed a wonderful* Midsummer Night's Dream.

O W : I am one of the two or three people in the world who don't like that production. As a production it's remarkable, but it's an insult to the play!

R M : *This play has been weighed down by pastoral tradition, and sets overloaded with greenery and leaves. Peter Brook managed to evade the pastoral tradition and replace it with another tradition, the circus.*

O W : Ah yes: Shakespeare's great enemy is the director!

R M : *It's true—but how can one do without him?*

O W : One needs a director who is perfectly measured, a true servant not only of Shakespeare but also of the actors. For a few years, I think, in Germany, Russia, and perhaps for a short time in England and America, there was a certain openness, an end to this impasse. The academic tradition is dead, I absolutely agree. But today—and I'm not speaking of cinema but specifically of theater—I feel that the director has become too strong.

R M : *Too strong for Shakespeare?*

O W : Yes, for Shakespeare, and also for theater. Because the basis of theater is the actor, and after the actor, the play. In that order.

RM: *The text doesn't come first? The actor takes precedence?*

OW: Absolutely. Because in the history of the theater, the text comes after the actor.

RM: *As in the* commedia dell'arte?

OW: But also in prehistoric times, in all countries, and even in pre-Shakespearean England. And Shakespeare himself was an actor, like Molière. It's no accident that he played Iago, the best role in Othello.

RM: *Are we sure he played Iago? It's not entirely certain.*

OW: I'm sure. There's a lot of proof. We are certain that he played the role of Hamlet's father.

RM: *The ghost?*

OW: Yes. For me, it's the second essential role in Hamlet, the most difficult role. I've never seen it done well or performed well, in cinema or in theater. [Welles himself interpreted the ghost at the Gate Theatre, Dublin, in 1932, and then in 1934 at the Woodstock, Illinois festival.]

RM: *This type of character is always hard to portray on stage, like the witches in* Macbeth.

OW: That's entirely different: the witches aren't ghosts. They're devotees of their religion, they're real. [In his 1947 film of *Macbeth,* Welles introduced a conflict between paganism and Christianity which does not figure in Shakespeare.] For me—I say *for me* because there are a million different opinions about *Hamlet*—Hamlet's father is first a man and only then a phantom. He's a man in rage, filled with fury, stronger than Hamlet, and he speaks violently, he's much more inventive than Hamlet. I am absolutely willing to believe that in the end the ghost exists only in Hamlet's head, at least that's one way to interpret it. But, in whatever way he exists, he's the greatest man in Denmark. And when Hamlet says in his apostrophe, *"Well said, old mole! Canst work i' the earth so fast?"* this earth is to be found in Hamlet's spirit. I have a theory (all directors have theories, like professors, like everyone . . .) that in each of Shakespeare's plays there's a role—not the principal role—that has to be played by the best actor of the company. And for me, Hamlet's father has to be played by the best. Only then does the play come alive.

RM: *But this reference to the boards of the stage ("canst work i' the earth so fast?") is also a way of communicating with the hall, because the audience was very close to the actors.*

OW: I don't think so. I'm sure he was in the balcony, not in the trap door. The voice came from above, and Hamlet had to tell the public that the ghost was under the stage. I don't think it was even possible to get a distinct voice to come from under the stage.

The question of magic always comes up in Shakespeare. There's always something supernatural. In *Julius Caesar,* there's a real ghost, a thoroughly supernatural vision. And all those magic things in *A Midsummer Night's Dream* that were completely butchered by Peter Brook in his famous and influential production which, in my opinion, was a *coup de théâtre* and a tremendous blow against the theater.

RM: *All the more so because in that production Titania and Oberon were also Hippolyta and Theseus, such that the whole play takes on the supernatural aspect of these characters.*

OW: In Shakespeare's time, England—like all of Europe—was essentially rural. Two steps from London and you were in the country, and Shakespeare is filled with the mystery and lyricism of nature. But to put the out-of-date pastoral vision to rest, one doesn't need a sterile vision of nature.

RM: *Still, it's in killing off or displacing the pastoral tradition that Brook managed to bring all those Athenian characters to life, while most previous productions render them in very uninteresting ways.*

OW: That too is a *coup de théâtre,* because in fact those characters aren't interesting! Shakespeare is right, they aren't interesting. It's only Peter Brook who, as a director, found a way to make them interesting, to their advantage. It's the fairies and the artisans who hold our attention. The truly profound role is Bottom. And Bottom, for Peter Brook, is just a comedian like any other.

RM: *Emphasizing the artisans and their facile comedy is the traditional way of directing the play.*

OW: For me, it's a rather judicious way. That's the right way to stage it. I know I'm going to speak paradoxically, but in my eyes, tradition is better than experimentation in theater, in general.

RM: *However, the way you've staged* Macbeth *for both stage and screen runs entirely counter to tradition.*
OW: I don't know . . .

RM: *In 1936 you did a black* Macbeth, *a voodoo* Macbeth.
OW: It was just a way of communicating with the audience; I didn't change the play's intentions, as I saw them. In other words, the difference between Peter Brook's *Midsummer Night's Dream* and my *Macbeth* is that Brook deliberately introduced a new intention into the comedy, whereas I used Haiti, voodoo, etc., to foreground what I thought was represented in the play.

RM: *Still, it was a way for you to make it accessible to a certain public.*
OW: But the intention belonged to the play.

RM: *All the same, you did change the text a little, didn't you?*
OW: Absolutely not.

RM: *It was unabridged?*
OW: Unabridged? Never! I cut, cut, cut, oh yes.

RM: *But in cutting, aren't you changing the general balance of the play? Especially a play like* Macbeth, *which is relatively short.*
OW: That's true. We didn't cut much in *Macbeth* because, as you say, it's the shortest play. I would like to say this: any director who directs a Shakespearean play or film can only realize a small part of it. Shakespeare is the greatest man who ever lived, and we are poor moles who work underground. All we can do is grasp at or bite off a little bit, but what we grasp must be true and undistorted. I am entirely against distortion in a Shakespearean production.

RM: *All the same, there are questions of interpretation: what one finds true, another sees as distorted.*
OW: Let's take *Macbeth*. In Shakespeare's times, Macbeth wore an Elizabethan costume, with a fraise and all that. And for two hundred years, he was dressed as a romantic: that's the romantic visual tradition, which has become prehistoric! If I find a way of creating a primitivism which moves the public, which communicates with them without touching the play, at least the little part that I am able to understand, why not do it? Macbeth poses a particu-

larly interesting problem: no actor in the history of theater has ever been a great Macbeth. Why? Because there has never been an actor who could perform the first and second parts of the play. For this play has a great defect, an imperfection: the Macbeth who is the victim of Lady Macbeth is not the one who then becomes king. No actor has ever been able to play both parts equally well. The actor must be brutally simple and completely natural to play the first part, and extremely cerebral to play the second part. In other words, Laurence Olivier would have to play in the first part, and John Gielgud in the second.

R M :   *In your film, you modified certain things, like the relation between the witches.*
O W :   I was making a film!

R M :   *One has the impression that Macbeth is an instrument in the hands of the witches. The witches mold a little clay figure in the image of Macbeth, and there seems to be a sort of magic at work, and from that moment on he acts like a man hallucinating, like a pure instrument of evil.*
O W :   Not like a pure instrument of evil, because he's a Christian. The forces of evil are fighting to win him over, but the battle isn't won at the beginning of the film, nor is it won at the end. Even at the end, Macbeth remains a member of the Christian world and continues to fight to save his integrity. The fact that he's destroyed by evil doesn't mean that he is its plaything, as the forces of evil wanted him to be. Finally he falls, he collapses. His wife, because of her ambitions for him, also uses him. Everyone uses him. It's the same Christian conscience that Shakespeare gives to his villains. When Hamlet's uncle, the king, says, *"O, my offense is rank . . . It hath the primal eldest curse upon't, a brother's murder,"* this is absolutely a part of Christian tradition, the Catholic tradition which Shakespeare, I think, whether he was a believer or not, belonged to by virtue of his culture. So scoundrels had to speak and act like this, and all the way through the play Macbeth acts like a man of conscience.

R M :   *From the beginning to the end of the film, then, you think of him as a man possessed of his free will . . .*
O W :   And who is trying to use it, but forces more powerful than he—a woman endowed with a stronger personality, historic forces and everything

else—get the better of him. But he's not a mere instrument of evil going to his downfall.

R M :   *One has the impression that from one end to the other he is possessed, he is hallucinating.*
O W :   He is hallucinating, of course, but it's the hallucination of a member of the Christian community. And the forces of evil, according to me—not according to me in general, but in my specific design for this film—are not necessarily evil. They represent ancient religion, paganism. Just as ambition is not necessarily evil. And his wife represents evil.

R M :   *In this specific case, ambition is an evil.*
O W :   Let's consider it in the historical context. What is ambition? Take the story of William the Conqueror at an earlier era, or the story of Henry II [who ordered the murder of Thomas Becket] and men like him who were assassins. If Richard III had found a horse at Bosworth, the Plantagenets would still be reigning in England and Richard would not be a villain because Thomas More would not have written the bitter pamphlet against him! [This unfinished history served as a source for Shakespeare.]

R M :   *Yes, but in this particular kind of evildoing do you only see a sort of literary creation? Or do you think it goes farther than that? In the play, the portrait of Richard is an act of propaganda against a defeated monarchy, but isn't Richard also the incarnation of evil?*
O W :   *Richard III* isn't really a play about evil. It's a play about a delicious villain. It has a marvelous role for a great actor, that of a fascinating felon. The role of Macbeth is very different. It's the story of a weak man. This is why Macbeth has never been the great role of a great actor. To play it requires an actor of great physical and intellectual power, capable of incarnating a weakling. However you interpret Lady Macbeth or the witches—and there are thirty ways to do it—Macbeth is always a weakling. The nature of his weakness remains to be found. He's not a strong man who is defeated and collapses. He's sick from the outset.

R M :   *But at the beginning of the play, when he appears as a glorious general who just defeated a rebel, he doesn't give that impression.*

o w : He's not as glorious as all that. These battles which were waged so often, at intervals of a few weeks, were a sort of permanent guerilla war and not very glorious. Yes, Macbeth brought home a victory. But he's not glorious like a Coriolanus, or a Julius Caesar, or a Mark Antony. There's not a single line in the play which gives him this kind of seductiveness. He simply won a battle, and that's all that can be said.

R M : *And the witches immediately tempted him?*
o w : They put an idea into his head. And he's so stupid that it wouldn't have come to him otherwise! As I often say, most of Shakespeare's heroes are noble and stupendous, grandiose, and imbeciles! Hamlet, Richard II . . .

R M : *And* Julius Caesar? *You staged it at the Mercury Theatre in 1937, and strongly underlined certain political themes of the play, which, by the way, is a political work.*
o w : Yes, it was overtly anti-fascist. It was a period when fascism wasn't a matter of a little discussion in a cafe, a little disagreement. At that time fascism was the most important thing in our lives. An anti-fascist theatrical work was an important thing. I admit that there were certain misrepresentations in the staging, because we were living in those times.

R M : *You accentuated the negative characteristics of Julius Caesar.*
o w : He's also negative in the play, no?

R M : *Brutus, too. That is, in a different way . . .*
o w : No, no, he's a liberal, and he's so intelligent and sympathetic . . . Terrifically difficult to play, very interesting. No, for me he isn't unsympathetic. Now Cassius, on the other hand, is unsympathetic.

R M : *But the play has often been interpreted as being about a man who assassinates his best friend, that is, his father. In some respects, Brutus betrays his own affections.*
o w : And he may have been Caesar's illegitimate son, but that's not in the text. What we have in the text is Brutus's great crisis of conscience. It's also a very difficult role, like Macbeth, because he is rather weak, and, in this case, extremely intelligent.

R M : *When you presented* Macbeth *in Harlem, there was a certain agitation among the blacks. Was it really the first Shakespeare play performed by blacks?*
O W : There were others, I think, but it was the first important production. In any case it was the most chic premiere of my whole career. I'd never seen anything like it. The Lafayette Theatre, this enormous theater, was filled with anyone who was anyone in Harlem and in New York, dressed in suits with white ties, standing because there was no more room. It was the most chic, elegant and lively atmosphere I've ever seen. And at the end of the play there were so many curtain calls that we finally left the curtain open and the audience came onto the stage.

R M : *At the time, the play was acclaimed by militant blacks. I found this clipping from critic King Otley: "The black actor is tired of bearing the burden of the black face assigned to him by whites. In* Macbeth, *he finally has the opportunity to play a universal character. The Harlem community attended a production in which the Black was neither taunted nor ridiculed. We attended the production of* Macbeth, *happy to know that the show would not once again give us the odious feeling of being dirty Negroes* [Amsterdam News, 18 April 1945]." *This is extraordinary, because it was a precocious manifestation of . . .*
O W : It was. It was a great political event.

R M : *There were riots in Harlem . . .*
O W : And also a riot that night! The police were everywhere because a large portion of the black community thought we were ridiculing blacks by having them perform Shakespeare and that the public had come to mock them. So there were hundreds of policemen to stop people from throwing bricks. There was a rumor that it was a kind of burlesque show. But it was just the opposite. The rehearsals lasted a very long time. I've never rehearsed a play so long: three months. And during all these rehearsals, I never once suggested an intonation to the actors. The blacks invented the whole diction of Shakespeare. It was very interesting and very beautiful. I didn't suggest anything about Shakespearean tradition or the white way of reciting Shakespeare. But their sense of rhythm and music is so great and their diction so good that they found their own way of reciting Shakespeare. It was astonishing!

R M : *Apparently there was a real sorcerer in* Macbeth.

o w :   Fourteen! We brought them from Dahomey—we couldn't find any in the Antilles—and while we prepared they killed goats on the stage and made the sorcerer's tom-toms.

R M :   *You had a large number of actors.*
o w :   Yes, an enormous cast. The scenery was very ugly, but the rest was extraordinary.

R M :   *Who designed the scenery? You?*
o w :   No, alas. After this I started making my own sets. [However, Welles used the same designer, Nat Karson, for the next two plays he directed.] Someone else designed it. It looked a bit like a musical comedy. I am ashamed of the photographs of the scenery. But I designed the lighting so no one could see it.

R M :   *The theater operated under the auspices of the Federal Theatre . . .*
o w :   . . . which was a marvelous thing.

R M :   *Could you say something about it? Because no one knows about it . . .*
o w :   No one knows anything about it now, not even in America. They've all forgotten what it was. There were millions of unemployed people who wanted to work. And rather than handing out money, Roosevelt created the Works Progress Administration. He gave painters jobs painting frescoes in public buildings; he set writers to work at all kinds of useful things that allowed them to express themselves as they pleased. I don't know how many theaters he opened, but there were theaters all across the country. It is the only *national* theater in the history of the United States.

R M :   *Then it could possibly be compared to . . .*
o w :   To [Jean] Vilar? Most certainly. But Vilar's theater, though it was very popular and addressed to young people, just like ours, still drew on the old traditions of national theaters in France and central Europe which were sub-sidized by the government. While in our case, we had to go up against Congress every day, because the idea that we would be subsidized to produce plays disgusted the members of Congress. When I staged *The Tragical History of Doctor Faustus,* a member of Congress stood up and denounced me as a

notorious communist because everyone knows that Christopher Marlowe was a member of the Komintern!

R M :   *In fact, your black* Macbeth *was attacked on political grounds. Someone said: "Black theater, a scion of the federal government and one of Uncle Sam's experiments, gave us a luxurious representation yesterday . . ."*
O W :   Yes, yes.

R M :   *But didn't the activities of the Federal Theatre disintegrate rather quickly?*
O W :   No, it lasted three years and produced a number of directors, including Joseph Losey, as well as the two most important theaters, I think, up until 1950, the Mercury Theatre and the Group Theatre. There were also the plays done by the Living Newspaper [theatrical political presentations in the manner of agitprop], which were very interesting theatrical experiments. And also, of course, a number of stars. But in all of America, people who had forgotten what a play was could see plays and actors at work. In Harlem, we didn't only stage *Macbeth,* there were around fifteen plays, and we brought together the whole world. You can't imagine the flourishing of life in Harlem. I was practically living in Harlem. [. . .]

    King Lear is a historic play, or else it is Brechtian, but I don't think it's universal. I don't think that any play can be universal unless it's given a particular reading for an audience. There are a hundred ways of performing this play. But we were speaking of my feeling that Shakespeare is a man of the country. He emerged from a pastoral world and he never stopped believing that the court represents evil. You find this in *Hamlet,* in *Lear,* . . . The idea that there is something essentially corrupt in the political confrontations of the court pervades his whole oeuvre. And one can understand these feelings by reading the history of England of the period.

R M :   *But he always tries to give some justification to his kings . . .*
O W :   To his kings, not to the court! There's a big difference, because in his mind the mystique of the king of England dated back to the origins of time. Now, we know this is false. But he had no way of knowing that the idea of the divine essence of kings was relatively modern, that it only dated back one hundred and fifty years. He couldn't know what we know about the anxieties of Richard II, of Henry V, of Henry IV. The idea that the crown was sacred, that around the crown corruption reigned but that the crown itself,

whoever wore it, was a sort of Holy Grail—for Shakespeare, this idea was very real.

R M :   *He always creates a kind of tension. He portrays Richard II as a corrupt king.*
O W :   Yes, he's corrupt, weak, what have you. But he is very complex. One shouldn't oversimplify. Only directors oversimplify.

R M :   *You published a revised edition of some of Shakespeare's plays. Were you trying to make his works more accessible to the public?*
O W :   Yes. I edited these plays for high school students, with many illustrations. The text was cut so as to leave only a minimum of things that wouldn't be understood. Because it seems to me that the first thing to do for a student at school is to make him love Shakespeare, not to make him hate it. He can learn to love Shakespeare by staging it himself in a simplified form. This edition was designed to allow a student to get into costume and perform. I thought that if he could do this, he wouldn't be afraid to read the complete texts of Shakespeare as he grew up, or to see more refined productions. But I did this when I was very young. These books were still in print almost two years ago.

R M :   *You yourself performed Shakespeare at school?*
O W :   Yes, at a marvelous boy's school [the Todd School]. It was very old-fashioned and very modern at the same time. The owner-director was an old man, and his youngest son [Roger Hill] brought new ideas. It was marvelous because there were no educational principles. All he wanted to do was to make people active, awaken their spirit of discovery. He is a famous man in the domain of education. I only stayed a few years but it was a marvelous experience.

R M :   *In your revised edition, you wrote a chapter on the stage at the time of Shakespeare.*
O W :   It was just to try to explain the kind of place where the plays were performed. Of course, the more we read and the more we discover today, the less we know about this subject. The nature of the Elizabethan stage has become one of the greatest mysteries of the world! But we know its main features and we can imagine the atmosphere.

R M :   *Has your knowledge of the Elizabethan stage had any influence on your theatrical work?*

O W :   I don't think so, because after the invention of the Italian-style stage, all this knowledge was erased. And when we emerged from the Italian-style stage—whether this was a good idea is still an open question—when we returned to the enclosure of the Middle Ages, to the altar or to some track in a sports stadium, as long as we went no further than imitations of salons with framed stages, nothing that concerned the physical representation of Shakespeare could be performed without being marked as precious, without becoming precious archeology. I think the only exception is Copeau, who created—not specifically for Shakespeare—a kind of theater where anything at all could be represented.

R M :   *I'm surprised at what you say about the Italian-style stage. It has almost entirely disappeared in our time. There are obviously a certain number of theaters which still use this convention, but in general modern theaters don't use it, and you seem to regret this.*

O W :   Yes. I think that the first experiments designed to eliminate the Italian-style stage were more successful than those of today. Because I think that theater, today, is essentially an anachronism, it's dead. I don't think it's necessarily dead forever, for theater is like the seasons. Now it's in its winter, but I don't think we're experiencing a true spring. And if there is one, I haven't discovered it yet. For me, we're in the age of film. Film is at the heart of life, and theater is like opera. I love theater, I love opera, but they belong to a certain world, and as long as the theater doesn't become truly popular, not an intellectual form pretending to be popular . . . This was our fault, this was everyone's fault . . . After all, in the first days of the Works Progress Administration and of the Mercury Theatre, it was easy for us to talk about popular theater, for we had an enormous population of Russian Jews and Polish immigrants and workers from central Europe who were poor and graced the cheapest seats with all the culture of a European education. We could not have done this in Indiana. And those who think they could have done it are dreaming, you know . . . [. . .] I wonder if Shakespeare is ever epic. I don't think he is. I think he belongs to an age of melodrama, comedy and farce, and that he never wrote a tragedy.

R M :   *And* Coriolanus?

O W :   That comes the closest. But every one of his plays is a melodrama interrupted by great tragic scenes. He's a dramatic writer who is too popular to be
truly tragic. True tragedy would never have had such sway over an Elizabethan or Jacobean public. And Shakespeare was certainly part of his time; he
was an actor who belonged to his audience. In my opinion, he couldn't have
written epic plays.

R M :   *Let's say that there are some epic tones in his work . . .*
O W :   Epic tones, certainly! But this doesn't authorize one to eliminate the
gigantic melodrama in Renaissance style, which is the basis of his work. I
love purely epic plays, but I don't think Shakespeare wrote any. I think he
wrote melodramas with an epic basis. Filled with farce, buffoonery, comic
themes, everything . . . And, of course, the context in which he was writing
allowed him to go the extremes of horror, magnificence, nobility, tenderness, lyricism, comedy. None of this would be possible in purely epic theater.
This is why I don't think it's right to stage his plays in the epic mode. In my
opinion, epic theater is nothing more than a slogan, a kind of cultural pollu-
tion engendered by the distorted notion that some have of what Brecht was
trying to do. Brecht was one of my close friends; we collaborated on *Galileo*.
[In 1946, Charles Laughton asked Welles to direct him in the title role. A year
later, the production was handled by Joseph Losey instead.] I am very pro-
Brecht. I am totally against his disciples. But I am against most disciples.
Look what they did to Christianity!

R M :   *But in* Falstaff *you eliminated certain epic tones.*
O W :   There aren't any in those plays.

R M :   *There's the chivalrous battle . . .*
O W :   It's heroic . . . Now I'm playing tricks with the English language, but
the heroic tones are much stronger than the epic foundation, you see. The
idea of chivalry is not epic. In English, the word *epic* applies more to Greek
tragedy than to the heroic nature of Shakespeare's political or historic plays.
Shakespeare was a precursor of novelists: everyone is complicated. Any play
can be reduced to a theory, but when this has been done, there is always a
remainder. If a book with the complete plays of Shakespeare were a single
play, you'd try to develop the best *mise en scène* that ever existed. And if you

did, the whole book would still be left because of its incredible richness. It's much easier to stage an epic play because the form is much simpler.

You see, it's like the difference between *kabuki* and *nô* theater. I don't think we live in an age when true epic theater squares with popular taste. That's just a slogan, it's snobbism. This wasn't the case, I think, during the years of Brecht's great productions. Then the word meant something. And epic theater was profoundly popular and, at the same time, filled with melodrama. There was a sort of austerity and the word *austerity* encircled the epic. What Peter Brook tells us about, and what is so wonderful about him, is his obsessive taste for ritual. In his production of *King Lear,* the most extraordinary aspect is the silence of the first four minutes, when no one speaks, when they take off their gauntlets and prepare themselves: it was absolutely magical. But King Lear was performed as if he were Gloucester, which is a great role and should be performed by the best actor of the troop. This has always been my theory: for the play to truly work, Edgar and Gloucester are the roles that must be played by the actors with the most talent, because almost anyone can play Lear. It isn't a difficult role; it performs itself. But then try to perform Gloucester!

R M : *There are some productions in which Gloucester is performed better than Lear. The role is more melodramatic—Gloucester suffers in his flesh—and perhaps a modern public understands his sufferings more than Lear's.*
O W : That's an excellent theory. He is physically annihilated, but if that's what you mean by melodrama, it's not an appropriate use of the word, because the protagonists of true tragic Greek theater are also annihilated physically, their eyes are gouged out . . . Not on stage, granted, but they come back in a mask covered in blood.

R M : *There's a slight difference . . .*
O W : Yes: *"Out, vile jelly* [Cornwall to Gloucester as he gouges out the latter's eyes, in *King Lear*]!" I suppose that's the difference, but it seems to me that Gloucester doesn't hold any attraction for the audience. He's the worst kind of old man. He's truly infantile, and today no one likes old people! The only thing he has is Edgar's love, which is sentimental and brings him a bit closer to us.

R M : *You say that today no one likes old people. Is this why you made a film about an engaging old man like Falstaff?*

o w : No, I didn't make it to reverse a universal tendency, but because it's a role which I've always thought of as one of the two or three greatest roles in Shakespeare, and I wanted to perform it four or five more times because there are four or five other ways to interpret it. This film developed a certain theme. There are so many other ways to approach it. Once someone wrote that Falstaff was a Hamlet who never returned from his exile in England, and became old and corpulent. The truth of Falstaff is that Shakespeare understood him better than the other great characters he created, because Falstaff was obliged to sing for his supper. He had to earn everything he ate by making people laugh. It's not that he was funny; he had to be funny.

R M : *But in Shakespeare, Falstaff also has a rather repulsive side . . .*
o w : I think that in all of Shakespeare, he's the only good man.

R M : *But as a recruiting officer, for example, he lets the rich off by making them pay him and then only enrolls the poor.*
o w : Doubtless, but you are transposing the social concerns of the twentieth century onto this epoch. This scene is simply a terrible and funny joke. I don't think it shows him to be a bad man. In fact, it doesn't show anything except that he is an engaging rascal.

R M : *I still think you magnify Falstaff's goodness.*
o w : I don't think so. I really don't. And I'm certainly not the only one to say this—a good number of Shakespeare specialists agree with me. I think that Falstaff is the only great imaginary character who is truly good. His faults are so minor. No one is perfect, and he's filled with imperfections, physical and moral defects, but the essential part of his nature is his goodness. That's the theme of all the plays he appears in.

R M : *You said once that you admire the ambiguities of Shakespeare and that things are not entirely clear.*
o w : With Falstaff, there are two very ambiguous moments and I performed them as forcefully as I could. One is the brutal recruiting scene, and though I played this scene gaily it is no less brutal. On the English stage, of course, it would never have been performed as anything other than a comedy. It's a scene which makes the audience laugh, after a long moment, because it comes after an interminable chain of civil wars. So rightly or wrongly, I did

nothing but follow classical tradition. But in doing this, I was not trying to pass Falstaff off as an honest man. He is certainly a swindler. But there are good swindlers . . .

R M : *Was this acceptable in the Elizabethan context?*
O W : By all means! After Shakespeare, who was the greatest man in England? I'd say it was Francis Bacon.

R M : *As a man, he was horrid.*
O W : And yet he's still one of the greatest authors of all time. He was also the perfect example of what was happening at the top and bottom of the social ladder during the reign of the Tudors. If Bacon was ultimately con-demned for being a swindler, then why would poor Falstaff, without a coin in his pocket, act any differently than his compatriots? This, I think, the dark humor of it all, is an image that reflects the entirety of the society, an image that Shakespeare would never have dared show in another way. Coming from him, it's a truthful critique of society, not only of the corruption of his time, but of the way things had worked for hundreds of years.

R M : *And yet he still justifies Prince Hal in all sorts of ways.*
O W : He couldn't do otherwise. Prince Hal is an official patriotic hero. But he makes him extremely ambiguous.

R M : *Yes, but you don't! In your film the prince is so cold . . .*
O W : He loves Falstaff, but he prepares a betrayal necessary from a Machia-vellian point of view. I'm speaking of the Machiavellianism, that of the real Machiavelli that we know and who is so far superior to the one Shakespeare judged to be so sly. Hal is certainly a great Machiavellian prince. He loves Falstaff and, still, is ready to betray him from the get-go.

R M : *What kind of necessity are you thinking of?*
O W : The necessity of a great king. How could he have forced the respect of the English court and the people if he had kept vulgar acolytes as his play-mates? But this kind of betrayal is still an infamy, even if it's a Machiavellian necessity. You can judge it severely or indulgently, but for myself, I find it impossible to be accommodating with the prince. From the point of view of

State rationality, I understand what a prince has to do, but I can't love him
for it.

R M : *But you know the modern audience . . .*
O W : Ah, but I was making a film, and a film is never made for an audience.
A dramatic work is made for an audience; a film is made for itself.

R M : *You never think of the people who will see it?*
O W : Never!

R M : *In other words, it's a kind of solipsism for you?*
O W : It's entirely personal, because the audience of a film doesn't exist. It's
impossible to conceive of it. It's made up of two hundred Berbers on the
other side of the Atlas Mountains. It's made up of a group of intellectuals at
the Athens film archives. It's made up of seven hundred bourgeois who voted
for Nixon. It's made up of a single person watching television. The audience
doesn't exist. And I'm also writing my bit of film for posterity, when there
will be other kinds of audiences that I can't foresee. It is impossible to address
yourself to an audience, unless you address a well-defined audience, as
Godard, Fellini or Bergman did. When I stage a play, I address an audience
this year in *this* city. When I make a film, I make a film and that's it.

R M : *Even when you're filming in the United States?*
O W : Certainly.

R M : *So* Citizen Kane *wasn't oriented towards an American audience?*
O W : You can orient things as you like, but what will the American audience
think about them? I hadn't the slightest idea. It's not out of disdain for the
audience, but because the audience of a film is inconceivable. Sixty percent
of an audience will never hear the words we say because the film will be
dubbed. Maybe ten million people will see it later, when we're all dead.
They're poor, they're rich, they're big, they're little. We don't know who the
film audience is, thus we can only make something we believe in. So when I
play Falstaff, I play a Falstaff who I think will be the center of a good story.
It's not *Henry IV, Part 1*, which would have been another film, or *Henry IV,
Part 2*, or *Henry V*, which would be yet another film. But by joining all three,
I created something new. And here's a new distinction: I have a very strong

feeling that a film made of one of Shakespeare's works is not at all what the stage version would be. Because Shakespeare was writing for a living public and not for film. And when I make a film, I feel as free as Verdi or any other adapter who borrows a Shakespearean subject. I feel no obligation to Shakespearean tradition. I may be its victim or prisoner, but I don't accept it as a constraint. [. . .]

I think there are a thousand ways to put Shakespeare on the stage and I'm not dogmatic about it. I simply defend my way of doing it, which isn't the only way, and I think it's possible to shoot a Shakespearean film, which is, in fact, a theatrical play. This is what Laurence Olivier has always done and it works very well. Why wouldn't it work? It's equally possible not to use a single word from Shakespeare.

R M : *Not a single one?*

O W : Yes, why not? All variants are possible, but I think that when one adopts film, this brand new medium of expression, one is free to decide to what point one will remain Shakespearean and to what extent one is making one's own film—I don't think this is a question that comes up in theater.

R M : *In that case, if I may come back to Prince Hal whom you criticize so severely, what did you try to represent through him?*

O W : He is the Machiavellian prince, the son of a usurper with no right to the throne. He is obliged to be an official hero. And I think that the obliged hero is one of the most disagreeable characters of all. He's also a man who is chided in no uncertain terms by his father because he's not acting enough like a king. And Henry IV, of course, is more anxious than a real king about what a prince should be because he isn't a real king: he's nothing more than Bolingbroke, who deposed the last legitimate king of England, that is, Richard II. And I think that the whole tetralogy should be understood in the context of usurpation or, rather, it *shouldn't* be, especially if you're free not to use the story of Henry V. When I staged *Five Kings* for the theater, we used the story of Henry V. And Henry V, that is, Prince Hal turned into a king, was interpreted very differently because he had to deliver the famous speech at the end. But the role was conceived as that of a demagogue who plans to become a great popular hero. And there's this brutality in him which, in my opinion, characterizes him, along with something fundamentally vulgar. I think that the scene where he's courting Katherine, which Olivier performs in his film as if Henry were an Italian prince, bypasses the comedy it should have, because Henry is a sort of Gary Cooper forcing himself to speak Italian and not an Italian prince trying to speak French. In the spirit of Shakespeare, he was a rugged Anglo-Saxon, in both the good and bad senses of the word. What Stalin called a sense of history, as well as all the violence which originated from his father and so many other things . . . all this imposed a great historic role on him by frustrating the best part of himself. His good nature, his good angel, was Falstaff, and his bad angel was the king. Even though he had an obligation to be king, this obligation was implicated in the illegalities of the end of a civil war. It's a very complex political situation.

R M :   *Would you say that in a certain way Hal uses one father against the other?*
O W :   I don't think he uses them. I think that Shakespeare uses them, yes, and very visibly. When he has Falstaff play the role of King Henry IV . . . He takes great trouble to show the audience that there are two fathers.

R M :   *The scene where Henry V rejects Falstaff is one of the most moving scenes you have ever filmed.*
O W :   Isn't it one of the most terrible scenes in literature?

R M :   *That depends on the way it's done.*
O W :   "I know thee not, old man . . ." After this kind of line, it's very hard to make the man who spoke it seem good. Because a good prince would have said: *"Take this man somewhere, I want to speak with him."* But *"I know thee not, old man"* has a demagogic cruelty to it, it's terrible. The role was played marvelously by Keith Baxter. He was extraordinary because his own heart broke too. The necessities of power . . . We know that power corrupts, and that it's a much deeper corruption than that of relieving a few travelers of their money or allowing rich people to avoid the army. Shakespeare adores parody. He loves it when one character in the play is the parody of another. Gloucester is a parody of Lear and, in my opinion, the recruitment scene is a parody of the struggle for power in the court. Shakespeare likes showing things in simple terms, or in crazy terms, in any terms, showing the same thing twice, a mirror image of this or that thing. Parody is specifically Shakespearean.

R M :   *You've used the theme of betrayal in other films. People betray their friends for various reasons, or else they betray the values they believe in.*

O W : Yes. In your mind, which is worse?

R M : *I suppose it's worse to betray the values you believe in . . .*
O W : There we go! Now we know how we differ! For me, betraying a friend
is the worst thing. I wouldn't stake my life on it, but it defines our positions.

R M : *If it weren't for the fact that, in all honesty, I have little belief in values . . .*
O W : Now you've got me! That's a Falstaffian response!

R M : *In the world as it is, it's very hard to believe in values. Thus the only value
left, I think, is friendship. And when a man betrays a friend . . .*
O W : Brutus and Caesar . . .

R M : *Yes, or, in* Touch of Evil, *Menzies who betrays Quinlan. In a sense, it seems
that he does it because he believes in the law, he believes that Quinlan was essentially wrong.*
O W : This is what I think, too. In the film, I'm as ambiguous as possible, and
you've been very clever and caught me in a trap. Because most of my friends
and most critics who comment on *Touch of Evil* believe Quinlan has an essential goodness, while I think he's a scoundrel. The fact that he's human, that
one can understand him in his humanity, all this is fine. But I for one have
a profound belief in the primacy of law. And I think that a corrupt policeman
is society's worst creation.

R M : *This doesn't contradict what you said earlier?*
O W : But of course, that's what I'm saying, you got me, you've caught me in
a terrible trap! I think that Menzies' betrayal of Quinlan is horrid, but that
his motivation is good. Here we are back with Hal who is about to take
power. Except that Menzies destroys himself: he didn't make himself chief
of police. Isn't there a small difference?

R M : *Why are you so fascinated by the image of the traitor?*
O W : I'm not! [. . .]

R M : *You were saying that Vargas applies the law mechanically, that he's a tech-
nocrat of the law.*

O W : Yes, the creature, the new man. We've seen him emerge in all countries, we don't need to specify his nationality, he's the modern man who
won't stir up the masses, no, he's a well programmed computer. He could
have been one of the great chiefs of the CIA, it's easy to imagine him in this
context. Here, he's Mexican. Mexico is a country born of the fermentation
of a deliciously corrupt humanity which enters in a brand new technocracy
and produces Vargases, who, strangely enough, are not paper-mâché heroes
but are actually like that.

R M : *The theme of betrayal is also essential in Shakespeare, no?*
O W : Of course, politically, it was essential then. Because they didn't know
who would engineer what project. There were so many revolts, so many con-
spiracies . . . It really was one of the great preoccupations of the time, as it
has been in Eastern Europe for forty years.

R M : *I'd like to cite a few lines from a Canadian critic: "The traitor is much more
disturbing than the coward or hypocrite. [. . .] The coward goes on living in society,
however shamed and disgraced. The traitor suggests the nothingness, the sense of
annihilation, inherent in the dissolving of a social group. This nothingness, or non-
being, is an abyss far deeper than death, for death in itself affects only the individual, and the individual is not, in this conception, the form of human life. [. . .] The
traitor remains more inscrutable. His motto is Iago's 'Demand me nothing; what
you know, you know.' " Do you agree with this definition?*
O W : Yes. It's said very beautifully and I agree. Who said it?

R M : *Northrop Frye, in a book on Shakespeare's tragedies called* Fools of Time.
O W : But, to be a little tricky, I actually think the question is whether Iago is
in fact a traitor. *"Demand me nothing; what you know, you know"* is a wonderful
definition of the traitor. But to know if Iago is actually a traitor is one of
those excruciatingly boring discussions. I don't think he is. I think he's faithful to himself. He never was Othello's friend.

R M : *He pretends to be . . .*
O W : He feigns friendship like a bootlicker, a sycophant. He's the non-com-
missioned officer who is trying to rise in rank. At the beginning, Othello
treats him with contempt, and he only treats him with respect when his own
evil forces, his own bile, are liberated by Iago.

R M : *I read somewhere that you wanted to unite Iago and Othello in a single murderous image.*

O W : No, that's not the case.

R M : *You made their relationship as close as possible . . .*

O W : That, yes.

R M : *But in doing so, didn't you accentuate the private person, the individual, rather than man in society?*

O W : Ah, but I think it's a question of a *domestic* tragedy. *Othello* is unique in Shakespeare's oeuvre because it's the only tragedy—we've seen that he didn't like tragedy, but what I mean by tragedy—which doesn't take place in the court, where the characters aren't kings who determine the course of history. In Shakespeare everything is comic unless the protagonists wear crowns and wage battles. Here, the play is domestic: everything takes place in a house and everything concerns man and his wife. If he's a great general, it's because the audience would never have taken any character seriously unless he were someone important.

R M : *In Shakespeare, the joint responsibility of Iago and Venice is suggested by the first scene, in which Brabantio accepts Iago's racist discourse from the beginning. You, on the other hand, have entirely shifted the accent. You begin the film by showing Othello and Desdemona dead, and then a crowd in the streets when Iago is being taken to his cage. Why did you put the end of the tragedy at the beginning?*

O W : Why not? I like putting the end of a tragedy at the beginning because it's hard to do in the theater, and can't be done within the framework of Shakespeare's form. But I find that it adds a lot. Later, I staged the play in London [1951], and I didn't do anything of the kind. Iago occupied his most traditional place. The play had exactly what I considered to be its Shakespearean form. Iago was very well performed by Peter Finch, a very different way of interpreting the role. I've been much better on stage than I've been on screen, or much less bad, let's say. But no one is good . . . How can one be good in the role of Othello? But I agree with what you say about Iago. All the accents that I placed were modifications I introduced for the specific needs of the film I wanted to make.

R M : *In your production of the play, it's impotence rather than Mephistophelism . . .*

O W : Mephistophelism is terribly out of fashion, you know . . . It was more
or less destroyed in the nineteenth century with the red stockings and trap
doors rigged up on stage.

R M : *Do you think that impotence explains his wickedness?*
O W : I hope so! That's all we could find. The other way to do it, as Olivier
did when he interpreted Iago with Ralph Richardson, is to make him a
homosexual. In the end, this seems weaker than impotence, but you have to
manage somehow . . . In reality, in Shakespeare, Iago is a scoundrel. Now, in
life I know some villains, simple villains, inscrutable villains, but the audience doesn't want to believe it. So you have to add a little something to say:
"He's impotent" or "He is this or that." I, for one, agree with Shakespeare:
one doesn't need to provide him with motivations.

R M : *In other words, you used impotence to dissimulate the mystery of Iago's villainy rather than eradicating it by explaining it?*
O W : Exactly. I didn't want to eradicate it. I simply wanted the audience to
believe that it could exist. These days people simply don't believe in villains
anymore. Since Freud, they think that everyone is sick!

R M : *So you believe in the mystery of iniquity?*
O W : The "secret power of iniquity" [phrase from II Thessalonians, used by
Melville to characterize Claggart in *Billy Budd*]: Yes, I believe in it. I believe in
the existence of that which is designated by the most old-fashioned word in
the world; that is, evil.

R M : *Individual evil? How do you conceptualize it?*
O W : I don't know. It's inscrutable. I've been confronted with evil all my life
and I think it exists. But I've never tried to portray it, in film or in theater,
pure evil, evil in itself, because I think that others wouldn't understand it.
They've all been brainwashed by Freud's successors. There are demons in the
air, you know!

R M : *Once you said that in your films there is always a quest, a pursuit. The
inscrutability of the traitor approaches the inscrutability of every human being . . .*
O W : We find this in the most ancient novels of the Middle Ages, which are
absolutely the source of my way of thinking. There's always inscrutable evil,

and there's always a quest. It's at the very heart of our folklore, which, for me, begins in the high Middle Ages, for which I have a strong affinity, and it goes through the beginning of the Renaissance. This is what I understand best. I have less understanding of the end of the Renaissance, even though I'm a baroque film director—or at least, I was. I'm not anymore. I don't consider myself to be a man of the Renaissance.

R M : *People generally say that you are!*
O W : I know. I don't see myself that way at all. The Renaissance is filled with people I'd love to dine with, but I prefer the beginning of the fourteenth century!

R M : *You say that power corrupts, and it's illustrated well by most of your films, but there's another kind of corruption that is provoked by age, poverty, physical decline . . .*
O W : The weakness of age, sickness, misery, etc. This kind of corruption comes from a sort of disaster. It's a very innocent form of corruption, as innocent as the corruption of the flesh after death. It seems to me to be a part of the cycle of nature rather than the inscrutable.

R M : *Have you ever tried to stage* The Tempest?
O W : No. I sketched out a way to stage it, or rather, I traced out the broad lines of action and Pavel Tchelitchew designed the sets and the costumes. [He had been asked in 1937 to design sets and costumes for a *King Lear* that Welles did not produce. There are no known traces of the *Tempest* project.] And before producing it I realized that it would be very beautiful and very chic but it wouldn't have anything to do with *The Tempest.* I love this play more than almost any other. We were just saying that I don't feel at all like a man of the Renaissance. Of course, Prospero, in a sense, is the man of the Renaissance *par excellence,* except that he throws his book into the sea and doesn't go to hell like Doctor Faustus. In any case, he isn't Faustian. I'm very attracted by him. Obviously, the problem is Caliban, but Caliban can be performed marvelously. In my childhood I saw an extraordinary interpretation by Werner Krauss in Max Reinhardt's production. [Theater listings of the time cite no such production of *The Tempest* which Welles could have seen in this period.] It truly evoked the forces of nature, something very grandi-

ose. He made Caliban into a real character, and a character you could believe in. So I know it's possible.

R M : *How would you portray Caliban?*
O W : I don't know. Having seen Werner Krauss . . . It's terrible to watch an actor do the perfect and definitive interpretation of a role; in a way it brings something to an end. Finally one sees someone perform a role as he thinks it should be performed, and the only thing left is to turn the page and say, "Good, let's move on." But I would love to stage that play or make a film of it. I think it could be a marvelous film.

R M : *And television? Do you think there are specific problems for Shakespeare on television?*
O W : The specific problems of television are budget problems. One could make *The Tempest* a magnificent play if there were a television company in the world ready to grant three cameras and six weeks of rehearsal to film it.

R M : *We only have one camera here!*
O W : It's a cinematographic camera. I'm speaking of theater recorded at the television station, filmed for television, and television finances are such that what you're doing each time isn't a dress rehearsal but the first rehearsal in front of the audience. It's that simple. I'm not criticizing French television, it's a world-wide problem. Among all the forms of spectacles throughout history, television has the largest audience and the smallest budget. And to stage a worthwhile *Tempest* would require a lot of money. Without money, one would have to be content with speaking in front of a white backdrop.

R M : *We're running out of film. Was it to economize that you yourself performed the role of black Macbeth one night?*
O W : The play was performed for three years on tour, all over, even in Texas, can you imagine, in the South! And one day Macbeth fell ill and no one knew the role. So I dove in, I blackened my face like I did for *Othello* and I played Macbeth! It was a marvelous experience. What a shame that the black theater couldn't continue!

R M : *I think it disappeared rather quickly.*

O W : Yes. Now there is a new school and heaps of talented people. But what
I tried to do with *Macbeth* and with *The Tragical History of Dr. Faustus* was to
show that blacks aren't necessarily actors merely for folklore, that they don't
necessarily have to speak with a Southern accent or be comic. [Welles cast
Jack Carter, his Macbeth in Harlem, as Mephistopheles.] It's truly a shame
that it couldn't continue, because in Harlem there was an authentically popular audience. People went to see *Macbeth* and the voodoo made them stamp
their feet. Voodoo and black magic work very well. It kills critics, you know.

R M : *It kills critics?*
O W : We received only one unfavorable review. The day after the performance, I went to see the actors to congratulate them on their great success,
and in the afternoon I had a few changes made to the show. And the chief
sorcerer of Dahomey said to me, "But there's a bad man who wrote about
us." I answered, "Yes, but don't go out and hit him." And he said, "Should
we put beriberi on him?" I said, "Yes, go ahead, put beriberi on him." And
he went tom-tom. And twenty-four hours later, the critic was dead. It's the
truth! After that, I was very polite to the sorcerers.

Five Days in the Life of Commander Welles

MICHEL BOUJUT/1982

MONDAY, FEBRUARY 22. First sequence. Hôtel Crillon, Place de la Concorde. Interior. The end of the day. Central lights and spot lights for maestro Orson's press conference. Sweating and serene, O.W. gives himself up to a ritual whose mechanism he has fully mastered. The darkness suits this debonair ogre. In the case of Welles, film has given birth to a mountain. He's a torso behind the green baize of the conference table, juggling para-doxes in the flickering of flashes and the rattle of irises. His voice is clear and deep. His eyes sparkle and there's a sort of sly candor on his face. He doesn't seem bored. Anything that touches Orson Welles is cinematic. What started off as a glamorous gesture by George Cravenne to re-open the César cere-mony has molted into a non-stop celebration of Welles's genius.

"Before the war," pronounced a lady colleague, *"you scared your compatriots with your radio show* The War of the Worlds. *How would you scare them today?"* Welles answered, *"The problem is that they can no longer be scared! Even if they have very good reasons to be scared—the end of the planet, the extinction of the human race, this is no small affair!"*

He is asked about the meeting he will have the following day with François Mitterrand. *"I've already met a good number of heads of state in my life and I've received a good number of decorations. Including, alas, a few from the hands of*

The "five days" recorded here occurred in Paris, in February and March 1982. From a special Welles issue of *L'Avant-Scène Cinéma*, July 1982. Translated for this collection by Alisa Hartz. Reprinted by permission of *L'Avant-Scène Cinéma*.

despicable tyrants in South America, during the time when I was unofficially representing President Roosevelt. I've never worn the medals, except for one time at a dinner, and that was just to make Laurence Olivier jealous!" His laugh is enormous, cavernous, Falstaffian. *"Lee Strasberg? Yes, he was one of our great men in theater. The two of us disagreed on many things. But the number of actors he trained speaks for itself. He knew how to give an actor strength.*

"French film? Hum! I think French films are a little too French. Perhaps today you don't have directors like Pagnol, Renoir, Duvivier or Carné whose films are shown everywhere. It's also the case that the U.S. is becoming very provincial once again. Be that as it may, I don't go to the movies very often. Anyhow, I don't like talking about directors very much. But I'll make an exception to tell you that I admire Scorsese, Bertolucci and Warren Beatty whose film Reds *has a lot of character."*

There's as much click-clackity noise as ever, like electric shocks, which bothers everyone except him. *"I prefer acting to directing. I act for money. And God knows that no one has made more bad films than I have, as an actor!"*

After a few jests in response to prankster questions, he talks about death: *"Since I was nine, I've always felt death to be very close to me. My interest in it has not diminished with age."* About Spain, where he lived for a long time: *"It elates me."* About happiness: *"I don't know what it is! The box of paints is too expensive to make the films one wants to make. And I wish the ones I've made were better!"* And the final word: *"A film about my life? Help! No, thank you."*

TUESDAY, FEBRUARY 23. Second sequence. 6 P.M., the presidential Palais de l'Elysée. Wainscoting and gold leaf. *"Today we finally meet,"* begins President Mitterrand. Facing him is Citizen Welles, moved and perspiring, in the middle of a large circle of ministers and celebrities. *"Affection, respect . . . He is one of the few who has attained the universal, through art."* With the sash of the *Légion d'honneur* around his neck, Orson looks like a fat conscript "ready to serve." The two men kiss each other and embrace. Mitterrand may have just lived his greatest cinematic moment since the spectacular gesture of bringing roses to the Pantheon [on the tomb of the resistant Jean Moulin]. Outside, night has fallen. But the Elysée palace is still not Xanadu. *"My name is François Mitterrand."*

* * *

WEDNESDAY, FEBRUARY 24. Third sequence. Cinémathèque de Chaillot, interior, night. Welles makes his promised visit to the students of the IDHEC [elite, government-sponsored film school] and other Parisian film schools. The students are there in crowded rows, at the base of a stage where King Orson the First is enthroned—the word is accurate—in Henri Langlois's chair. He's not, for all that, giving a master class, but freely digressing on film.

"I've never set foot in a film school. And I'd never set foot on a set before filming Citizen Kane. *No doubt I was touched by the grace of total ignorance. I learned everything in three hours, not because I'm smart but because film is simple! You've surely spent too much time watching films. Don't shut yourselves up in the film universe, like a tin of herring. Dream up your own films, instead. And give your attention to the charms of the most perverse of muses . . . The decadence of film is the result of the glorification of the director. The actor is more important. Today the director is the most overestimated artist in the world. Think of the great moments of film: they're in black and white. The more technique progresses, the more the creative spirit declines. And I fear that electronics will only help make third-rate films.*

From the balcony, a student asks an inaudible question about Elia Kazan. "Chère mademoiselle, *you have chosen the wrong metteur en scène,"* Orson suddenly intones, *"because Elia Kazan is a traitor. He is a man who sold to McCarthy all his companions at a time when he could continue to work in New York at high salary, and having sold all his people to McCarthy, he then made a film called* On the Waterfront *which was a celebration of the informer."* Silence, and then, *"In other respects, he's one of our great directors."*

Outside, in the cold, about a hundred of us are waiting for him, to watch him board his gray Bentley. A sedan-chair brings him up the few stairs that lead from the sunken hall of the Cinémathèque to the fresh air, not because of one of his whims, but because the state of his legs makes any staircase dangerous. It's a strange spectacle which isn't far removed from the idea of royalty. Orson Welles: the only director in the world carried on a sedan-chair.

THURSDAY, FEBRUARY 25. A room on the ground floor of Fouquet's for the Union of Film Critics luncheon, in honor of Orson Welles. The menu is appropriate: crayfish salad from *The Lady From Shanghai,* green asparagus à la *Falstaff,* turbot à la royale from *Mr. Arkadin,* a cheese plate from *The Third Man,* a *Magnificent Ambersons* dessert, not to mention the red Bordeaux from *Touch of Evil* and rolls stamped with coat of arms from *Citizen Kane!*

There were about fifty of us surrounding the hero of the day, as if for a Last Supper, or for the banquet in *Citizen Kane.* He was at his ease, smiling and in brilliant form. Yes, he was once tempted by politics: *"Roosevelt encouraged me to run for Senator of Wisconsin, my home state, which is in the hands of very reactionary milk producers. But as a leftist I had no chance at all. And I cowardly declined, especially because I was divorced. Well, who was elected but the dreadful Joseph McCarthy. Today I tell the story saying that if I had run, McCarthyism would never have existed! What a responsibility. President Mitterrand made a strong impression on me. He has a lot of dignity, warmth and irony. Plus, he's a real film aficionado. As for Churchill, he saw only one film in his whole life, but he never tired of it. It was* Lady Hamilton *with Vivien Leigh! Nixon swore by* Patton. *And Franco, he made cartoons!"*

During dessert, my colleagues and I were still hungry for answers. About his projects, he said, notably, *"I have two this year. A film about an American politician. No, not Reagan, because there's not enough material there for a feature-length film! And* The Dreamers, *a nineteenth-century romance. I'm also keen on finishing my* Don Quixote, *if I'm still among the living."* An angel passed by and Orson rose up, as supple as a ballerina disguised as Moby Dick.

SATURDAY, MARCH 27. Fifth sequence. Salle Pleyel, for the awarding of the Césars for French film. Orson is still Olympian, applauded by our fifteen or twenty French movie stars, sitting in the orchestra. What followed was enough to make one blush, a muddled and sinister charity "party," to which the inevitable Thierry Le Luron brought an additional dose of vulgarity. In short, the scene turned ridiculous, like those lugubrious celebrations of film and television. With one lovely image, though, in the wings: Welles and Wajda pressing their hands for a long while, without saying a word. *So long, Citizen Commander!*

Interview from *The Orson Welles Story*

LESLIE MEGAHEY/1982

LESLIE MEGAHEY *[introducing the telecast with a film clip from* Follow the Boys, *featuring Orson Welles's magic show]: In 1944 Orson Welles was twenty-nine years old. He's been working his magic now for another forty years, and we talk to him tonight about his life and work, his major triumphs and his biggest disappointments.*

ORSON WELLES: I've never had a friend in my life who wanted to see a magic trick, you know. I don't know anybody who wants to see a magic trick. So I do it professionally; it's the only way I get to perform. There are people in the world who say, "Show us a trick," you know. I went once to a birthday party for Louis B. Mayer with a rabbit in my pocket, which I was gonna take out of his hat. And on came Judy Garland and Danny Kaye and Danny Thomas and everybody you ever heard of and then Al Jolson sang for two hours and my rabbit was peeing all over me, you know. And the dawn was starting to rise over the Hillcrest Country Club as we said goodnight to Louis B. Mayer and nobody'd asked me to do a magic trick. But the rabbit and I went home.

LM: *What makes a good magician? He said seriously.*

Leslie Megahey's interview was filmed in Las Vegas in 1982 as the centerpiece for *The Orson Welles Story*, a two-part documentary telecast in the United Kingdom on the BBC's *Arena* program, 18 and 21 May 1982. In its original format, the program incorporated an array of film clips and stills, interviews with others, and Megahey's voice-over commentary. Brief excerpts from the latter are retained here to contextualize some of Welles's responses. Published by permission of Leslie Megahey, Oja Kodar, and the BBC.

O W :   Seriously, what makes a good magician is a man who can get that rabbit out in time. [reacting to a device employed in the filming of his interview:] Oh, my goodness. I never saw that before. All right.

L M :   *You want one?*
O W :   Yes. That's wonderful. Technology has finally reached the movies . . . after forty years of paralysis. Yes.

L M :   *I was interested in a phrase you used in fact to Huw Wheldon. You said that when you arrived in Hollywood you had the confidence of ignorance.*
O W :   Yes.

L M :   *Can you tell me what that meant?*
O W :   Well, it's pretty much like my beginnings in the theatre: I had the confidence of ignorance. Not knowing anything about it, there was no basis for fear. In other words, if you're walking along the edge of a cliff and you don't know it's the edge of a cliff, you have perfect confidence, you know. And I didn't discover the cliff in the theatre or in films until after I'd been in it for a while.

L M :   *What happens then, when ignorance turns into experience?*
O W :   Then you have to be very careful not to listen to anybody, you know. Because . . . you have to remember your old ignorance and ask for the impossible with the same cheerfulness that you did when you didn't know what you were talking about.

L M :   *It does seem that you tried to re-create a sort of innocence in your approach to every single film.*
O W :   I like that very much. I think that's true. And I seldom like anything that's said about my films, so we're off to a good start.

L M :   *Didn't you play King Lear at the age of nine?*
O W :   No. Certainly not.

L M :   *Is that a biographical . . .*
O W :   One of those exaggerations. I played Mary the Mother of Jesus at the age of thirteen.

L M :   *Even better.*

O W :   Yes. Very good in drag. But no, didn't touch King Lear until later on.

L M :   *How much of this, of the whole business of the child prodigy is . . .*

O W :   The musical part of it is true. I was one of those abominable little creatures, you know, with a baton and I played the violin and I played the piano and there's nothing more hateful on earth. I was one of those. And my mother, who was a professional musician, died when I was nine and I stopped playing immediately. A kind of trauma, traumatic shock from her death, combined with, I think, essential laziness—the delight of not having to go on doing those scales. And I abandoned my career in music, because that's what I was supposed to be destined for.

L M :   *But all the other stuff about being studied as a child prodigy . . .*

O W :   Yes, I was spoiled in a very strange way as a child. Because everybody told me from the moment I was able to hear that I was absolutely marvelous. I never heard a discouraging word for years, you see. I didn't know what was ahead of me. I painted and they said nobody's ever seen such painting, you know. I played, nobody's ever played like that. And there just seemed to me no limit to what I could do.

L M :   *Now I've got here what Micheál Mac Liammóir writes about you in his autobiography. It's the story of when you arrived at the Gate Theatre in Dublin.*

O W :   I know. I know that story.

L M :   *"We found a very tall young man with a chubby face, full powerful lips and disconcerting Chinese eyes. He moved in a leisurely manner from foot to foot and surveyed us with magnificent patience as though here was our chance to do something beautiful at last, and were we going to take it? He had some ageless and superb inner confidence that no one could blow out. That was his secret."*

O W :   It's a wonderful description when you consider that the author was in London at the time this was happening in Dublin. Micheál was in London the first six weeks that I was in the Gate Theatre, and I got my job only with Hilton and Micheál never saw any of the stuff that he writes about. But he couldn't have told the story as well if he hadn't put himself in as an eye witness so that's perfectly all right.

L M : *But you were saying you were, what, eighteen years old?*
O W :   Yeah, it varied from eighteen to twenty. When I couldn't explain how I got to be that famous at eighteen, I would raise it up a little. That's why I smoke a cigar. I got cigars and smoked them that day in order to look older and kept a cigar in order to seem like an older actor. In fact, I played mostly old parts in Dublin.

L M : *Yes, and then in America too, when you went back to America, the . . .*
O W :   Well, yes, because there were no parts for anybody with such a baby face.

L M : *Now there was one other thing you appeared in about this time, also as an old man, and I think that was your very first film,* Hearts of Age.
O W :   Oh, it's not a film at all. It was a little joke one Sunday afternoon. We'd all seen either Buñuel or Cocteau or somebody's surrealist movie. We said, "Let's make one." And from two o'clock in the afternoon until five we shot some dumb stuff and put it together just to amuse ourselves. And it's terrible and it's suddenly found its way into the oeuvre, you know . . .

L M : *[following a synopsis of Welles's work in the New York theatre]: And then Welles astonished New York with a lavish production of* Macbeth, *which broke all the conventions of the Broadway stage, and used an all black cast.*
O W :   I wanted to give the black actors a chance to play classics without it being funny. Or even exotic. Just . . . there it is. And I directed *Macbeth* without ever giving them a reading. And none of them had ever seen a Shakespearean play. And it was extraordinary . . . how good Shakespeare is if it's spoken by somebody who's never heard somebody say it before. And we had some marvelous effects and of course it was a big production. We had, I think, almost two hundred people on the stage and we had voodoo drummers and witch doctors from the West Coast of Africa and . . .

L M : *Real ones?*
O W :   Oh, real ones, yes . . . By all odds my great success in my life was that play . . . the opening night there were five blocks in which all traffic was stopped; you couldn't get near the theatre in Harlem. Everybody who was anybody in the black or white world was there. And when the play ended, there were so many curtain calls that finally they left the curtain open; the

audience came up on the stage to congratulate the actors. And that was, that was magical.

L M : . . . *The Mercury Theatre was living from hand to mouth and Welles had to begin a hectic double life.*
O W : I'd been contributing from my radio salary. I kept putting in a thousand dollars or so every week, so we'd get the show on. And we got all our plays on before anybody else because I was doing radio all day long. Soap operas and everything else. I used to go by ambulance from one radio station to another, because I discovered there was no law in New York that you had to be sick to travel in an ambulance. So I hired the ambulance and I would go from CBS to NBC. They'd hold an elevator for me; I'd go up to the fifth floor, go into the studio, whichever I was booked for. I'd say, "What's the character?" They'd say "eighty year old Chinaman," and I'd go on and do the eighty year old Chinaman, and then rush off somewhere else. And I had been for a year and a half auditioning hopelessly as an actor. Never could get a job on radio. Suddenly, I got one part and in about a month I was making, in those days, tax free, about fifteen to eighteen hundred dollars a week, as an unknown radio actor, without my name being mentioned.

L M *[following audio clips and commentary relating to* The War of the Worlds *broadcast]: The next morning, the name of Orson Welles was headlines all over America . . .*
O W : The thing that gave me the idea for it was that we had a lot of real radio nuts on as commentators at this period. People who wanted to keep us out of European entanglements, and fascist priests called Father Coughlin, and people believed anything they heard on the radio. And I said, "Let's do something impossible and make them believe it. And then tell them, show them, that it's only radio." So that was what started it. And then, of course, they passed a lot of laws. Now you can't do it. You can't give a news broadcast, say this is the news, without . . . all that. But the people who tried it in other countries were all put in jail. And I got a contract in Hollywood; it really is the truth.

L M : *That was a year before you made* Kane, *is that right?*
O W : Yes, and that year I was busy preparing to make *Heart of Darkness*. I wrote the script and we designed the sets and we were all ready to go and we

couldn't get the fifty thousand dollars off the budget so they wouldn't let me do it. So that was the first film I was going to make. The contract was negotiated in New York. And this superb contract only happened because I didn't much want to make a movie. And I thought the only way I could possibly make it would be without anybody interfering. So I asked for things nobody'd ever had. And nobody has ever had since. Written out. They have that kind of power now because once you let a director loose with forty million dollars there's nothing you can do about it. But in my case I was given a limited budget but unlimited control and the studio wasn't even allowed to see the rushes, if you can believe such a thing.

L M : *Because you were twenty-five and you had this amazing contract, did you sense an enormous amount of resentment around Hollywood?*
O W : Oh, yes, of course, big resentment. Ward Bond cut my tie off in the middle of Chasen's restaurant. And we went out in the parking lot and had it out. There was tremendous resentment . . . of course. Because nowadays every star has directed a movie. Even the TV stars direct some of their segments. It's perfectly normal for actors to direct themselves. But nobody had done that since von Stroheim. And it was unheard of. And then that I should be the author and absolute producer. Now of course, the producers hated me most because if I could do all those things, then what is the need for a producer?

L M : *Were you able just to barge through it? Did it affect you personally?*
O W : No, because I was very lucky, you see. I had brought all my Mercury actors with me so I had a little world of my own. And I thought that would be a great thing in a movie, to have nobody in the film you'd ever seen before. Because those were the days when every studio made a hundred and twenty pictures a year and the faces were all so well known and I thought to see a movie in which everybody is new . . . and I liked my people and we got along well together and we'd been in the theatre and radio together, so why not in films?

L M *[Incorporated into the next section were interviews with Peter Bogdanovich and Robert Wise]: You also got along very well with Gregg Toland?*
O W : Oh, yes. He came to me, you know. I didn't ask for him. One day in the office they said, "There's a man called Toland waiting to see you." And he was, of course, the leading cameraman. And he said, "I want to make you

a picture." And I said, "Well, that's wonderful. Why? I don't know anything about movies." And he said, "That's why I want to do it." He said, "Because I think if you're left alone as much as possible, we're gonna have a movie that looks different. I'm tired of working with people who know too much about it." And . . . we came to a moment in the first week of shooting where—no, the second week—where I suddenly was told by somebody that it was not the job of the director to do all the lighting. Till then I had been doing all the lighting with Toland behind me balancing and so on and saying, "Don't tell anyone," you see. Then I had to go and apologize to him and everything. Then another awful moment came when I didn't understand directions. That was because I had learned how to make movies by running *Stagecoach* every night for a month. Because if you will look at *Stagecoach*, you will see that the Indians attack left to right, and then they attack right to left and so on. In other words, there's no direction followed, every rule is broken in the picture. And I sat and watched it forty-five times. So of course when I was suddenly told in an over-shoulder shot that I had to look camera left instead of camera right, I said "no," because I was standing . . . that argument, you know. So we closed the picture down. And about two in the afternoon I went back to my house and Toland showed me how that worked. And I said, "God, there's a lot of stuff here I don't know," and he said, "There's nothing I can't teach you in three hours." And that's when I said— which has been taken as a very pompous statement—that I learned everything in three hours. It was Toland's idea that anybody can learn it in three hours. And then he taught it to *me* in three hours. Everything else is if you're any good or not.

LM: *In fact, which came first? Was it the story of* Citizen Kane *or was it the idea of looking at a life from a lot of different . . .*

OW: *That* was what came first. But my co-author, Mankiewicz, took off with me on the idea of making it based on some big American figure. And we thought of a President; that was because [Howard] Hughes had got us started thinking that way. And I wasn't going to play Hughes, because I wouldn't have been good at it. It was gonna be Cotten who would have played Hughes. And we said, "Well, let's get a part I can play," and, finally, before we decided what sort of big man it would be, we began on this idea of seeing it from various points of view. And the original scripts or at least story lines had much more dramatic differences of point of view. It was much more of a trick. It was much more *Rashomon* than it ended up being. In other words, the story got a little better than the gag.

L M :   *What sort of things were they?*
O W :   Well, just that . . . For instance, the man who hated him, you would then see a scene in which Kane was totally hateful. Somebody who loved him, you would see him totally loveable. And that isn't so in the movie, you know. We see what he is all the time, I think. At least we tried to do it.

L M :   *You said once that Kane seemed to you to have been really quite close to parody as a character . . . rather close to burlesque. I didn't know if you meant the way you played him or the way he was perceived.*
O W :   I don't know what I meant by that. Maybe that comes from one of those foreign language interviews where I pretend I understand the question and say "yes," you know. There's a whole lot of things I'm supposed to have said that really come from not hearing very well or not being as good a linguist as I pretend to be. And there's a kind of interviewer—and you're not one of them—who tends to make a statement and then say, "Isn't that true?" And if I get very bored or . . . I say, "well, absolutely, yes." And that may be how come the parody because I can't imagine what I would have had in mind.

L M :   *. . . Marion Davies, the actress, was to Hearst what the singer Susan Alexander was to Kane. Except that Hearst had found himself a devoted life-long companion, a woman admired by everyone for her talent and her intelligence.*
O W :   I thought we were very unfair to Marion Davies. Because we had somebody very different in the place of Marion Davies, and it seemed to me to be something of a dirty trick, and does still strike me as being something of a dirty trick, what we did to her. And I anticipated the trouble from Hearst for that reason. It was the opening night of *Citizen Kane* in San Francisco and I found myself going to the Top of the Mark, high in the elevator with Mr. Hearst, and I introduced myself. This strange dinosaur, you know: He had ice-cold blue eyes and a very high eunochoid voice like that. And I said to him, "Mr. Hearst"—I didn't bother him with my father or any of that—I just said, "I have some good tickets for the opening of *Citizen Kane*. Would you like to come?" And he didn't answer, and I got off the elevator thinking, as I

still do, that if he had been Charles Foster Kane, he would have taken the tickets and gone.

L M : *And he didn't say anything?*
O W : No.

L M : *But you seem much more open now, perhaps with the passage of time, to be talking about Hearst at all in connection with* Citizen Kane.
O W : Well, Hearst, you see, lodged such an attack on us, particularly on me, or his minions did. It was kind of "Can no man rid me of this . . ." and so on. And I was once—well this will get terribly long and anecdotal but I'll try to tell it very quickly. I was lecturing in Buffalo and after the lecture I was with some people having dinner and a waiter said, "There's a policeman wants to see you," and I turned white. I always feel guilty when policemen want to see me. The cop turned out to be very nice. He said, "Don't go back to your hotel room." I said, "Why?" He said, "They've got an underage girl undressed and photographers waiting for you. It's a setup." So I didn't go back to my room that night. I just stayed up, took the plane in the morning. But that was as far as they were prepared to go. I would have gone to jail of course. And they had the producers in Hollywood ready all together to pay RKO to burn the negative. It was nip and tuck, you know, whether the negative would be burned and the picture never shown.

L M : *There's another legend that seems to have attached itself to you over the years and that's that you're a profligate spender, that you go way over on your budget and your shooting schedule.*
O W : I've never gone over schedule or over budget.

L M : *Not on* Kane?
O W : No. In fact, we were under budget on *Kane* and under schedule, but we did that by a trick, Because I said, "I don't know anything about movies so for about ten days I'm just gonna shoot tests." What we did was shoot *Kane.* And we shot ten days of *Kane* before we admitted we were actually shooting. But we would have been under schedule anyway.

L M : *Do you get upset these days—there's now so much literature on you. Do you get upset by some of those legends, particularly the ones to do with people, the ones that suggest that you've behaved irresponsibly towards . . .*

O W : Very badly. I'm much too upset about them. All my loving friends keep
telling me to stop brooding about it but it bothers me terribly. Anything that
has to do with my behavior. I don't mind how they criticize what I do, but
the total lies about me bother me much more than they ought to. I don't
know why I'm so touchy about it. I went into Mr. Chow's restaurant in London once, to have lunch alone. I like to eat lunch alone or dinner alone. I'd
brought a book. And they have Italian waiters there, you know. An Italian
waiter came and said to me in Italian, "Did you ever make a picture after
Citizen Kane?" And I had just been told by Huw Wheldon that I was out of
fashion, in one of his famously tactful moments. So this came at the wrong
moment. And I said patiently to him, "Yes, after *Citizen Kane,* I made *Magnificent Ambersons,*" and then I listed my pictures. Now Joan Didion wrote a
piece in *Esquire* a few months afterwards in which she described me coming
into Mr. Chow's with impressive silence and how all heads turned. I opened
a book and sat reading it, studying the book and so on. And then, suddenly,
the silence was broken by me saying I made *Citizen Kane* in 1940 and so on.
Well, you know, I've been brooding about that thing for six years now. That
I just sat and delivered a monologue to the audience of lunchers at Mr.
Chow's about the pictures I'd made, you know. So those kinds of things do
make me brood a bit. But that's the worst of them. That's my real obsession.
The picture of somebody sitting by himself in a restaurant and suddenly
reciting his screen credits [laughter].

L M : *Right after* Citizen Kane *you made* The Magnificent Ambersons.
O W : Yes, yes.

L M *[Comments from Robert Wise and Peter Bogdanovich were incorporated into
the next section]: Welles doesn't appear in his second film. But from the start the
voice of the storyteller is unmistakable.*
    Were you deliberately looking for something in which you wouldn't appear?
O W : Yes.

L M : *Why was that?*
O W : Well, I didn't want to be—I made a mistake, I shouldn't have done it.
I was obsessed in my hot youth with the idea that I would not be a star. That
I would only incidentally play great roles. Now there's no such thing as inci-
dentally playing great roles. Because you're not gonna get them offered to

you or anything. And I was in a position to promote myself as a star, and I should have. I should have gone back to New York and played Hamlet . . . as long as it was going. I didn't. I had this idea that I wanted to be known as a director. That was it. And I loved *Ambersons,* wanted to make a movie of it. The real point of *Ambersons,* everything that is any good in it, is that part of it which was really just a preparation for the decay of the Ambersons.

L M : *You'll never see that part of the film. These stills are all that remain of three or four missing reels. The film was cut by the studio in Welles's absence. At least forty-five minutes of his version have totally disappeared.*

O W : It was thought by everybody in Hollywood while I was in South America that it was too downbeat, famous Hollywood word at the time. Downbeat. So it was all taken out, but it was the purpose of the movie to see how they all slid downhill, you see, in one way or another. And how their relationships—how they turned away from each other and all of that kind of thing.

L M : *Let me just get it clear. You couldn't do anything about it. You didn't have the same sort of contract as on* Kane?

O W : No, I could do nothing. Because while I was in South America, RKO was sold to Howard Hughes and another group of people. And a new studio head came in. And they asked to see the movie and they previewed it out in Palmdale or something, in a rough-cut, and said it was downbeat and they started cutting it . . . There are three scenes at the end I didn't even write or shoot.

L M : *One of their solutions was to shoot and tack on a happy ending for the Ambersons, set in a hospital corridor where Agnes Moorehead and Joseph Cotten seem all set to walk into the sunset. Not Welles's style and certainly not his intention.*

O W : There's no scene in a hospital, nothing like that ever happened in the story. And the great long scene which was the key long scene at the end, which was Aggie Moorehead in a third-rate lodging house, near where an elevator was passing and they're playing a comic record—"Two Black Crows"—on a gramaphone, some old people in the back who are playing cards, and Joe Cotten has come to see how she is. That was the best scene in the picture. That was what the picture was about. Gone, the whole end of it, the whole, an actual plot was changed. In other words, about the time Major Ambersons dies, the picture starts to go, to become another picture, becomes their picture.

L M :   *Do you ever get over something like that?*
O W :   Not really, you don't, you don't. But, you see, I was in terrible trouble then because I was sent to South America by Nelson Rockefeller and Jock Whitney. I was told that it was my patriotic duty to go and spend a million dollars shooting the carnival in Rio. Now I don't like things like carnivals and Mardi Gras and all that, but they put it to me that it would be a real contribution to inter-American affairs in the Latin American world and so on. So without a salary but with a budget of a million dollars, I was sent to Rio to make up a movie [*It's All True*] about the carnival. But in the meantime comes the new government. RKO has now a new government and they ask to see the rushes of what I'm doing in South America. And they see a lot of people, black people, and the reaction is "He's just shootin' a lot of jigger-boos jumpin' up and down, you know." They didn't even hear the sound of music because it hadn't been synched up . . . So I was fired from RKO. And they made a great publicity point of the fact that I had gone to South America without a script and thrown all this money away. I never recovered from that attack. They had also promised me that when I went to South America they would send a Movieola and cutters to me and that I would finish the cutting of *Ambersons* there. They never did. They cut it themselves. So they destroyed *Ambersons* and the picture itself destroyed me. I didn't get a job as a director for years afterwards. So then I did *Jane Eyre.*

L M :   *Did it look at that stage as if people were kind of breathing a sigh of relief, saying "Thank God we've got Orson Welles into acting?"*
O W :   Oh, yes. RKO had its stationery that year, its official stationery, RKO Pictures and its slogan for that year. Printed on every piece of paper that went out from RKO was "Showmanship Instead of Genius." In other words, the reason you should buy an RKO picture was that you didn't get Orson Welles. The genius came from—I never said I was a genius. Nobody ever called me a genius seriously, certainly not in those days. But Louella Parsons called me "the would-be genius." And she called me that—she was a Hearst columnist; she called me that so often that this terrible word got stuck to me. So "Showmanship Instead of Genius," you see. And that was their big selling

point: They didn't have me anymore. And then the next picture I did do was *The Stranger*. And I did that to show people that I didn't glow in the dark, you know. That I could say "action" and "cut" just like all the other fellas.

L M :   *. . . Welles originally told the studio he wanted a woman for [Edward G.] Robinson's part, Agnes Moorehead.*
O W :   I thought it would have been much more interesting to get Boorman [Kindler, Welles's role] tracked down by a spinster lady than by Eddie Robinson, but they wouldn't agree to it.

L M :   *And Robinson wasn't actually a crony of yours, or a . . .*
O W :   No, I didn't know him at all. And he had gone into a big sulk the first week. I couldn't understand what it was about and he said, "You keep shooting me on my bad side." Now can you imagine Eddie Robinson having a bad side? And I was shooting him that way because Loretta Young's side was the other one, you see. So I told her about it and she said, "All right, shoot me on my bad side and keep him happy." [laughter] But he was an immensely effective actor. And he was very good in the picture.

L M :   *Welles's favorite sequences in* The Stranger *are the scenes of small town life. Like Robinson's visits to the drugstore and his dialogue with the bit part player Billy House. Robinson wasn't so keen on those scenes.*
O W :   He was very unhappy about the drugstore situation. He kept going back to the drugstore and playing checkers with the druggist, who never moved, always sat in his chair. And that was Billy House, a burlesque comedian that I found and put in the movie. And Billy House had a very unhappy first week too, as well as Eddie. I saw him mournfully standing around between takes. I finally took him away and said, "Billy, tell me, what's troubling you?" And he said, "Either give it to me or to the other son of a bitch but let's decide." And it was his stand-in. He thought the stand-in was there to play the part in case he wouldn't be good enough. He just saw that other fat man. He said, "Give it to him, I don't care. Just let me know where I am." He was a sweet man. So he cheered up a lot after that. But Eddie's point was that he was a supporting actor and why should a scene go to him? Scenes didn't go to supporting actors in Hollywood in those days unless they were featured players, so well beloved and so highly paid by the week by the studio that they had to be given. So if they were, you know, any of those won-

derful people—there were an awful lot of great character people. But here was an unknown actor, given great hunks of scenes that should have gone to the money, you know. And he was very unhappy about that. I tried to persuade him that it wouldn't cost him anything.

L M :   *And that's the first time you came up against that kind of star?*

O W :   Yes, yes. Well, I was working with two stars. And I had to decide. You see, when you work with stars you have to make love to them. It's the business of the director to carry on a continual courtship with the people he sticks in front of the lens. And when you deal with stars, you know, *real stars,* you have to . . . you have to *really* make love, you know. And it seemed to me natural to direct my attentions to Miss Young. And so there was a little jealousy there between Eddie and . . . particularly because she allowed me to hold her arm. There's a shot where I hold her arm, and she's five stories above and she really is. I'm holding her arm. And Eddie was too scared to put his feet over the edge, you see. So there was a lot of unhappiness about that. There was nothing we could do about the fact that he was scared. Except double him, you see.

L M :   *That was a real clocktower in fact?*

O W :   That was a real . . . we built a clocktower.

L M :   *And it was as high as that?*

O W :   Where now some skyscraper stands. We were running around on that, yeah. We had one shot where we would put poor John Russell out on a flagpole, hanging on to this camera. And it was the one shot where I fall and it could never be duplicated because the stunt man and all that got paid so much for doing it. And the next day at rushes we put in all the sound effects over black film in order to make Russell think he'd forgotten to rack over. That's the sort of cruelty that was common on the sets in those days. And we were all very forgiving—doesn't matter, we'll do it again tomorrow night. He'd been so scared.

L M :   *In 1943, Welles and Joseph Cotten had co-written and starred in a Grand Guignol thriller,* Journey into Fear, *and there were rumors that Welles had taken more than a passing interest in the direction.*

OW: The books about me which give me credit for that picture are wrong because it really is Norman Foster's picture and he deserves any credit that's going. And if you'd seen the picture before they cut out what didn't advance the action, you would have realized what a good movie he made. Yeah, in spite of my very hammy performance. But it was supposed to be a hammy performance. It wasn't unconsciously so. That's all I can say about that.

LM: *Well, that's interesting. It always seems as if there's something missing from* Journey into Fear. *I don't know what . . .*
OW: Well, some of the things are plots. Plot points. At one marvelous moment a man who's been killed in the third reel looks through a porthole. So it naturally confuses you.

LM: *It's the humor in* Journey into Fear *and little naturalistic bits of humor, little jokes that don't . . .*
OW: Yeah, we'd rehearsed all that before I left. We'd rehearsed all that. And a lot of that is Joe Cotten too. We'd been working together so long in the theatre, we developed a kind of Mercury Style. And you know, when I keep nagging on about this cutting, against that cutting, I'm not a director who likes to linger on things. You know, most of the directors of the generation after me—particularly European directors and now Americans too, every-body—they stay on a shot forever. If somebody's going to walk down a road, my God, they walk down the whole way. And you say to yourself, "You've got to see this right off the horizon." Yes, Antonioni's the king of it—they all do it—I get away from it. My pictures are pretty fast moving, I think.

LM: *. . . When he first viewed* Lady from Shanghai, *producer Harry Cohn offered anyone in the room a thousand dollars to explain the plot to him. Not even Welles took him up on it. The gossip columns had a field day. Welles's co-star was his recently divorced wife, Rita Hayworth. And the circumstances of the making of the picture in the first place are almost as bizarre as the story. Welles had actually left the movies for a year and returned to the theatre to lose a lot of money putting on a new musical. It was called* Around the World in Eighty Days.
OW: I put all my money into it and before the opening in Boston the cos-tumes were sitting in a railway station and there was fifty-five thousand dol-lars to pay for them or they wouldn't go to the theatre for the opening night. So I was in the box office and I was trying to think who in Hollywood could

send me fifty-five thousand dollars before—in the next three hours. And I thought, Harry Cohn. Only one with the courage to do it. I called him up and I said, "Harry." He said, "What is it? What do you want?" I said, "I've got the greatest story you've ever read," and I turned the paperback around that the girl in the box office was reading. It was called *The Man I Killed*. I said, "It's called *The Man I Killed*," written by such and such, "a paperback, buy it." I said, "You get me fifty-five thousand dollars to Boston in two hours and I'll make the picture. I'll write it and direct it and act in it." Fifty-five thousand came. I did *Around the World in Eighty Days*. Lost a fortune on it. But we had a musical that Brecht went to see seven times and was, I think, the best thing I ever did in the theatre. But it was a financial disaster. So I went back to Hollywood to pay my debt. And I intended to make a 'B' picture. I hadn't said I'd be in it, that was wrong, I shouldn't have told you that. I was gonna direct it. And so I had a French girl that we'd seen a picture of in *Life* magazine. We got her over and were all set to shoot it in about four weeks. And I had been divorced from Rita, and she came to me and said, "I want to make your picture. I want you to come back with me." And Harry sent for me and said, "I want you do that with Rita, for her sake." Well, that turned it from five weeks to a big super movie. And the essential plot is the plot of the book that I pointed to. Which I had never read. So the theory which has been printed a thousand times, that this was an act of vengeance against Rita, that it was a great device in which I was going to degrade her and so on, is nonsense, because all that's in the book. She'd read the book and wanted to play this character to show she was an actress.

L M :   *You built her up as this . . . all this soft focus . . .*
O W :   Yes, all of that. Then put her in the gutter at the end.

L M :   *You do seem to need that edge all the time, don't you? It's a sort of balancing act between drama and melodrama and parody almost.*
O W :   Yes. And I'm bored with stories that don't seem to be balanced dangerously like a, you know . . . when you walk down a highway with a story instead of on a tightrope. I'm bored with it, you know.

L M :   *Were you to some extent, though, setting out to make a critique, the very kind of film that the studios wouldn't like? Because you had a leading man who was*

stupid enough to get himself into the situation, the part you played. You had a sort of sex goddess playing a parody almost of a sex siren . . .
o w : Yes, of course, of course, there's that element. Oh, yes.

L M : *Welles's delight in subverting the classic scenes of melodrama runs right through* Lady from Shanghai. . . . *And this, by the way, was the film that Hollywood, the studios, and even Welles's friends thought was probably the worst thing he'd ever done. His reputation as a rebel, an uncontrollable kind of anarchist who didn't fit within the system, had grown so big that it looked as if no one would ever touch a Welles project again. And that reputation never left him.*
   I've never heard you or read you being bitter about Hollywood.
o w : No, I'm not. I'm not. It would be ridiculous to be bitter about Hollywood. Anybody who goes to Hollywood can see right away what the setup it. In my early days, it was much more fun. It was much more fun to outwit the dinosaurs than it is to outwit the college graduates from the conglomerates, you know. But Hollywood is Hollywood; there's nothing you can say about it that isn't true, good or bad. And if you get into it, you have no right to be bitter. You're the one who sat down and joined the game, you know.

L M : *Is it a clash, really a clash of temperaments between you and the system? I mean there have been fine films made within the Hollywood system.*
o w : Yes, indeed. Ford made all his films within the system but he outwitted the system. His taste and his instincts were such that he could make pictures which were sometimes in the mainstream and always marginally, the sort of pictures that the bosses wanted. He succeeded not by his originality but by the depth of his sensitivity. But the people who have done well in the system are the people . . . who want to make the kind of movie which producers want to produce. Not what the public wants but what the producers want to produce. The people who don't succeed, the people who've had long bad times like Renoir, for example, who is I think the best director ever, are people who didn't want to make the kind of pictures that producers want to make. Producers didn't want to make a Renoir picture even if it was a success. People don't realize that nobody in movies is interested in money. Everybody thinks Hollywood is interested in money because they talk about money all the time. Well, they talk about sex all the time and they don't do much of that. They're really interested in—it's all an ego trip they're interested in—in having produced this picture, in power, in status, all sorts of

things. Money is only the counters in the game . . . Nobody would go into the movies if they were really interested in money. If you're interested in money you'd go into a business in which you make bigger sums easier. The trouble with Hollywood isn't its money aspect and, as you speak of, a clash of temperaments, not at all. The pictures I like to make are not the pictures Hollywood producers, and particularly modern Hollywood producers, want to make.

L M : *Another project that Hollywood wasn't ecstatic about was Welles's 1948 version of* Macbeth. *Republic Pictures accepted it but they gave him only twenty-one days' shooting and a tiny budget.*
   Did the budget and shooting schedule dictate the way you . . . ?
O W : Yes, sure.

L M : *Quite clearly?*
O W : Sure and the set was badly executed . . . I made a careful model of it and by the time it was built it looked a little bit like the salt mine in the cereal, you know. And I wasn't too happy about that. Of course, the style of it was entirely dictated. It was done as a 'B' picture quickie.

L M : *Within the almost impossible limits he was set, Welles still manages to create an inventive and sometimes even witty version of* Macbeth.
O W : I thought I'd have a great success with it and then I'd be allowed to do all kinds of difficult things as long as they were cheap. But *Life* magazine came out that . . . they always . . . Martha Gellhorn always hated me anyway. She came out that week with "Help, Holy Murder, *Macbeth*," or something like that, you know. And it was a big critical failure. The biggest critical failure I ever had.

L M : *You have said that it poses great problems when you actually appear in films, in your films, because of your presence or your personality.*
O W : Yes, much more than in the theatre. I have a kind of personality which requires that I play certain kinds of parts. Or I discombobulate the scenes. And that's a kind of handicap. There used to be a division of actors in France in the *Comédie Française* who were called King Actors. They weren't necessarily the best actors; they were the actors who played the king, you know. And I'm a king actor, maybe a bad one, but that's what I am, you see. And I have

to play authoritative roles, but Truffaut is quite right when he says about me that I always show the fragility of the great authority and that that's the thing I do. I think I would be intolerable if I didn't.

A large company, the biggest company I've ever had as a director on location, about seventy people I think it was besides the actors and everything, came to Mogador on the West Coast of Africa to shoot *Othello*. And we arrived and got a telegram, the day after we arrived, that Scalera, the biggest Italian movie studio, with whom I had a contract to make the picture, had gone bankrupt. We had no money, we were in Africa and we had no costumes, nothing.

L M :   *. . . Welles got into the habit of suddenly leaving his crew on location, flying off to star in someone else's movie and rushing back weeks later with the money to shoot a bit more.*

The story has grown up that these unfortunate actors were left stranded while Orson Welles went off . . . I don't know what . . . and joins . . .

O W :   The actors love to tell that story because, of course, they were stranded, but what they forget is that they were stranded in the four-star luxury hotels of Europe. They were stranded in the Grand Hotel and the Europa in Venice, and in the Colon d'Or in the Provence and so on. And they were stranded only to the extent that I didn't want to send them home. I wanted to keep them together, and I went off to get money and left them, at great expense, eating and sleeping in luxurious conditions. I had a very good art director for that picture, Trauner, one of the best in movie history. But because of lack of funds we ended up shooting it mostly in real places, and there wasn't much for him to do. But he designed a wonderful *Othello* which somebody should do someday.

L M :   *The invention continued all over Europe, with Welles art directing on the run and creating marvelous set pieces like the fight scene filmed in a sewer in Portugal. And outside a citadel in Morocco on the edge of a cliff he found the setting for the funeral that makes a stunning opening for the film.*

O W :   It's quite a sequence, the opening of *Othello*. It was done entirely with never more than about sixty people. Except for one shot in Morocco where a lot of Jewish tailors run towards Micheál. They had to be Jewish tailors because it was Ramadan; the Arabs were all starving to death. So we had all the Jewish tailors who were busy making costumes for us, and when we needed that crowd scene we got them all out and we took sardine cans and flattened them out and tied them with string and so on so they would shine in the sunshine. And they came running forward, all the Jewish tailors and their sardine cans, for that one shot.

L M :   *The long filming schedule caused other problems. Welles often had to shoot his pickup shots in different locations. This fight starts in a street in Morocco. The final punch is delivered two thousand miles away, in Italy.*
O W :   We were in about, I don't know, at least seven or eight different cities, including . . . from Torcello to the South of Italy, just where there would be a little piece that would be right, you know. Didn't need something added to it. Then of course that determined the kind of cutting, which I wouldn't have done otherwise. I would have played longer scenes, but I had to . . . it had to be done in cuts because . . .

L M :   *I find the cutting early on a bit confusing in* Othello.
O W :   Yes, so do I. So do I. I don't like that. I don't like several bits there, in Venice. I think the weakest thing in the picture is Venice. Some of it's quite weak indeed, I think.

L M :   *Do you accept the label people have put on it? They've called it a flawed masterpiece because they've drawn attention to that and to the dialogue sound, which they find poor. That against these brilliant images . . .*
O W :   Yes, well, I don't know what happened to the sound. It was all right when we were done with it but something happened in making distribution copies or something. That did hurt it, so it's flawed to the extent that we weren't able to control the quality of the release print. It was actually all right as we did it. With awfully good music, wonderful music. I don't know flawed masterpiece, I don't know masterpiece either, you know. I can tell you things I don't like in all my movies and if that makes it flawed, then it's flawed; and I don't think I ever made a masterpiece, you know.

L M :   *But there are wonderful things in* Othello, *in its marriage of film and theatre, in Welles's use of his real life film set, and in his own performance. Can we go on to what we call the . . .*
O W :   I see that *Othello* is not one of your favorite movies. After one of those questions, "Would you agree that it's a flawed masterpiece?" . . . I love those questions. We then, after a slight pause, say, "Could we go on?" [laughter]

L M : *Could we go on to something else?*
O W : I think we'd better.

L M : *Mr. Arkadin.*
O W : That's a real flawed one, yes.

L M : *Is it?*
O W : Oh, yes, that's a disaster. It's a story about curious forms of vanity because here's a man who commits these terrible murders because of his interest in his image. In other words, nothing will happen to him. If any of the things which are found out about him are printed, nothing will happen to Arkadin. It's really about vanity and about people's preoccupation with their image. Even somebody as powerful as Arkadin, you see. But that film was taken away from me completely, and was totally destroyed in the cutting. That is the real disaster of my life, that one, you know. A flawed masterpiece, how are you this? There's your flawed masterpiece. It's *Arkadin.* I hate to think about it.

[Incorporated into the next section was an interview with Charlton Heston, who suggested that OW direct *Touch of Evil,* the film under discussion.]

So they quickly called me back again and said, "Will you direct this picture? We can't pay you any more." I said, "I'll direct it but if I also get to write it, every word of it, an entirely new script." They said, "Yes." So I had three weeks before we were supposed to start and I hired about twelve secretaries round the clock and made an entirely new script.

L M : *He must be physically the most grotesque character you've ever played?*
O W : Yes, yes, he's pretty grotesque. And I gave a dinner party not long after I started the picture for all my old producer friends and big star friends, the old Hollywood brigade. And my wife laid on a splendid meal and I was a little late so they were all there having their drinks before they would sit down. I came in, in order to arrive in time, in my make-up and costume. And they all said, "How are you, Orson? You're looking great!" And, you know, I was an absolute monster.

They didn't know they had Marlene Dietrich; she turned up in the rushes. They said, "That's Marlene Dietrich." And they called her up and said, "You're in this picture." She said, "Yes." And they said, "Well, what's your salary?" And she says, "You don't put my name on the picture, it's the minimum; you put my name on, see my agent." So they saw her agent. They were delighted. And it was roses all the way until that gate closed on me. It's still a mystery. I've no idea what it was about.

L M :   *Once again, Welles was barred from the post-production of his own film. And cuts were made in it. Why, again, in this case were you shut out from . . .*
O W :   I've no idea. It's never been explained. Because they loved the rushes. Every day the head of the studio came to me, wanted me to come to the office and sign a deal for several pictures, and, oh, it's great stuff. Then they saw a rough cut of it and they were so horrified that they wouldn't let me in the studio. And nobody's ever explained what horrified them. They tried very hard really to stop it. Heston had won an Oscar and was a great star and they released it without a press release, without press showing, second on the bill with a 'B' picture in America. And it was shown in Brussels right afterwards, at the World's Fair, where it got the prize for the best picture of the year. And the distributor, the Belgian distributor who had put it into the contest against the will of the studio, and had worked for Universal for twenty years, was fired. It then opened in a small theatre in Paris . . . where it ran for two years. And it's made a lot of money, even in America. To their tremendous rage, you know. The last thing they wanted was a success and nobody has ever explained it to me. Chuck Heston doesn't know, they never told him. They certainly never told me. We don't know what it is. It's too dark for them, too strange, too . . . I don't think we would have had that reaction now. A little too tough, a little too black. But that's a guess. I just don't know. Are we on?

L M :   *Yes.*
O W :   Yes, our viewers will know that, because this is on film, there are conversations that go on between reloading. And somebody said that *Touch of Evil* seemed very unreal and yet real. And I corrected that statement, said what I was trying to do was to make something which was unreal but true. And I think that's the definition of the highest kind of theatricality, the best kind. And that's the kind of theatricality that can exist in films too, as well as theatre. And I think . . . what is more unreal and stylized than Cagney? It's a totally stylized, unreal performance. No human being ever behaved the way he does. And every moment of Cagney's entire life in films is truth. He never had a second that wasn't true. He certainly was large than life. He did

everything dangerously and, you know, as though he were playing in Madison Square Garden. And it was always cinematically true. But unreal. That's the difference, I guess. *I* think.

L M :   *There's always, for the viewer anyway, a kind of moral ambiguity about the characters . . . and Quinlan's character, that although he's sort of . . .*
O W :   Well, you know what Renoir said? He said, "Everyone has his reasons." And that really sums it up, you know. There's no villain who doesn't have his reasons. And the bigger the villain, the more interesting it becomes . . . the further you explain his villainy—not psychiatrically, not because mama didn't love him, but because you humanize him. The more human you make the monster, the more interesting the story must be, it seems to me.

L M :   *Also Quinlan's instincts turn out to be right, even though the methods he used were wrong.*
O W :   That's right. You see, his method is totally wrong and my position in the political or moral sense is completely anti-Quinlan. I'm absolutely on the side of Heston. Myself, personally. But playing Quinlan and having a character like that, I had to make him a real person. I'd been trapped into a true person . . . or what I hope is a true person, a true monster. Because he was a successful cop, using means which do work but which are simply against every good instinct that we have in the democratic world. He's everything we hate. But *he* isn't what we hate, it's his method, and yet he would never have got those people behind bars if he hadn't done it. And it's that ambiguity which gives tension to a story, you know, that ambivalence rather.

L M :   *You also allow him this fantastic epitaph at the end.*
O W :   Yes, yes. Well, she was pretty good, pretty good casting for that.

L M :   *She was some kind of a woman.*
O W :   Yes, yes. It's her last great performance, no doubt about it. [clip from *Touch of Evil* featuring Marlene Dietrich's lines: "He was some kind of a man. What does it matter what you say about people?"] Got another flawed masterpiece?

L M *[introducing the second part of the telecast with a* Citizen Kane *clip]: Welles has always resisted attempts to find autobiographical references in his work. But there's one major theme in* Citizen Kane *that has been a lifelong obsession with Welles himself. During his Hollywood years, he was actively involved in politics, speaking at anti-fascist rallies, broadcasting political commentaries on the radio, writing his own daily column for the* New York Post, *and actively campaigning for Roosevelt.*

OW: I didn't run for the Senate for several reasons, the most cogent of which perhaps is the fact that I didn't believe anybody . . . you see, if you run for the Senate everybody who does in their hearts hopes that they might possibly get to the top, you know. I have to admit that if you're going to run for the Senate, you've got your eye on that big building. And I didn't think anybody could get elected President who had been divorced and who had been an actor. I made a helluva mistake—in both directions. [laughter] And the thing on my conscience is that if . . . Roosevelt was very anxious for me to run, and there was a study made . . . the Southern California Communist . . . Beverly Hills Communist division was against me. I was a dangerous revisionist. And I only had the North, and my advisor in California about how to run was Alan Cranston, who later became the Senator so I don't think he was totally disinterested. So it was finally discovered that the best place for me to run was Wisconsin, where I was born. We made a study of that and discovered that the dairy interests, who I felt I had to fight, were so powerful that I would almost certainly be beaten unless I was the greatest campaigner ever known. But now, supposing I *was* the greatest campaigner ever known . . . because if I had been, there never would have been Joe McCarthy. He was the candidate who ran on the Republican ticket and got in. So I have that on my conscience. Maybe I could have run and beaten him and there never would have been a McCarthy.

LM: *What happened to that political activity?*
OW: The political activity stopped when I had to go to Europe and earn my money to pay the taxes.

LM *[Incorporated into the next section were interviews with Anthony Perkins, star of* The Trial, *and Peter Bogdanovich]: In 1962, Welles was offered his choice of a subject for a film in Europe. He picked the novel by Kafka,* The Trial. *The film was seen by many critics as a kind of contest between Welles and Kafka, with Kafka coming off second best.*

O W : If you make an opera of *Othello,* you have a right, if you're Verdi, to make a great one, or if you're Bellini, to make a good one, or if you're Jack Chermulken to make a bad one. But you can make your own opera out of that play. And the same thing goes for movies. I don't believe in an essential reverence for the original material. It's simply part of the collaboration. And I felt no need to be true to Kafka in every essence. I'd thought it was necessary to capture what I felt to be the Kafka atmosphere, which is a combination of modern horror creeping up on the Austro-Hungarian Empire. I saw it as a European story, full of old European bric-a-brac, with IBM machines lurking in the background. And that was the way I wanted to present the picture.

L M : *The humor in the word play which happens early on, I don't know whether . . .*
O W : No, that's entirely mine.

L M : *That's Orson Welles?*
O W : There's nothing of that kind in Kafka. It's very solemn. It may be funny in German but it certainly isn't in English.

L M : *You were talking about working . . . making love to actors. I mean, I think, from what I hear of you from actors, you do it far more than any director, to the extent that you will stay up all night with your leading players, that you invite a kind of collaboration. That seems to me quite, really quite unusual . . . oh, we've run out of film.*
O W : You had me riveted! I loved it! Don't cut a word out of it! [laughter]

L M *[Incorporated into the next section was an interview with Jeanne Moreau, who appeared in* Chimes at Midnight*]: Welles as Falstaff. Perhaps his greatest performance. Certainly one of his finest films,* Chimes at Midnight. *Welles plays against the traditional Falstaff, the lying, drunken clown. He creates a character who's flawed and overindulgent but also intelligent and humane and his final rejection becomes the more poignant because of it.*
O W : Falstaff, I think, is the most unusual figure in fiction in that he is almost entirely a good man. He is a gloriously life-affirming good man, and there are very few gigantic silhouettes on the horizon of fiction who are good. They're always flawed, they're always interesting because of what is wrong with them . . . Somebody once said that Falstaff was Hamlet who

stayed in England and got fat, you know. Which is amusing to think of but I don't think it's true because Hamlet is not a good man, I don't think. There is hardly a good man in dramatic literature who dominates a whole scene and Falstaff is, I think, really Merrie England. I think Shakespeare was greatly preoccupied, as I am in my humble way, with the loss of innocence. And I think there has always been an England, an older England, which was sweeter and purer, where the hay smelt better and the weather was always springtime, and the daffodils blew in the gentle warm breezes. You feel nostalgia for it in Chaucer. And you feel it all through Shakespeare. And I think that he was profoundly against the modern age, as I am. I am against my modern age, he was against his. And I think his villains are modern people, just as they're likely to be continental. I always see that the villains in *Lear* are non-Anglo-Saxon. They're from over there. They represent the modern world, which includes gouging out eyes and sons being ungrateful to their fathers and all the rest of it. I think he was a typically English writer, archtypically, the perfect English writer, in that very thing, that preoccupation with that Camelot which is the great English legend, you know. And innocence is what Falstaff is. He is a kind of refugee from that world. And he has to live by his wits, he has to be funny. He hasn't a place to sleep if he doesn't get a laugh out of his patron. So it's a rough modern world that he's living in. But I think you have to see in his eyes; it's why I was also very glad to be doing it in black and white, because if it's in color he must have blue eyes, you know. You've got to see that look that comes out of the age that never existed but exists in the heart of all English poetry.

LM: *Then that rough modern world explodes into one of the most violent, I think, battles.*
OW: Terrible battle scene, yes, which is supposed to show the end of the chivalric idea, you know. It's supposed to show the way it's gonna be from now on.

LM: *Even the funny tin can running about, which is Falstaff in his armor, but it's funny pathetic. It's not a belly laugh.*
OW: Yes. It's supposed to be. Yes. The real fact is that Hotspur, another refugee from Camelot, is dead and the beady-eyed Tudor is getting ready to be an English hero, you know. And to build that establishment, under which Shakespeare must have struggled, because it was a very real establishment.

All that was done by terribly good technicians, you know. I was awfully lucky . . .

L M :   *And the cutting? The editing?*
O W :   Yes. Well, I did that. That's what it's made of, you know. If it hadn't been cut, it would have . . . you can't imagine . . . how sad the beginning and end of each shot was, you know. Pitiful in all the wrong senses of the word. Showing a lot of tired gypsy extras turning around, wondering where they were gonna eat, you know.

L M :   *It seems that* Chimes at Midnight *gives you particular pleasure . . .*
O W :   It's my favorite picture, yes. If I wanted to get into heaven on the basis of one movie, that's the one I would offer up. I think it's because it is to me the least flawed; let me put it that way. It is the most successful for what I tried to do. I succeeded more completely in my view with that than with anything else.

L M :   *Two years after* Chimes at Midnight, *Jeanne Moreau appeared in another Welles film,* The Immortal Story. *I kind of believe that the sailor's story existed before Karen Blixen, Isak Dinesen, wrote it.*
O W :   No, no, I've heard that story.

L M :   *You've heard it?*
O W :   I've heard it. Literally by a sailor, on a tramp steamer. That's what made my hair stand on end when I read it. I've heard it told as though it really happened, by a sailor, I swear to you. It's still being told. It is *The Immortal Story.*

L M :   *Mr. Clay can't accept that the story never really happened and he commits the folly of trying to bring it to life. It's very tempting to see Mr. Clay . . . almost . . . he's played by the director, but to see him as a kind of . . .*
O W :   As a director, as he is a kind of director, isn't he? Yes. And it could be very tempting to show it as the total uselessness of the director's job too.

L M :   *Do you actually, do you actually, think the director is over-rated?*
O W :   Oh, yes. Oh, yes. I think the exceptions are the exceptional directors. Of which there are very few up till now. But the actual job of the director in

ninety-nine percent of all movies is minimal. It's the only really easy job around. It really is, you know. And you can fool the people for years if you're a good producer. The director who is by nature a good producer can make a great name for himself and live to a great age, covered with glory and honors, and never be found out. Because a movie can be made by the actors, or by the cutter, or by the author. The best movies are made by the director.

L M :   *In 1949, Welles had acted in a film for the British director, Carol Reed. He created one of the most memorable anti-heroes of all time, the racketeer Harry Lime, in* The Third Man. *He dominates the picture although he's actually onscreen for less than ten minutes. He doesn't even turn up until the fourth reel, but when he does, it's one of the most magical appearances in cinema.*

O W :   Yes, you were saying about it being rare for directors to be very fond of actors and acting. And I was saying that Carol Reed—nobody ever loved acting more than he did. He was passionately interested in his actors and in the process of acting, without the remotest feeling that he was imagining himself in that position or imposing himself. He was the real actors' director. His joy was in your work, not in seeing something of his come to life. He was exceptional in that case.

L M :   *And did he invite your collaboration?*

O W :   Oh, yes, he invited everybody's collaboration, as I do. That's why I loved working . . . His style was so much like mine in the respect that he wanted any suggestion he could get . . . I could tell you scenes in pictures of mine that were suggested by members of the crew, you know. Anybody can make a suggestion. It doesn't mean they get to have it in the picture, but if it's good, it goes. And he welcomed it. In an earlier time when I was being interviewed in another language, I gave the impression that I'd somehow co-directed my scenes with . . . well, that's not true. And I never meant to say that or give that impression. I was, however, to a large extent, the author of the dialogue of Harry Lime, including the cuckoo clock and all that kind of stuff. But that is what I do when I act in other people's pictures. I never argue about the direction but I've usually come up with a re-written scene. That's the headache they have to put up with. And then, if they don't like it, I'll go back to the other. But I go back home at night and write next day's scene and hope they'll take it instead of what it is. But I never would tell a director, "Would you do that?" or something. Unless they asked me.

L M :   *Do directors often tell you how to do things when you're acting?*

O W :   Oh, yes, sure, sure. I had one director in England who . . . it was wonderful . . . about halfway through every take he'd say "cut, cut" and there'd
be a long silence and I'd look at him, you know. I said, "How would you like
me to do it?" "Just do it again." So we'd do it again and then there'd be this
. . . "cut." We went through the whole picture like that and I never knew
what was giving him this pain. Directors get up to such things, you know.
Some directors are great actors at being directors. René Clément, for example,
is absolutely superb. He's like Lenny Bernstein or von Karajan, you know.
When he tells you how to sit in a chair and so on it's just wonderful to watch.
And Huston is the most fascinating of all actor/directors, because his performance as a director is so awe inspiring and unnerving. It's absolutely marvelous because it's at once tremendously charming and attractive and
terrifying, you know. I've made a lot of pictures with him, made five pictures
with him and directed him in another. And in one of the last pictures he had
a penthouse above the stage. And while they were re-lighting, he'd go up to
his penthouse and then slowly there would get a silence on the set and we
would realize that John had come back. Then there would be a voice that
would say, "All right. Roll them. Action." Then "cut," and he would go away
in the darkness again. Well, everybody was speechless, you know. He could
get up to the damndest things you could imagine, you know. He was a virtu-
oso actor at being a director.

L M   *[following an interview with John Huston focusing on* Moby Dick*]: Have you
found yourself turning down really substantial parts because you wanted to get on
with directing?*

O W :   No, I haven't been offered them. I would have sold my soul to play
The Godfather, for instance. But I never get those parts offered to me at all.

L M :   *Why have you accepted so many parts, no matter how well you may have
done in the end, that were basically from bad scripts?*

O W :   To live. To live. I have to live in a . . . you know, if you're gonna try to
finance movies and live, you have to earn your money somehow. And most
of my movies have been movies I didn't want to make. I've never done a
movie that I disapproved of morally. The last star part that I was offered was
Caligula and I refused it on moral grounds. And yet there I would have been
playing the leading part in an eight million dollar picture. And it would have

been nice to do that, but I didn't even have a moment's doubt about not doing it. And the same thing would be for a political reason or anything like that. I've turned down a lot of things for those kinds of reasons. But no great parts. I haven't had any great parts offered me, only a few good ones in all these years. They hire me when they have a really bad movie and they want a cameo that will give it a little class, you know. So every time I do one of those things I chip off something more from me as an actor; it's a kind of . . . you know, you're in liquidation when you do that and that's why I hope to avoid it. Now it looks as though I have a chance to direct a couple more movies [knocks wood] and I've got a couple of good parts I've written for myself. Only way I know how to get them.

L M :   *If nobody else will . . .*
O W :   Yes. I've played all the great parts of the theatre by running . . . You know, there's an old Yiddish saying in the Yiddish theatre that the star's the man who owns the store. So, some of my stores have been rather small establishments but I was the star because I owned it.

L M :   *Have you also had bits chopped off you from doing commercials?*
O W :   No, I don't think so at all. That's an English attitude. Larry does commercials in America but not in England. Every time they write about me now in a performance in an English paper they talk about my sherry voice or something. I think that's nonsensical. You know, painters have always made posters. Why the hell shouldn't an actor sell a product that he thinks is a decent product and not a . . . when you aren't cheating the public. It's a perfectly legitimate use of your . . . of what you have to sell.

L M :   *Welles's most saleable commodity these days is himself. His own personality and his unrivaled skill as a storyteller. Well, in* F for Fake *you described yourself as a charlatan.*
O W :   Yes, well I describe myself as a charlatan in order . . . it was a complete trick, like everything in that movie, it was a trick, because I don't regard myself as a charlatan. Are we out of film? . . . Ah, no! I said I was a charlatan in order not to sound pompous talking about all the charlatans that were in the movie. And that's why I did the magic and so on. I thought by saying "charlatan" that will keep me from looking like some superior moral judge of tricksters. I didn't think I was a charlatan but a lot of very serious film

writers have taken that up and written at great length about Orson Welles as a charlatan, you see. Out of his own lips and all of that. But that was the trick too, it was all a trick. Everything about that picture was a trick.

L M : *It has that lovely magpie quality as well. I mean you got that film from another source.*
O W : Yes, BBC. And I rushed over to BBC to look at it and bought the film and bought also the outtakes. If I'd had more success with *F for Fake* in America I would have . . . by making only those kind of movies. When I finished *F for Fake,* I thought I had discovered a new kind of movie and it was the kind of movie I wanted to spend the rest of my life doing. And it was the failure of *F for Fake* that was one of the big shocks . . . in America and also in England, was one of the big shocks of my life. Because I really thought I was onto something. And it's a form, in other words, the essay, the personal essay, as opposed to a documentary, quite different. Not a documentary at all.

L M : *In* F for Fake *you appear as Orson Welles and you're the storyteller and I think—is it right?—in* Don Quixote *you appear as the storyteller?*
O W : Yes, and it's very interesting that Cervantes set out to write a short story. It's just by coincidence I set out to write, to make a short film. But the figure of Quixote seizes you, and Sancho Panza, and carries you forever. There's no end to them. But they have become ghostly; they're starting to fade, like an old movie, piece of old movie film. That's what I'll have to make. We were talking about the essay film and I haven't said that I'd like to take another shot at it, this time on the subject of Spain. Spain and the Spanish virtues, and vices, especially virtues. Because Cervantes wrote a figure of fun. A man who had gone mad reading old romances. And he ended up writing a story about a knight, a real one. When you finish up with Quixote you know that he's the most perfect knight who ever rode out against a dragon. And it has taken tourism, you know, and modern communications, and maybe even democracy, to destroy this, if not destroy at least to dim this extraordinary Spanish thing. That would be the subject of my essay on Quixote and Spain when I finish it. And I'm going to because it won't cost much money and it's going to be a great pleasure to do. And you know the title? *When Are You Going to Finish Don Quixote?* That's what it's gonna be called.

L M : *Because you've heard that somewhere before?*
O W : Yes, so many times before. Yes. And since it's my own little picture that I put my own money on, I don't know why they don't bug authors and say,

"When are you gonna finish *Nellie,* that novel you started ten years ago?"
You know, it's my business.

L M :   *It does sound as if since you started it, which is about twenty-five years ago,*
wasn't it . . .
O W :   Oh, God. Yes.

L M :   *But both actors have died now, is that right?*
O W : Yes, they're both dead. But I don't need them. I need them because I
love them but I don't need them for the movie.

L M :   *It sounds that the more time it takes the more time changes your attitude*
to it.
O W :   Of course. But Spain is changing, you see. Because for all the years of
Franco's Spain, Spain was paralyzed. In other words, everything good and
bad of the old Spain remained frozen as in a fairy story. You know. Nobody
came and kissed the sleeping princess. Everybody was left in the gestures that
they were making at the moment when Madrid fell. And I rejoice in what's
happening in Spain and like everybody in the world and the Spaniards in
particular who are my . . . I have more Spanish friends than anywhere else I
suppose. And all of them are absolutely astonished by the success of democracy in that country. But what happens to Quixote? It's very interesting.

L M :   *Could you describe to us at all any of the sequences that you might have shot*
that just won't work anymore to your mind because of the way time . . .
O W :   They're not very interesting if I tell them that way. I'm refusing the
question because my superior knowledge of the material, since you don't
know it, tells me that we're headed in a boring direction.

L M   *[Interviews with Jeanne Moreau and Peter Bogdanovich were incorporated into*
the final segment]: Welles has always refused to show any of Don Quixote *until*
he's finished it. And besides he admits he's not altogether sure where the various
bits of it really are. Jeanne Moreau starred in another Welles film that remains
unseen, The Deep, *completed in 1969 and never released. And John Huston acted*
in another unfinished project, this one held up by complicated legal tangles. It's
called The Other Side of the Wind, *the story of an aging and respected film*

director, surrounded by admirers but, with a typical Welles irony, unable to find
the money for his next picture.

o w :   I think I made essentially a mistake in staying in movies but it's a mistake I can't regret because it's like saying I shouldn't have stayed married to
that woman but I did because I love her. I would have been more successful
if I hadn't been married to her, you know. I would have been more successful
if I'd left movies immediately, stayed in the theatre, gone into politics, written, anything. I've wasted a greater part of my life looking for money and
trying to get along, trying to make my work from this terribly expensive
paintbox which is a movie. And I've spent too much energy on things that
have nothing to do with making a movie. It's about two percent moviemaking and ninety-eight percent hustling. It's no way to spend a life.

L M :   *Do you feel that's going to go on?*
o w :   Oh, I'm gonna go on being faithful to my girl. I love her. I fell so much
in love with making movies that the theatre lost everything for me, you
know. I'm just in love with making movies. Not very fond *of* movies. I don't
go to them much. I think it's very harmful to see movies for movie-makers
because you either imitate them or worry about not imitating them. And you
should do movies innocently. The way Adam named the animals the first
day in the garden. And I lost my innocence. Every time I see a picture I lose
something, I don't gain. I never understand what directors mean when they
compliment me, young directors, and say they've learnt from my pictures.
Because I don't believe in learning from other people's pictures. I think you
should learn from your own interior vision of things and discover, as I say,
innocently, as though there had never been D. W. Griffith or Eisenstein or
Ford or Renoir or anybody.

L M   *[voice-over with clip from* Citizen Kane*]: Jean-Luc Godard, writing about*
Orson Welles: "May we be accursed if we ever forget for one second that he alone
with Griffith, one in silent days, one sound, was able to start up that marvelous
little electric train. All of us, always, will owe him everything."

[Cut to Jeanne Moreau to conclude the program: And to me, Orson is so much
like a destitute King. A destitute King not because he was thrown away from the
kingdom, but on this earth, the way the world is, there's no kingdom that is good
enough for Orson Welles. That's the way I feel.]

Remembering Orson Welles

GORE VIDAL/1989

ALTHOUGH ORSON WELLES WAS ONLY ten years my senior, he had been famous for most of my life. I was thirteen when he made his famous Martians-are-coming radio broadcast. Then, three years later, when Welles was twenty-six, there was, suddenly, *Citizen Kane.* I was particularly susceptible to *Citizen Kane* because I was brought up among politicians and often saw more of my own father in newsreels than in life, particularly *The March of Time,* whose deep-toned thundering narrator—the voice of history itself—Welles was to evoke in his first film, whose cunning surface is so close to that of newsreel-real life that one felt, literally, at home in a way that one never did in such works of more gorgeous cinematic art as *All This and Heaven Too.*

Five years later, at the Beverly Hills Hotel, I first beheld the relatively lean Orson Welles. ("Note," Mercury Player Joseph Cotten once told me, "how Orson either never smiles on camera, or, if he has to, how he sucks in his cheeks so as not to look like a Halloween pumpkin.") On his arm was Rita Hayworth, his wife. He has it all, I remember thinking in a state of perfect awe untouched by pity. Little did I know—did he know?—that just as I was observing him in triumph, the great career was already going off the rails while the Gilda of all our dreams was being supplanted by the even more beautiful Dolores Del Rio. Well, Rita never had any luck. As for Welles . . .

For the television generation he is remembered as an enormously fat and

From *The New York Review of Books,* 1 June 1989. Reprinted with permission from *The New York Review of Books.* Copyright © 1989 NYREV, Inc.

garrulous man with a booming voice, seen most often on talk shows and in commercials where he somberly assured us that a certain wine would not be sold "before its time," whatever that meant. But Welles himself was on sale, as it were, long before *his* time in the sense that he was an astonishing prodigy, as Frank Brady records in *Citizen Welles,* a long biography which, blessedly, emphasizes the films in detail rather than the set of conflicting humours that made up the man.

Born in Kenosha, Wisconsin, on May 6, 1915, Welles was much indulged by a well-to-do, somewhat arty family. He was a born actor, artist, writer, magician. At fifteen, he ended his schooling. At sixteen, he was acting, successfully, grown-up parts for Dublin's Gate Theatre. At eighteen, he co-edited and illustrated three Shakespeare plays and a commercial textbook, *Everybody's Shakespeare.* At nineteen, he appeared on Broadway as Chorus and Tybalt in *Romeo and Juliet.* At twenty-two, he founded his own acting company, The Mercury Theatre, whose greatest success was a modern-dress *Julius Caesar* with Welles as Brutus. The Mercury Theatre then took radio by storm, dramatizing novels and stories, among them H. G. Wells's *War of the Worlds,* done in a realistic radio way, using the medium to report, moment by moment, the arrival of Martians in New Jersey. The subsequent national panic augurs ill for that inevitable day when some evil Panamanian tyrant drops his Señor Buén Muchacho mask and nukes Miami.

In due course RKO gave Welles a free hand, if a limited budget, to write, direct, and star in his first film. *Citizen Kane* began a new era in the movies. For those given to making lists, *Citizen Kane* still remains on everyone's list of the ten best films; often as the best film ever made. But for Welles himself things started to fall apart almost immediately. The Hearst newspapers declared war on him for his supposed travesty of Hearst's personal life. On Kane's deathbed, he whispers the word "Rosebud." This is thought to be the key, somehow, to his life. In the film it turns out to be a boy's sled, which Mr. Steven Spielberg recently bought for $55,000. In actual life, Rosebud was what Hearst called his friend Marion Davies's clitoris, the sort of item that producers of children's films tend not to collect. Although the next film, *The Magnificent Ambersons* (1942), might have been better than *Citizen Kane,* there was trouble with the editing—largely because Welles was in South America, failing to make a film.

For the rest of his life Welles moved restlessly around the world, acting on stage, in movies, on television. As director-actor, he managed to make *Mac-*

beth, Othello, Chimes at Midnight (the world from Falstaff's point of view). He also invented, as much as anyone did, the so-called film noir with *Journey into Fear* (1943), *The Lady from Shanghai* (1948), *Touch of Evil* (1958).

Everything that Welles touched as a director has a degree of brilliance, here and there, but he was always running out of money not to mention leading ladies, who kept mysteriously changing in his films, because he was often obliged to shut down for long periods of time, and then, when he started again, actors would be unavailable. In *Othello* Desdemona, finally, is a most expressive blonde wig. Meanwhile, Welles took every acting job he could to finance his own films and pay American taxes. We got to know each other in the Sixties, a period which Mr. Brady regards as "the nadir" of Welles's acting career. Well, all I can say is that there was an awful lot of nadir going around in those days. In fact, Welles acted in a nadir film that I had written called *Is Paris Burning?**

In later years we appeared on television together. "You see, I have to do the talk shows to keep my lecture price up at the universities." Orson always acted as if he were broke and, I suppose, relative to the Business, he was. He seemed to live in Spain as well as Hollywood and Las Vegas, "where I am near the airport," he would say mysteriously. "Also there are no death duties in Nevada unlike, shall we say, Haiti."

Orson's conversation was often surreal and always cryptic. Either you picked up on it or you were left out. At one point, he asked me to intervene on his behalf with Johnny Carson because there had been a "misunderstanding" between them and he was no longer asked to go on *The Tonight Show* and his lecture fees had, presumably, plummeted. I intervened. Carson was astonished. There was no problem that he knew of. I reported this to Orson in the course of one of our regular lunches at a French restaurant in Hollywood where Orson always sat in a vast chair to the right of the door. There was a smaller chair for a totally unprincipled small black poodle called Kiki.

---

*I was astonished to read in Frank Brady's *Citizen Welles* that Orson was offered the starring role in *Caligula*, "but when he read the Gore Vidal script and found it to be a mixture of hard-core pornography and violence, he peremptorily turned it down on moral grounds." Since Brady also gets the plot to *The Big Brass Ring* wrong, I assumed that he was wrong about Caligula, a part Orson could not have played even if my script for the picture had been used as written. But now, suddenly, I recalled Kenneth Tynan telling me that Orson had been upset by my original script. "You must never forget what a Puritan he is when it comes to sex."

"There is more to this than Johnny will ever tell you," he rumbled. "Much, much more. Why," he turned to the waiter with cold eyes, "do you keep bringing me a menu when you know what I must eat? Grilled fish." The voice boomed throughout the room. "And iced tea. How I hate grilled fish! But doctor's orders. I've lost twenty pounds. No one ever believes this. But then no one ever believes I hardly eat anything." He was close to four hundred pounds at the time of our last lunch in 1982. He wore bifurcated tents to which, rather idly, lapels, pocket flaps, buttons were attached in order to suggest a conventional suit. He hated the fat jokes that he was obliged to listen to—on television at least—with a merry smile and an insouciant retort or two, carefully honed in advance. When I asked him why he didn't have the operation that vacuums the fat out of the body, he was gleeful. "Because I have seen the results of liposuction *when the operation goes wrong*. It happened to a woman I know. First, they insert the catheter in the abdomen, subcutaneously." Orson was up on every medical procedure. "The suction begins and the fat—it looks like yellow chicken fat. You must try the chicken here. But then the fat—hers not the chicken's—came out unevenly. And so where once had been a Rubenesque torso, there was now something all hideously rippled and valleyed and canyoned like the moon." He chuckled and, as always, the blood rose in his face, slowly, from lower lip to forehead until the eyes vanished in a scarlet cloud, and I wondered, as always, what I'd do were he to drop dead of a stroke.

We talked mostly of politics and literature. At our last lunch, I was running in the Democratic primary for Senate. Orson approved. "I too had political ambitions, particularly back in the FDR days. I used to help him with speeches and I like to think I was useful to him. I know he thought I should have a serious go at politics some day. Well, some day came. They wanted me to run for the Senate in my home state of Wisconsin, against Joe McCarthy. Then I let them—another 'them'—convince me that I could never win because," and the chuckle began again, "I was an actor—hence, frivolous. And divorced—hence, immoral. And now Ronnie Reagan, who is both, is president." Eyes drowned in the red sea; laughter tolled; then, out of who knows what depths of moral nullity, Kiki bit a waiter's sleeve.

When I observed that acting—particularly old-time movie acting—was the worst possible preparation for the presidency because the movie actor must be entirely passive so that he can do and say exactly what others tell him to do and say, Orson agreed that although this might be true in general (we both excluded *him* from any generality), he had known two movie actors who would have been good presidents. One was Melvyn Douglas. The other was Gregory Peck. "Of course," he was thoughtful, "Greg isn't much as an actor, which may explain why he has so good a character."

During the last year of our occasional meetings, Orson and I were much preoccupied with Rudy Vallee. The popular singer of yesteryear was living in the mansion "Silvertip" high atop that Hollywood hill halfway up which I sometimes live. When the maestro heard that I was his neighbor, he sent me a copy of his memoirs *Let The Chips Fall*. . . . Like a pair of Talmudic scholars, Orson and I constantly studied this astonishing book. Parts of it we memorized: "Somehow I have never inspired confidence. I don't think it is due to any weakness particularly evident in my face, but there is something about me, possibly a quiet reserve or shyness, that gives most people the impression that I can't do anything very well."

Each of us had his favorite moments. Mine was the telegram (reproduced) that Rudy sent the relatively unknown radio announcer, Arthur Godfrey, in 1940, to show what a keen eye and ear Rudy had for talent (for a time Vallee ran a talent agency). Orson preferred the highly detailed indictment of Rudy's protégé, "The Ungreatfulcholy Dane," Victor Borge, complete with reproductions of inter-office memoranda, telegrams sent and received, culminating in two newspaper cuttings. One headline: VICTOR BORGE SUED FOR $750,000; the other: BORGE SUED BY THE IRS.

As professional storytellers, we were duly awed by Rudy's handling of The Grapefruit Incident, which begins, so casually, at Yale: "Ironically, the dean was the father of the boy who, nine years later, was to hurl a grapefruit at me in a Boston theater and almost kill me." Then the story is dropped. Pages pass. Years pass. Then the grapefruit motif is reintroduced. Rudy and his band have played for the dean; afterward, when they are given ice cream, Rudy asks, "Is this all we're having . . ."

"Apparently one of [the dean's] sons noticed my rather uncivil question . . . and resolved that some day he would avenge this slight. What he actually did later at a Boston theater might have put him in the electric chair and me in my grave but fortunately his aim was bad. But of that more later." Orson thought this masterful. Appetites whetted, we read on until the now inevitable rendezvous of hero and grapefruit in a Boston theater where, as Rudy is singing—"Oh, Give Me Something to Remember You By," "a large yellow grapefruit came hurtling from the balcony. With a tremendous crash it struck the drummer's cymbal . . ." [but] "if it had struck the gooseneck of my sax squarely where it curves into the mouth it might have driven it back through the vertebra in the back of my neck."

Of this passage, the ecstatic Orson whispered, "Conrad"—what might have been *if* Lord Jim had remained on watch.

Finally, in a scene reminiscent of Saint-Simon's last evocation of the Duchess of Burgundy, Vallee tells us how he had got the Chairman of the Board himself to come see his house and its rooms of memorabilia. Frank Sinatra dutifully toured room after room of artefacts relating to the master. Although an offending journalist gave "the impression that most of the pictures portrayed my likeness, actually, one third of the pictures are of neutral subjects or of personalities other than myself." Even so, "as Frank Sinatra rather snidely put it as we left this particular corridor, 'You would never guess who lived here.' "*

In literary matters, Orson was encyclopaedic, with an actor's memory for poetry. I have known few American writers who have had much or, indeed, any enthusiasm for literature. Writers who teach tend to prefer literary theory to literature and tenure to all else. Writers who do not teach prefer the contemplation of Careers to art of any kind. On the other hand, those actors who do read are often most learned, even passionate, when it comes to literature. I think that this unusual taste comes from a thorough grounding in Shakespeare combined with all that time waiting around on movie-sets.

When we had finished with politics and literature and the broiled fish, Orson told me a hilarious story of a sexual intrigue in Yugoslavia during the shooting of Kafka's *The Trial.* How was Orson to manoeuvre a willing young woman away from her escort in a bar that was connected by a dark and creaking staircase to Orson's room, and then . . .? Each detail of this labyrinthine tale was lovingly recounted right up until the final victory in the wrong bed or room—or something. Orson was a superb dramatizer. As an actor, he was limited by his unique physical presence and that great booming conman's voice. But when it came to storytelling, he was as exciting at a corner

---

*Rudy Vallee scholars will search in vain for the adverb "snidely" in *Let the Chips Fall . . .* I have taken the liberty of using an earlier version of the Sinatra visit as recorded in *My Time Is Your Time* (1962). Even though Rudy Vallee always wrote the same book, he was given to subtle changes, particularly in his use or omission of adverbs, reminiscent, in their mastery, of the grace notes in Bach. A synoptic edition of Vallee's three memoirs is long overdue, as well as a meticulous concordance.

table, talking, as he was on the screen itself in a work all his own. But the tragedy of Welles ("How," I can hear him say, eyes theatrically narrowed to slits in that great round pudding of a face, "do you define tragedy?") is that more time was spent evoking movies at corner tables than in a studio. Yet he was always seriously at work on a number of projects that he could never get the financing for.

"This time I've written a political script. Rather your kind of thing." He puffed on a cigar. He looked like Harry Lime. "You know Paul Newman. Can you put in a word for him? Because if I don't have one of the Six Bankable Boys, there's no financing. What one has to go through." He patted his stomach as if it were his dog. He looked like Falstaff. "They always ask me, aren't you glad, *cher maître,* that the old studio system is finished, that there are no more vulgar furriers controlling your films? And I say, my God, how I miss them! Even Harry Cohn. When you make fifty-two pictures a year on an assembly-line basis there is always room for an Orson Welles film. But now there is no room anywhere." He smoothed the dog's fur as if it were his stomach. Then he chuckled. "I have made an art form of the interview. The French are the best interviewers, despite their addiction to the triad, like all Cartesians." I took this well: triad = trinity, but *versus,* I would have thought, Descartes.

Orson was now in full flow. "They also have the gift of the unexpected letdown. The ultimate Zinger. 'There are only three great directors in the history of the film,' they will announce. I smile shyly." Orson smiles. Cotten was right. Though he doesn't seem to be sucking in his cheeks, the corners of his mouth are drawn not up but down. "There is D. W. Griffith. I roll my eyes toward Heaven in an ecstasy of agreement. There is Orson Welles. I lower my lids, all modesty—little me? Then," his voice drops, basso profundissimo, "there is—Nicholas Ray!" Orson erupts in laughter. We meditate on the interview as art form as well as necessity for Orson, "because I don't lecture any more."

"Then why," I asked, "did you ask me to ask Carson to get you back on *The Tonight Show* so that you could get more lecture dates when you've given up lecturing?" He looked at me in true surprise. "Surely I told you I've stopped lecturing because I can't walk from the airport terminal to the gate." "You can use a wheelchair," I said. "But that would be the end of me as an actor. Word would spread I was terminally ill. Besides there is no wheelchair large enough unless I bring my own, which would make a truly bad impression."

Orson never knew that I knew how, the previous week, Orson's driver had delivered him to the restaurant's parking lot, only to find that Orson was so tightly wedged in the front seat that the car had to be taken apart so that he could get out.

"If not Newman, there's Nicholson or Beatty. Warren has consented to give me an audience. But Nicholson would be better. The story's called *The Big Brass Ring,* about a senator who's just been defeated by Reagan for president—two years from now, of course. Really right down your alley . . ."

Three years after our last lunch, Orson died at the age of seventy. He had not been able to get one of the Bankable Boys to agree to do *The Big Brass Ring* and so it is now just one more cloudy trophy to provoke one's imagination. What would Welles's *Don Quixote* have been like if he had been able to finish it? But then it is pleasurable to imagine what he might have done with any theme because he was, literally, a magician, fascinated by legerdemain, tricks of eye, forgeries, labyrinths, mirrors reflecting mirrors. He was a master of finding new ways of seeing things that others saw not at all.

Happily, I now know something about *The Big Brass Ring,* which was published obscurely in 1987 as "an original screen-play by Orson Welles with Oja Kodar." Wellesian mysteries begin to swirl. Who is Oja Kodar? The dust jacket identifies her as Welles's "companion and collaborator (as actress and screenwriter, among other capacities) over the last twenty years of his life. She is a Yugoslav sculptor who has had one-woman shows in both Europe and the US. The lead actress in *F for Fake* [which I've never seen] and *The Other Side of the Wind* [unreleased], she collaborated on the scripts of both films as well as many other Welles projects" . . . all unmade.

Orson never mentioned her. But then, come to think of it, except for bizarre dreamlike adventures, he never spoke of his private life. In all the years I knew him, I never set foot in any place where he was living, or met his wife, Paola Mori, who died a year after he did. I invited Orson several times to the house where I lived within megaphone distance of the Rudy Vallee shrine and he always accepted, with delight. Then the phone calls would start. "I know that it is the height of rudeness to ask who will be there, so my rudeness is of the loftiest sort. Who will be there?" I would tell him and he'd be pleased to see so many old friends; finally, an hour before the party began, he'd ring. "I have an early call tomorrow. For a commercial. Dog food, I think it is this time. No, I do not have to eat from the can on camera but I *celebrate* the contents. Yes, I have fallen so low."

Further mysteries: there is an afterword published to the script by Jonathan Rosenbaum, who tells us that Welles left two estates, "one of them controlled by his wife Paola Mori and daughter Beatrice, . . . the other controlled by Kodar." Now the two estates appear to be in equilibrium; hence, "the publication of *The Big Brass Ring* represents a major step forward in the clarification of the invisible Orson Welles, even though it comprises only a piece of the iceberg (or jigsaw puzzle, if one prefers)." I prefer jigsaw puzzle. And now, for me, an essential piece is at hand: the screenplay, which is purest Welles. He is plainly at the top of his glittering form, which was as deeply literary as it was visual.

What, precisely, is "purest Welles"? Although every line sounds like Welles, we are told that he based some of the story on an autobiographical sketch by Kodar. Thus, they collaborated. But the germ of the story, one of Welles's few "originals" (a word in this context never to be let out of quotes), was first expressed by Welles in a conversation with the film director Henry Jaglom. Welles said that there was a story that "he'd been thinking about for years, about an old political adviser to Roosevelt who was homosexual, and whose lover had gotten crippled in the Spanish Civil War fighting the fascists. Now he was in an African kingdom, advising the murderous leader—and back in the US, a young senator who'd been his protégé was going to run against Reagan in 1984, as the Democratic nominee." So far so Wellesian. The fascination with politics, particularly the New Deal; with homosexuality to the extent that it involves masks and revelation; and, finally, with the relationship between the teacher and the taught.

The action is swift. A series of images—fading campaign posters: the defeated presidential candidate, Pellarin, walks through a restaurant where he is recognized and cheered; he is a combination of Texas Good-Ole-Boy and Harvard Law School. The wife, Diana, is edgy, long-suffering, rich. Then we are aboard a yacht. Pellarin is bored. Diana plays backgammon with a woman friend. Pellarin goes into their bedroom and finds a girl—a manicurist—stealing his wife's emerald necklace. To his own amazement, he tells her, "Keep it." With this Gidean *acte gratuit* the story takes off. When a shipwide search for the necklace begins, Pellarin realizes that it will be found on the girl; so he makes her give him the jewels; then he promises her that he will turn them over to a fence at the next port, which is Tangiers.

At Tangiers Pellarin books a flight to the African country where his old mentor, Kimball Menaker, is advising the local Idi Amin. At the airport, he is ambushed by Cela Brandini, a superb portrait of the dread Oriana Fallaci in the terminal throes of requited self-love. "I am Cela Brandini," she declares with all the authority of a bush afire. "Of course you are," he says, mildly. Brandini: "And I have never asked you for an interview." Pellarin: "Guess I'm just plain lucky." Now Welles can use his second art form, the interview with tape recorder. Brandini has just interviewed Menaker, a figure that Pellarin must never see again because . . . The plot of the emerald necklace crosses with that of the search for Menaker, to be played by Welles at his most oracular, not to mention polymathematical.

As they wait in the airport lounge, Brandini plays for him some of Menaker's dialogue on her recorder, a nice narrative device. Menaker: "A message? Do I wish to send a message to the Senator from Texas? ex-chairman of the Foreign Affairs Committee? former vedette of the Hasty Pudding Club Review, our future President, and my former friend?" Brandini has interviewed Menaker as background for a piece she wants to do on Pellarin. She is aware that Menaker is the skeleton in Pellarin's closet. Had they been lovers? What glorious scandal! Brandini: "The way he speaks of you—he seems to think he's your [father]." Pellarin is pleased. She strikes, "And yet, politically—he almost killed you off." Pellarin demurs: "He didn't quite do that, you know—He killed himself." Mysteries within mysteries. A quest. Nothing now is what it seems. Pellarin, pilgrim.

Pellarin finds Menaker in the Batunga Hilton; he is in bed with a sick monkey while two naked black women play backgammon as they keep guard over him. Although the scene is about finding a fence for the emeralds (Menaker is the author of *The Criminal Underworld Considered as a Primitive Culture—An Anthropological View:* "I'm an authority on everything," he says), the subtext concerns a woman, Pellarin's lost love, a Cambodian beauty, last seen by Menaker in Paris.

Pellarin departs with the sick monkey knotted about his neck, hiding the emeralds. He joins the yacht at Barcelona. Brandini is also there. She declaims: "I'm an anarchist." Pellarin: "I wish you were a veterinarian." Brandini: "I do not think that monkey has very long to live." Pellarin: "Neither do I." Brandini: "Interesting." Pellarin: "Death? The subject doesn't capture my imagination." Brandini: "I know something about it, Pellarin. I've seen it in Vietnam, Central America—in Greece." Pellarin: "I know. There's a lot of that stuff going around." Back on the yacht, Pellarin tries to get the monkey off his neck: it falls into the sea, the emeralds clutched in its fist. How is Pellarin to get the money he "owes" the girl?

Meanwhile, Menaker is out of Africa and again in the clutches of Brandini. A reference is made to Menaker's Harvard rival, Henry Kissinger, "chief brown-noser to the Rockefellers." Menaker is concerned about Kissinger because: "He *is* getting *shorter*—Have you noticed that? He's positively *dwindling* with thwarted ambition: Metternich as the incredible shrinking man. They ought to give poor shrinking Henry one last go at State. As a foreigner, there's no higher he can go—and who knows how much smaller he can get." They speak of Menaker's influence on Pellarin. Menaker seems to him triumphant despite their association, not to mention that of Harvard. These are only minor limitations. Brandini: "You've spoken of his limitations—What are yours?" Menaker: "I'm an old man, Miss Brandini—and a faggot. I couldn't use another limitation."

Pellarin and Menaker meet. Menaker says not to worry about the emeralds: they are false. Diana sold the originals to help get Pellarin elected to Congress. She has worn paste copies ever since. So Pellarin must cash a cheque in order to give money to the girl for the worthless jewels that she stole and Pellarin lost. This is exquisite Welles. And he brings it off with Wildean panache.

Now the story of the emeralds again crosses the story of the lost love in Paris. Apparently, she is in Madrid. She wants to see Pellarin. Menaker will take him to her. Meanwhile they meditate upon identity. Menaker: "Even the great ones must have sometimes felt uncomfortable in their own skins. Caesar must have dreamt of Alexander, and Napoleon of Caesar." Pellarin: "Shit, Professor—I couldn't make their weight." Menaker: "Then think of poor Dick Nixon—mincing about inside his fortress in the Oval Room, all bristling with bugs—hoping a playback would eventually inform him who he was . . . He told us often what he *wasn't,* but he never really got it figured out." Pellarin: "Neither have I . . . You sly old son of a bitch, so *that's* what you've been getting at." Menaker: "In a perfect world, all of us should be allowed some short vacations from our own identities. Last week you were Bulldog Drummond, gentleman jewel thief. Soon you'll be hoping to sneak down that rabbit hole again to where it's always Paris in the spring." Orson

Welles, who was known to all the world as Orson Welles, could never be anyone else in life but, in art, he could saw a lady in half, pull a rabbit from a hat, arrange shadows on celluloid in such a way as to be any number of entirely other selves.

Menaker leads Pellarin to "The Old Dark House." A *feria* is in progress; fireworks. Only Pellarin goes inside the house: "The scene is strange, almost surreal . . . (The action must be given in synopsis . . . The climax of this sequence is strongly erotic: to spell out its specific details would be to risk pornography) . . . A man searching and searching—up and down, from floor to floor, from room to room of an empty house, comes to discover (in a lightning flash of fireworks breaking through a shuttered window) that all along there has been someone watching him:—naked, in a shadowed chair." This is much the same scene that Orson told me at our last lunch as having happened to him. Did it? Or was he trying out the scene on me? She is found; they speak in French; make love; then she vanishes. Although the film was to be shot in black and white, Orson intended the fireworks to be in color; at the scene's end "The colored lights fall into darkness."

Pellarin faces Menaker in the street. Menaker never delivered the letter that Pellarin had written asking the girl to marry him. Menaker did not deliver it because he wants Pellarin to go to glory. Pellarin: "Screw Pennsylvania Avenue." Menaker: "Boysie—There's nowhere else for you to go." Later, the ubiquitous Brandini strikes. She tells Pellarin that "during his sexual fantasizing about you—Dr. Menaker would masturbate into a handkerchief . . . Then, when it was stiff with his dried semen, he mailed it to his crippled friend, as . . . I don't know what: a sentimental souvenir." I must say that even at the lively funcourt of Tiberius and of his heir, Caligula, neither Suetonius nor I ever came up with anything quite so—dare I use so punitive a word?—icky. But Orson needed an emotional trigger for a nightmare flight through the city and an encounter with a blind beggar who menaces Pellarin and whom he kills. Let it come down. The police suspect but cover for him.

Pellarin re-enters the world. A speech must be given in Brussels. Menaker is on the train, which Brandini satisfactorily misses—"dressed as usual: semi-safari with a strong hint of battle fatigues." They sing, jointly, Menaker's "hit number from the Hasty Pudding Show of nineteen twenty-nine." Then Orson adds, with his usual flourish: "If you want a happy ending, that depends, of course, on where you stop your story."

In a statement to Henry Jaglom (May 20, 1982), Orson wrote of Pellarin.

He is a great man—like all great men he is never satisfied that he has chosen the right path in life. Even being President, he feels, may somehow not be right. He is a man who has within him the devil of self-destruction that lives in every genius . . . There is this foolish, romantic side of us all . . . That is what the *circumstances* of the film are about—the theft of the necklace, the situation with the monkey, etc. All these idiotic events that one's romantic nature leads one into.

But of course Orson is describing Menaker, not Pellarin, and, again of course, Orson is describing his own "romantic nature" which led him down so many odd roads, to our enduring delight if not always his.

I have a recurring fantasy that if one were to dial the telephone number of someone in the past, one would hear again a familiar voice, and time would instantly rewind from now to then. I still have Orson's telephone number in my book (213-851-8458). Do I dare ring him and talk to him back in 1982, where he is busy trying to convince Jack Nicholson to play Pellarin for two not four million dollars? Should I tell him that he'll not get the picture made? No. That would be too harsh. I'll pretend that I have somehow got a copy of it, and that I think it marvelous though perhaps the handkerchief was, from so prudish a master, a bit much? Even incredible.

"Incredible?" The voice booms in my ear. "How could it be incredible when I stole it from *Othello*? But now I have a real treat for you. Standing here is your neighbor . . . Rudy! Overcome 'that quiet reserve or shyness.' *Sing.*"

From out of the past, I hear "My time is your time," in that reedy highly imitable voice. The after-life's only a dial tone away. "What makes you think that this is the after-life?" Orson chuckles. "This is a recording." Stop story here.

INDEX

Conversations with Filmmakers Series

Peter Brunette, General Editor

The collected interviews with notable modern directors, including

Robert Altman / Theo Angelopolous / Bernardo Bertolucci / Jane Campion /
George Cukor / Clint Eastwood / John Ford / Jean-Luc Godard / Peter Greenaway /
John Huston / Jim Jarmusch / Elia Kazan / Stanley Kubrick / Spike Lee / Mike Leigh /
George Lucas / John Sayles / Martin Scorsese / Steven Soderbergh / Steven Spielberg /
Oliver Stone / Quentin Tarantino / Billy Wilder / Zhang Yimou